The VICTORIAN HOMEFRONT

TWAYNE'S
AMERICAN THOUGHT
AND CULTURE SERIES

Lewis Perry, General Editor

The VICTORIAN HOMEFRONT

American Thought and Culture, 1860–1880

LOUISE L. STEVENSON

Twayne Publishers • New York
Maxwell Macmillan Canada • Toronto
Maxwell Macmillan International • New York   Oxford   Singapore   Sydney

The Victorian Homefront: American Thought and Culture, 1860–1880
Louise L. Stevenson

Copyright © 1991 by Louise L. Stevenson

Twayne Publishers   Maxwell Macmillan Canada, Inc.
Macmillan Publishing Company   1200 Eglinton Avenue East
866 Third Avenue   Suite 200
New York, NY 10022   Don Mills, Ontario M3C 3N1

Macmillan Publishing Company is part of the Maxwell Communication Group of Companies.

Library of Congress Cataloging-in-Publication Data

Stevenson, Louise L.
     The Victorian homefront: American thought and culture,
1860–1880/ Louise L. Stevenson.
          p.   cm. — (Twayne's American thought and culture series)
     Includes bibliographical references and index.
     ISBN 0-8057-9053-5 (hc : alk. paper). — ISBN 0-8057-9058-6 (pbk.)
     1. United States—Civilization—1865-1918. 2. United States—
Intellectual life—1865–1918. I. Title. II. Series.
     973.8—dc20   91-21297
                                                                         CIP

The paper used in this publication meets the minimum requirements
of American National Standard for Information Sciences—Permanence
of Paper for Printed Library Materials, ANSI Z39.48-1984. ∞™

10 9 8 7 6 5 4 3 2 1 (hc)
10 9 8 7 6 5 4 3 2   (pb)

Copyediting supervised by Barbara Sutton.
Book production and design by Janet Z. Reynolds.
Typeset by Compset, Inc., Beverly, Massachusetts.

Printed in the United States of America.

For Philip

Contents

LIST OF ILLUSTRATIONS   ix
FOREWORD   xi
ACKNOWLEDGMENTS   xiii
INTRODUCTION   xv

ONE
Around the Parlor Table   1

TWO
Serious Reading and Reading Seriously   30

THREE
Beyond the Parlor: Cultural Institutions in Small Towns and Big Cities   48

FOUR
Preparing for Parlor Life   71

FIVE
Leaders for Parlor and Public Life   101

SIX
In Pursuit of Truth   137

SEVEN
Intellectuals and the Public   156

EIGHT
Centennial Milestones: 1876 and Beyond   182

CHRONOLOGY   201
NOTES AND REFERENCES   205
SUGGESTED READING   220
INDEX   231

List of Illustrations

Victorian home: front elevation   16
Victorian home: plan of first floor   17
President Lincoln and Family Circle   18
The Bancrofts of Wilmington, Delaware   19
Advertisement for parlor furniture   20
Trade card of Mason & Hamlin Organ & Piano Co.   21
Winslow Homer, *The New Novel*   21
Central Park, The Drive   67
Page from *McGuffey's Reader*   80
Page from *McGuffey's Reader*   80
Page from *The Freedman's Second Reader*   81
Public school merit award   87
Assembly-Room at Hampton Normal and Agricultural Institute   129
College Row, Franklin and Marshall College   130
Vassar College   131
Senior parlor, Vassar College   131
Chatauqua Lake montage   159
Statue of a freed slave, Centennial International Exhibition   193
Women's Pavilion, Centennial International Exhibition   197

Foreword

The American Thought and Culture Series surveys intellectual and cultural life in America from the sixteenth century to the present. The time is auspicious for such a broad survey because scholars have carried out so much pathbreaking work in this field in recent years. The volumes reflect that scholarship as well as valuable earlier studies. The authors also present the results of their own research and offer original interpretations. The goal is to bring together books that are readable and well informed and that stand on their own as introductions to significant periods in American thought and culture. There is no attempt to establish a single interpretation of all of America's past; the diversity, conflict, and change that are features of the American experience would frustrate any such attempt. What the authors can do, however, is to explore issues of critical importance in each period and those of recurrent or lasting importance.

Today the culture and intellectual life of the United States are subjects of heated debate. While prominent figures summon citizens back to an endangered common culture, some critics dismiss the very idea of culture—let alone American culture—as elitist and arbitrary. The questions asked in these volumes have direct relevance to that debate, which concerns history but too often proceeds in ignorance of it. How did leading intellectuals view their relation to America, and how did their fellow citizens regard them? Did Americans believe that theirs was a distinctive culture? Did they participate in international movements? What were the links and tensions between high culture and popular culture? While discussing influential works, creative individuals, and major institutions, the books in this series place intellectual and cultural history in the larger context of American society.

In this book Louise Stevenson takes up the challenge of prominent critics and theorists who have argued that culture cannot be understood by looking solely at the motives and contentions of the most articulate writers, philosophers, or politicians. This is a book on Victorianism as a culture for middle-class Americans during the Civil War and Reconstruction. It does not address Victorian culture primarily through analyzing the utterances of men like Abraham Lincoln, Henry Ward Beecher, or Walt Whitman. Stevenson focuses instead on the reception of ideas—on the parlors where books were read and on the reading habits of ordinary men and women. She shows us the patterns in domestic intellectual life, then moves on to consider the impact of "parlor life" on public institutions, including freedmen's schools and clubs for urban women. Along the way she analyzes best-selling novels, intellectual movements, and American culture as reflected in 1876 Centennial celebrations. But even when she turns to such topics, which are more conventionally associated with intellectual and cultural history, her vision remains focused on the audience for Victorian ideas. Thus, she familiarizes readers with the prevalent meanings of American Victorianism and with the currents of change in private life during a period of great public conflict.

LEWIS PERRY
Series Editor

Acknowledgments

Every scholarly book has at least three ingredients—time for research and writing, the assistance of colleagues, and inspiration. I would like to thank those people and institutions who supplied these essentials.

For time to pursue research and write, I am indebted to Franklin and Marshall College for granting me a sabbatical leave and a year's leave from teaching. In addition, the college Committee on Grants provided funds to defray costs and a Hackman Grant for a summer research assistant. While I was on leave, the Spencer Foundation provided me with support for work on chapters 3 and 4, and Winterthur Museum and Gardens named me a Henry F. du Pont Fellow.

For their assistance, special thanks go to the staffs at the Winterthur Library and the Shadek-Fackenthal Library at Franklin and Marshall College. In the rare books and manuscripts collections of the Winterthur Library, the librarians and archivists generously shared their knowledge of the collections and made possible investigation of the relationship between material culture and domestic intellectual life. At my home institution, the interlibrary loan department and reference department patiently responded to my many inquiries, and their resourcefulness made many questions stop nagging. At both institutions, so many librarians were vital to my work that I have named none. I hope that each one reading this passage realizes my profound appreciation for his or her help.

An interdisciplinary work requires that an author depend more than usual on the expertise of others. I am most grateful to Stephen M. Clement, David D. Hall, Kirk Savage, David Schuyler, and Robert Scholnick, who furnished copies of unpublished papers. Appreciation also goes to Aileen S.

Kraditor, David Schuyler, and Kay Smedley Yellig, who read and criticized portions of the manuscript. In addition, Clifford Clark, David Hall, Catherine Hutchins, and Barbara Sicherman read the entire manuscript. The perceptive comments of all these colleagues made this a better book with a more explicit and precise argument. Still the book would be even stronger if I had had the time and imagination to respond completely to all their suggestions. The knowledge that they shared and the support that they offered made the phrase community of scholars have real meaning.

I also would like to thank the people involved with Twayne Publishers' American Thought and Culture Series. Lewis Perry, the general editor of the series, had faith in this novel approach to intellectual history. I wish to thank him for giving me the opportunity to write this book and for helping me shape the manuscript. Senior Editor Anne Jones supervised this project from idea to finished book, and I thank her for encouragement and good humor throughout the process.

Many people contributed technical assistance in the production of *The Victorian Homefront*. Student Marjorie Kwah helped to compile a preliminary bibliography, and Peggy Bender supervised student workers in the history department, who checked facts and duplicated drafts for mailing to readers and the publisher. John Herr photographed much of the art work. My thanks go to them for their capable assistance.

The inspiration for this book springs from debates in graduate school. Then, a certain student of material culture and I, an intellectual historian, used to argue the relative merits of our fields. In the late seventies, material culture studies seemed to be one of the waves of the future and intellectual history a backwater. As the years progressed, social historians began to reel in many of the benefits of material culture studies, and I started wondering how intellectual historians might share the bounty. *The Victorian Homefront* results from these reflections, and the student who started me wondering about material culture is now my husband. With the arrival four years ago of our daughters Lila and Katie, Philip's relationship to this book transformed. He made its writing possible by encouraging me and sharing responsibility for the children and household. So, Philip, with love and appreciation, I thank you.

Introduction

At 4:30 on the morning of 12 April 1861 Confederate cannons boomed. Their missiles bombarded the Union garrison defending Fort Sumter in the harbor of Charleston, South Carolina. Americans on the West Coast had to wait 10 days for the news until a pony express rider brought the mail, but other Americans heard about the encounter remarkably fast. Reports went to cities and towns over telegraph lines, and newspapers, in their multiple editions, put the story into the hands of readers on the same day. Then that extraordinarily effective communications system—word of mouth—took over and informed most other Americans who did not buy newspapers or did not read. Men might have learned about the Confederate assault at their jobs or enroute to or from them. Middle-class women might have heard the news from tradesmen, from friends, or from their husbands or fathers when they returned from work with the newspaper. Within the next day or two, almost everyone probably would have discussed the meaning of the event with family and friends, read editorials in the newspapers and newspaper reporters' interviews with prominent politicians, or gone to church and heard the minister comment on the confrontation.

This is just one example of how great events intrude upon everyday life. To understand extraordinary events like the Confederate bombardment of Fort Sumter, midcentury Americans drew upon the ideas that their culture held in its intellectual storehouse. To show how ideas moved from that storehouse into real life is the objective of *The Victorian Homefront*.

Many entities make up American intellectual life. No historian has yet been so ambitious as to try to recapture its wholeness. Such a book would have to encompass all the culture's participants—the upper, middle, and working classes; African-Americans; and all religious sects—and comprehend all its institutions, public and private. This book is not such an endeavor; it is an in-depth exploration of the intellectual life of one crucial group of Americans.

In my research for this study, I followed a program intended to reveal how ordinary Victorians in this country conducted their intellectual lives. First, I read published and unpublished diaries, journals, and collections of letters from all regions of the United States. Most authors were middle-class residents of towns and small cities; two were from rural farm families. While reading these materials, I noted what people discussed, where and what they read, and what institutions they participated in and supported. Because more than one-fifth of these writers mentioned reading *Harper's Weekly*, I surveyed that journal between 1860 and 1880. I also consulted periodicals with which I was not previously familiar, such as the *Phrenological Journal*. Then I read or reread all the best-sellers from these years, such as Augusta Jane Evans Wilson's *St. Elmo* (1867). Although my direct quotations from these primary sources are few, their eyewitness accounts have guided my description of the institutions that shaped their authors' intellectual lives.

In addition to exploring the ground usually covered by intellectual historians, I examined the domestic workings of Victorian life. Scholars who investigate material culture have shown that people express themselves when they decorate their homes and that the decoration of homes shapes the way people live. Analysis of material culture can reveal the ever-present but unarticulated ideas and assumptions of everyday life. My sources from the mid-century years seem to have conducted much of their intellectual life in their parlors. To learn more about the decoration of that room, I surveyed advertising cards and manufacturers' and merchants' trade catalogs of furniture, stereographs, photographic reproductions, books, and household objects; although I focused on catalogs published during the years 1860–80, I did include catalogs published from 1880 to 1885 when the catalog copy suggested little change had been made in the product.[1]

From 1860 to 1880 and throughout much of the nineteenth century, Victorians tried to dominate public discourse in the United States, and their voices often drowned out those of others. Victorians were among the innovators of their day. They created new private and public institutions, including libraries, magazines, and museums, and they reformed others, including schools and colleges. These institutions are the great-grandparents of many of the institutions that shape intellectual life to this day.

Many of the books useful for studying the years between 1860 and 1880 focus on either the Civil War and Reconstruction or the continuities of Victorian American life. Although the Civil War and Reconstruction, which directly affected the everyday lives of many Americans, dominate the foreground in any portrait of these years, I have pushed these great events aside to reveal the less dramatic but equally important happenings in the background.

This portrait of midcentury Victorian American intellectual life is concerned with the point at which cultural and intellectual history overlap. It is more than a history of how elite Victorians thought and advised other Victorians to think and act, and it is much less than an ethnographic study of Victorian folkways. It is neither a history of great ideas nor a study of the rituals of public holidays. It is a history of intellectual life, revealing how Victorian Americans recognized one another as members of the same tribe, how some of the institutions of everyday life, such as schools and parlors, embodied their ideas and purposes, and how other institutions were intended to guarantee the survival and prosperity of their world.

As primary sources from all over the United States quickly reveal, not all Victorian Americans shared the same intellectual resources for understanding their world and its events. Southerners and northerners, women and men, African-Americans and whites, big-city residents and small-town residents, Presbyterians and Methodists—all had different resources. Yet all shared one vocabulary and one set of key assumptions about life. This book will focus on the essential resources in the Victorian intellectual storehouse while also noting the different ways that different Victorians drew upon and used them.

During the past decade intellectual historians have turned to the word *discourse* to make their discussions more precise.[2] A history of discourse tells the story of discrete worlds of ideas, of groups of people in socially and historically specific situations talking among themselves. Historians often assume that participants in a discourse are among the idea-makers of their day. They were the significant individuals who largely defined, say, what republicanism meant in the 1790s, or what evangelical scholarship meant in the mid-nineteenth century. A most valuable history of the discourse of intellectuals during the 1860s and 1870s is George Fredrickson's *The Inner Civil War: Northern Intellectuals and the Crisis of the Union* (1965), which relates how one group of intellectuals changed their thinking about the nation and about their influence on its destiny.

Because this study takes as its subject a larger piece of the past than did *The Inner Civil War* and other histories of discourse, it is more properly described as a history of intellectual life. The term "intellectual life" is similar to "discourse" because of its focus on specific participants in specific historical situations. But it has a broader scope in two ways. A history of intellectual life may include an investigation of how people who were not intellectuals by role or profession participated in the intellectual culture of their times. Also, a history of discourse implies an analysis of written or verbal communication; a history of intellectual life attends to a third dimension of communications—the institutions and situations through which ideas are disseminated and received. A history of intellectual life is thus more than a history of the ideas of the age's most articulate individuals, for these individuals communicate with their publics through certain institutions and in certain situations. Therefore, historians of intellectual life have a two-fold task: to tell how people received ideas into their lives, and how the men and women who spoke for their age communicated with their publics.

Most historians of intellectual life, recently Lewis Perry in his informative *Intellectual Life in America: A History* (1984), focus almost exclusively on intellectuals and their means of communication. This study joins recent path-breaking histories of the mid-nineteenth century that attempt to describe both aspects of intellectual life. Michael Denning's *Mechanic Accents: Dime Novels and Working-Class Culture in America* (1987) tells how working-class readers understood dime novels, and Katherine C. Grier's *Culture and Comfort: People, Parlors, and Upholstery, 1850–1930* (1988) suggests how members of the middle-class interpreted the material culture of their parlors.[3]

The two major divisions of this study cover the two aspects of intellectual life. The first part describes those institutions that made up the intellectual life of Victorian Americans, who would quickly tell you that the center of their intellectual world was the home. Taking them at their word, I have organized this book to follow Victorian Americans from their homes into public life. Chapter 1 shows how Victorian women shaped intellectual life in the ways they decorated their parlors. Besides having many social functions, the parlor was also the central room for intellectual activities. The second chapter is devoted entirely to reading, which was a primary parlor activity. Chapter 3 deals with the institutions that Victorians participated in when they left their homes: literary clubs, lyceums, museums, parks, and libraries. The fourth and fifth chapters cover the educational life of Victorians from childhood through adulthood, from common school through college.

In the second part the focus shifts to the spokesmen and women of the day. Chapter 6 analyzes the key words and issues of their discourse and the differences in the ways intellectuals communicated with their publics. Chapter 7 describes the different stances of four groups of Victorian American intellectuals. While southerners were coming to terms with Confederate defeat, most northern intellectuals were embracing Victorian America and its institutions. In contrast, liberal intellectuals denigrated those institutions as havens of mediocrity. Women intellectuals were devising tactics and strategies for participation in public discourse. To conclude the portrait, chapter 8 looks at how Victorian Americans celebrated the centennial of the signing of the Declaration of Independence.

Skeptics will see this study as a mere history of institutions and the elites who sponsored them. Leaving inveterate doubters aside, let me invite other readers to view it as a more comprehensive portrait of Victorian Americans' intellectual life. Previously unperceived details of that life come to light in this study because of its novel approach and its particular combination of sources—not only diaries, letters, journals, best-selling books, and popular periodicals, but popular songs, hymns, and common school penmanship books and readers. This study does not make distinctions between private and public life. Instead of relegating analysis of museums, parks, higher educational institutions, and lyceums to the province of intellectual historians and analysis of the home, women's reading clubs, and freedmen's schools to that of social historians, this study presents an integrated analysis of these institutions, in keeping with the wide embrace of Victorian America and the consensus that supported its institutions.

I also hope to show that educated elites were participants in the cultural life of Victorian America. When I started graduate school, I was skeptical whether any intellectual ever ventured out of the ivory tower. But after studying Victorian America for 15 years, I have put my skepticism to rest. We can appreciate the special interests that elites had as elites, while also seeing how similar they were to the other members of their culture. As anthropologists have shown, even the intellectual leaders of a culture live in it, and no one can escape it. In addition, divorcing Victorian American elites from their culture overlooks the fluidity of their middle-class society and the complex interests of its members. Most intellectuals, for instance, changed their paid employment several times during their careers, and many ordinary people contributed to the intellectual endeavor of the day. The pages of all but the most prominent newspapers and journals contained the contributions of never-famous authors.

As I was writing this book, Lawrence W. Levine's *Highbrow, Lowbrow: The Emergence of Cultural Hierarchy in America* (1988) appeared in bookstores. Levine engagingly explains how the cultural distinctions "highbrow" and "lowbrow" came to be by the early twentieth century. He seems to admire the first half of the nineteenth century as "the good old days." Its cultural life, he finds, was lusty, shared, and participatory. Audiences felt free to demand that actors adjust their performances to their whims, and the works of William Shakespeare were an everyday cultural resource for both working people and the middle classes. In the second half of the nineteenth century, Levine argues, some Americans changed their understanding of culture and began to define art as something removed from everyday life. As the newly founded zoological societies of the day captured lions and tigers and let rats run in the streets, museums and symphonies caged artworks and classical music and left mundane and ordinary cultural artifacts outside their walls.

My story and Levine's differ in several key ways. We disagree about the relationship of elites to cultural life. We have also read the primary sources differently. Because of the terms on which women participated in the public life of antebellum America, I question Levine's whole-hearted embrace of that period. Finally, other differences stem from the particular focuses of the two books. By comparing public institutions such as museums and libraries to private and semiprivate institutions such as parlors and reading clubs, my study demonstrates how Victorian American public institutions could serve both elitist and democratic purposes.

The period 1860–80 falls in the middle of the reign of Queen Victoria (1837–1901), the English queen who gave her name to the second two-thirds of the nineteenth century. Although people who lived during that period had no special name for themselves, historians frequently have applied the term "Victorian" to them and to the events of both Britain and America during those years. British and American Victorians shared many ideas, and the institutional development of the two countries was similar. This book, however, is concerned only with the United States. Following the practice of leading contemporary scholarship, I apply the term "Victorian" exclusively to the largely middle- and upper-class members of the public who held certain characteristic ideas and tried to govern their lives by them.

The Victorian public defined itself primarily by its values and beliefs.[4] They seriously believed that life should be a preparation for some higher or greater purpose. Most often this purpose was religious in nature and described in terms of the beliefs of a Protestant denomination. Being "serious" meant not doing anything for its own sake; Victorians believed that every task ultimately served a moral purpose. For example, reading could uplift and educate, the study of an architectural style could recall the desirable qualities of an earlier historical period, and the practice of certain conventional behaviors could suggest an admirable inner self. Serious or moral behavior was not, however, an ideal always embodied in real life. Women might give in to their material desires and make or have made extravagant dresses; men might yield to their sexual desires and patronize prostitutes. Historians are coming to understand these lapses not as exceptions to but as integral parts of Victorian culture. Every culture has its own way of allowing people to express their humanity.

Even though people were serious, they still retained a sense of humor and had fun. At home, Victorians entertained themselves and their guests with parlor games that could be as simple as buzz, the game we know as telephone, or with elaborate hoaxes. A young Pennsylvanian tells in his diary how he and his fiancée played Animal Show. The two persuaded guests that they would see an animal of their choosing when they looked through a drapery. A gullible guest entered the viewing room, parted the draperies of a tabletop tent, and discovered merely a backlit self-reflection in a mirror. Once in the know, the duped person added to the hoopla by helping to raise the expectations of the next victim.

Victorians also enjoyed stories that poked fun at those who took the conventions of Victorian life too seriously. In *The Adventures of Tom Sawyer* (1876), Mark Twain (Samuel Clemens) contrasted the underlying virtue of the hero with the superficial values of the townspeople who merely practice propriety. Humor columns were also standard features in publications of all sizes—from magazines with circulations of over 100,000 to hand-copied weeklies and monthlies that schoolgirls, college men, and Civil War soldiers passed among themselves. In all these publications, the conundrum, a riddle with a pun in its answer, was a favorite form of joke. An elaborate one that southern diarist Mary Chesnut recorded for a young friend suggests the delight that punning afforded: "What are the points of difference between the Prince of Wales, an orphan, a bald-headed man, and a gorilla? Answer— Prince of Wales, an heir apparent. Orphan, ne'er a parent. Bald-headed man, no hair apparent. Gorilla has a hairy parent."[5]

Serious people made judgments using absolute standards of right and wrong. They believed that standards of morality were divine in origin and timeless in nature. People could read these laws in the Bible's Old Testament lessons and Ten Commandments and in the New Testament teachings of Jesus. To the Victorians, "civilization" was a world founded on moral law. In a civilized world, social, political, and cultural institutions rewarded the good and condemned the bad. Judging cultures by the degree to which they lived up to their ideal of civilization gave Victorian Americans a basis for evaluating their own culture as well as those of other peoples.

In the mid-nineteenth century, countries white, Protestant, and Anglo-Saxon in origin most fully embodied their ideal of civilization. Other peoples living outside the influences of civilization were thought to be savages—brutish, out of control, ruled by their passionate and animal natures. Victorians called the native peoples of sub-Saharan Africa and the American West savage and uncivilized. Also uncivilized were the immigrants to the United States who were illiterate, intemperate, and fond of violent pastimes. Drunkards and prostitutes deviated from the ways of the civilized world, with its respectful, civic-minded men and domestically oriented women. Indeed, one source of the previous conundrum's popularity was its juxtaposition of apogee and nadir, of civilization and savagery. The Prince of Wales resided in Buckingham Palace; a gorilla hung out in the jungle.

Although Victorian Americans often were smugly self-confident about the superiority of their values, that self-confidence impelled some of them to action. They initiated humanitarian and educational crusades to bring the benefits of their civilization to others. During the years of the Civil War and Reconstruction, some committed men and women left their northern homes and ventured into the still-hostile South, where they founded schools and colleges to bring literacy and the tools for self-sufficiency to the recently freed slaves.

Victorians believed that civilized people should be punctual, industrious, neat, modest, and temperate—in other words, self-controlled. Self-control regulated the interaction between people, ensuring that they would be free both to compete with one another and to develop their better natures. If all were self-controlled, the world would be orderly. Individuals who worked hard would succeed because of their admirable personal traits, not because of chance. Stories and books of the period express these themes. A young person might be lucky and find a gold coin in the street, but his or her exemplary behavior with that coin, not the money itself, would guarantee success. An honest young woman might find the coin's rightful owner and so meet her perfect match. A generous young man might give the coin away to a needier youth whose father would turn out to be a millionaire. He would reward the young man's generosity with a position as a clerk in his thriving merchant firm.

Finally, Victorian Americans saw themselves as members of the middle class, which they identified as the largest and most important class in society. Henry Williams and Mrs. C. S. Jones, advisers on home decoration, defined the middle class as "great and highly respectable" and saw its members as those "who by industry and economy have amassed moderate wealth."[6] It was the hope of Victorian advisers and their audience that civilization in the United States would embody their ideals, not those of the rich or poor. The material circumstances of both the upper and the lower classes could tempt them away from desirable behavior.

At one extreme, the rich might allow their wealth to lure them away from proper, serious behavior. Best-selling novels often had wealthy men as major characters. For example, in *Sevenoaks* (1875), J. G. Holland created the hateful character of a prosperous manufacturer who treats the people of his town with disdain, refuses to recognize the obligations of charity, and ignores his wife and children. At the novel's conclusion, the manufacturer flees to Canada as a penniless and friendless fugitive from the law. A lawyer—a representative figure of the moral middle class—had successfully prosecuted the immoral rich man for stealing the plans that had made possible his manufacturing venture. At the other extreme, people could be so poor that their wretchedness blinded them to civilized standards. Victorian charities gave aid to people this destitute in quantities designed to offer help but not to discourage work. For example, families would receive necessary household items and holiday meals, but not a weekly stipend.

Nonetheless, material circumstances did not absolutely rule behavior. Those with enormous wealth were not necessarily immoral, and the poor were not necessarily virtuous. Charity workers investigated the lives of applicants for aid. If they found the applicant to be immoral, as defined by Victorian standards, they recommended no assistance, calling such a person one of the "vicious poor." The obituaries of prosperous men show that they were admired in their public lives for having had no "sharp" dealings and in their private lives for fulfilling their obligations to church, family, community, and charity.

To a large extent, but not entirely, Mr. Williams and Mrs. Jones were correct: the Victorian social world of the 1860s and 1870s was, by and large, the world of the middle class. Still, being Victorian was a matter of values and beliefs; belonging to the middle class had more to do with economic position. People could be Victorian without belonging to the middle class, or they could belong to the middle class without being Victorian. Besides a middling economic position, there are other factors that reliably predict membership in the middle class.[7]

In 1860 most middle-class men earned a living as farmers, professionals (ministers, professors, doctors, lawyers, surveyors), agents for businesses, small entrepreneurs, or clerks in small businesses. With the exception of clerks, who were mostly young men preparing for independent pursuits, middle-class men were their own bosses; their occupations allowed them large degrees of independence. Members of the urban middle class earned between $500 and $2,000 a year, whereas unskilled manual workers earned about $250 a year or less. Skilled manual workers could be middle-class if they were craftsmen who owned their own shops in a prosperous line of work. Jewelers or furniture makers were more likely to be middle-class than shoemakers or tailors, who had more modest incomes. Higher-paid middle-class men never had to rely on the earnings of wives and children and could accumulate savings and afford one or more live-in servants. Lower-paid middle-class men could not save, had little discretionary income and no servants, and had to send their wives and children to work when economic downturns, like the depression of 1873–78, caused wage cuts and, even worse, unemployment.

Even excluding male nonmanual workers in highly paid, prestigious positions—such as merchants and bankers—male nonmanual workers accumulated wealth far more frequently than male manual workers in high-paying lines of work. Stuart Blumin's research on Philadelphia shows that 62.2 percent of male skilled manual workers over 18 years of age reported owning no real or personal property in the 1860 U.S. census; merely 49.5 percent of low-paid nonmanual workers had no property. Further, merely 17.2 percent of skilled manual workers had more than $500 of real and personal property, as compared with 36.9 percent of nonmanual workers in lower paid and less prestigious positions.[8]

Since Victorians assigned distinct roles to men and women, very specific criteria were used to determine whether a woman belonged to the middle class. It was woman's duty to provide for her family's needs within the home. In their extremely popular advice book, *The American Woman's Home (1869),* the sisters Catharine Beecher and Harriet Beecher Stowe wrote that woman is the "chief minister" of the family state and that "to man is appointed the out-door labor."[9] Because almost all Victorians agreed with this general sentiment, merely a tiny percentage of married Victorian women worked for pay outside their homes. It is safe to say that, with the exception of writers and teachers, married women earning money did not belong to the middle class. If they did have paid positions, married women thought of them as vital to the support of their families, which usually were in extreme need.

Although paid employment outside the home was inconsistent with the ideal for married women, young single women were free to pursue certain employments. Some found positions in the textile and shoe factories of New England and the mid-Atlantic states. Others became teachers because of the prevalent belief that teaching was a proper job for a young woman and because teaching was one of the few middle-class jobs open to them. As many as 25 percent of the women in antebellum Massachusetts had worked as teachers at some time in their lives, usually after they completed their schooling and before they married. During the Civil War and Reconstruction years, however, new opportunities for women arose. As government offices and private businesses grew in size and complexity, they needed increasing numbers of clerks. Since offices seemed to be more desirable workplaces than factories, women entered these positions, though employers were reluctant to hire them at first.

The salaries of women teachers and clerks were so low, about one-third those of men in the same jobs, that middle-class status for women was particularly dependent on the noneconomic standards of behavior and deportment. To be full members of the middle class, unmarried working women had to be moral and serious.

Members of the middle class tended to join religious and voluntary associations. Although some Protestants, mostly Methodists and Baptists, were not middle-class, most middle-class people in 1880 belonged to Protestant churches. Membership in a Protestant congregation, especially one with a high percentage of other middle-class members, and participation in church-related activities such as Sunday schools and missionary societies were strong signs of middle-class status. Middle-class women and men also supported benevolent and charitable endeavors and many of the reform movements of the mid-nineteenth century. Temperance had the broadest support across the entire United States; other reform efforts, such as the antislavery movement, education for freed slaves, and woman's rights, drew their supporters exclusively from the North. Young men and women often joined institutions that were stepping-stones to the middle class. The Young Men's Christian Association (YMCA), the Young Women's Christian Association (YWCA), mechanics' institutes, lyceums, and other organizations permitted young people to pursue their education informally and to network with people who shared their ambitions.

To middle-class people, the term "family" referred exclusively to the social unit of a husband, a wife, and their children. In almost all middle-class families, marriage was supposed to be, and was, a lifetime bond. Family structure changed only because of birth, death, or marriage, or because a couple boarded or took in boarders.

To raise their families, middle-class Victorian parents adopted a different strategy from that of their grandparents. The predominant midcentury religious thinking included the belief that children are naturally innocent. Families believed that childhood should be an extended, protected period that allowed children to develop their innate goodness and to acquire the skills necessary for their eventual participation in the larger society. To devote more attention to each child, midcentury parents had fewer children. The birth rate in 1860 for white women surviving to menopause was approximately five children, down from seven in 1800. To limit family size, members of the middle class tended to marry in their midtwenties and to practice sexual continence.

Although only a tiny number of Americans, less than 2 percent, went to college, most middle-class families informally pursued education as a lifelong endeavor. Intent on self-improvement, they read purposefully, attended public lectures sponsored by lyceums, joined reading groups, and enrolled in summer institutes. To be middle-class was to be literate. Because of the importance parents placed on education, they did without the potential wages of their children. Most middle-class boys and girls completed the elementary grades, and some received a high school education. In Philadelphia in 1860, 78 percent of 15-year-old children with fathers in high-paying, prestigious nonmanual positions and 67 percent with fathers in low-paying, low-prestige, nonmanual positions attended school, compared with 49 percent of 15-year-old children with fathers in high-paying manual jobs.[10]

Increasingly in the midcentury years, middle-class families lived among other middle-class families in residential neighborhoods distant from urban business and manufacturing sections. Families also began to move to the suburban areas that were accessible to the central cities by horse-drawn streetcars. For most middle-class families, the goal was to own a single-family house, and in fact, during the 1860s and 1870s home ownership became a real possibility for more and more of them. The middle class was increasing in both size and prosperity as real wages increased.

Moreover, to families who could not afford a single-family house, middle-class suburbs and urban neighborhoods offered a variety of housing forms, including townhouses, apartment houses, boardinghouses, and double houses. To stretch the husband's salary, young couples frequently boarded with relatives, or they took in boarders themselves once they owned a house. In some cities as many as 25 percent of families had boarders. Taking in boarders was one way that middle-class women could add to the family income without leaving their homes.

Middle-class families expressed their Victorian beliefs in the ways they transformed their houses into "homes." In lectures, as well as in gospel hymns, novels, and sermons, the home was often called "a little heaven on earth." Outside its doors, people encountered fear, violence, and temptation. Inside the walls of the home, it was believed, God's love was manifest in husbands' love for their wives, and in parents' love, especially that of mothers, for their children. From these protected and nurturing homes, people ventured forth to make the world a better place. In her *From Attic to Cellar* (1879), Mrs. Maria Oakley described the impact of home and family: "God has placed us in families. Let us feel and prove ourselves grateful for so great a gift, and remember, that from these families, of whatever grade or position, all the influence of the world comes."[11] Mrs. Oakley and other Victorians believed that boys would eventually influence the world directly through their adult jobs and voluntary activities, and girls indirectly in their role as mothers, the makers of the next generation's ideal homes.

The idea that women influenced the world through their children had arisen during the American Revolution, when some statesmen and some well-educated women were arguing for reform of women's education. What was new in the Victorian period was that this idea, called "republican motherhood," became accepted throughout the middle class. In the first years of the Victorian period, women antislavery activists and moral reformers had argued that women should participate in reform activities, such as those of temperance and antislavery associations because they could extend the moral values of the home to the world. By 1873 the proposition that the home influenced the world had become so accepted that a woman reformer could argue that the sons of enlightened mothers were "benevolent, just, and virtuous individuals whose animosities and selfish passions will never call for the conflict of sword and bullet, and whose moral rectitude will make jails and prisons, brothels and dramshops impossible evils."[12] A few women went further and used this idea to argue for the enfranchisement of women. Giving women the vote, they believed, would extend their influence directly to the world and correct its wrongs.

Most women found that the concept of republican motherhood helped them to gain control over their own lives. They took charge of the education and discipline of their children and the management of their homes. Since Victorian men increasingly worked at a distance from their homes, women assumed responsibility for the purchase of most consumer goods, including furnishings and food. By midcentury women had assumed primary responsibility for the decoration of their homes. As they exercised this new responsibility, their influence would be felt in the private lives of Victorians and would have far-reaching effects on the public world. Mrs. Henry Ward Beecher, the wife of one of the most influential preachers in mid-Victorian America, told women that there was no "higher, nobler, more divine mission that in the conscientious endeavor to create a *true home*."[13]

one

Around the Parlor Table

All Victorian houses had parlors. Northern and southern families had parlors, as did western and midwestern families, rural families and urban families, Protestant and Catholic families, middle-class white families and African-American families. The houses of both the lower and upper middle classes had parlors. As the household advice book authors Mr. Williams and Mrs. Jones observed, a parlor could be either "the elegantly furnished apartment of some lordly dwelling, or the one room of the poor mechanic."[1] A family of modest means whose house had first floor rooms only for eating and preparing food showed its Victorian aspirations when the first room that it added was a parlor. The houses of very well-to-do people had so many rooms that the many functions of the parlor often were divided among a library, a music room, an art gallery, and an upstairs study. Although a moderately prosperous family could not afford a house with so many special-purpose rooms, it could often afford one with two parlors, one for family use and another for entertaining guests and more formal occasions. Whether formally or informally used, whether elegantly or simply decorated, all parlors had similar purposes.

Victorians could not have been Victorians without their parlors. Here families assembled, met their guests, and entertained themselves and others through conversation, playing games, putting on plays, viewing stereographs, singing and enjoying music, writing letters, and engaging in the paramount parlor activity, reading.[2]

The parlor was Victorian in the sense that it was a serious setting for serious events. Although they gave immediate pleasure, every parlor entertainment and every decoration had the potential to remind people of the

1

ultimate world to which they belonged. A midcentury household adviser suggested the overriding intellectual dimension of parlor life when she wrote that the room was to be pleasant, that it should have "a good light, quiet, beauty of surroundings, and occupation for the mind." The first items in her list form the setting for the last, "occupation for the mind," which was clearly the most important purpose of the room.[3]

The focal point of parlor life was its center table. In the universe of the parlor, it was the sun pulling family members and their visitors into its orbit. Surrounded by several chairs and sometimes a sofa, it usually stood about 30 inches in height and was round and covered with a rich-looking fringed cloth. The table cover and the deeply colored rug on which the table stood added visual interest to parlor decor. The table held some combination of various books and objects: a Bible, recent magazines, a carte-de-visite album, travel books, books of poetry, or a stereoscope and slides (stereographs). Some parlors and their center tables were much more modest. In Montana in 1864 a pioneer family considered itself settled when it had converted a flour barrel into a center table and placed upon it the family Bible and photograph album.[4]

Although a kerosene lamp usually sat on the center table, a large lamp often hung above it. Some homes still relied on oil and kerosene lamps at this time, while recently constructed or remodeled ones had built-in pipes that supplied gas fuel to the parlor lamp. Parlor tables may have been placed in the centers of rooms so that people would not bump their heads on the lamps above them. Only expensive homes sometimes had wall-mounted gas lighting devices set at a height to make reading in chairs beside them possible. The kerosene- or gas-fueled lamp on or over the center table helped to make domestic intellectual life a communal experience, for after dark people gathered around its light.

One wall of the parlor sometimes had a fireplace and hearth, which gave the room a second focal point. Fireplace mantels often contained recessed mirrors and frames with various shelves, nooks, and crannies to display objects. Freestanding shelves, sometimes called whatnots, stood in corners, in architectural niches, and in other decorative places against the walls and were used for the storage and display of books, ornaments, and mementos.

The style and arrangement of parlor furniture suggest that Victorians valued individuals but wished to contain any expressions of individualism within the family group. To furnish their parlors, families often purchased an entire set or suite of furniture, consisting of a sofa, two armchairs, and several side chairs. The armchairs and two or three of the side chairs usually surrounded the center table. The sofa was either placed at the center table or set apart for private conversations.

The placement of separate chairs around a center table allowed groupings to change as people varied their activities. They could move their chairs to be with others or to be alone; unity and diversity were simultaneously possible. One person could read aloud while some listened and others pursued quiet activities, such as sewing or looking at stereographs. Grownups could converse while sitting in one grouping while children gathered in a different part of the room to amuse themselves.

The various furniture forms within a parlor suite reveal one way that Victorians recognized gender differences. Parlor suites usually contained at least one large armchair with full arms. Manufacturers liked to call it a gentleman's or "gent's" chair and frequently paired it with a smaller lady's chair. The half-arms of a lady's chair accommodated women's dresses and petticoats while discouraging a slouching or unladylike posture, though etiquette required an erect posture for both men and women. Manufacturers also offered special options. When a suite contained two armchairs of the same design and size, buyers sometimes could substitute a lady's rocker for one armchair. Thus, manufacturers did not always consign women to a lady's chair of uncomfortable design.

Although parlor suites had other special-purpose chairs, none were designed for children. They sat on full-sized furniture, and when their elders preempted it, they sat on footstools. Other chairs, however, designed for special activities. In the mid-1870s, for example, manufacturers began to offer a reading chair as part of a parlor suite. Also called a student chair, it was a low-backed, upholstered armchair that supported the arms and the back. Parlor suites thus recognized individual seating differences and preferences. But their uniform design suggested that all individuals were part of a whole no matter where they were seated.

The design of the parlor sofa confirms that Victorians wanted the material world to direct people into desired behavior. Sofa backs were curved so that two people had to face one another. Sofas thus were called tête-à-têtes—têtes, for short—the French phrase for an intimate conversation. Nevertheless, neither the design of objects nor the names that manufacturers gave them absolutely controlled people's behavior.

In addition to unity and diversity, another dualism characterized parlor life: historicity and contemporaneity. Furniture catalogs of the 1860s and 1870s all display furniture styles related to historical periods. Among the more popular styles were Gothic, Renaissance, and French Empire. By choosing a suite in a particular style, buyers were expressing their personal taste. But their choice set them apart in a superficial way because all these furniture styles were associated with a European historical period or civilization, all buyers were choosing a fundamentally similar style of furniture. Each style reflected cultural creativity, religious unity, or the glory of empire.

Although they were linked to the European past through the historical references of their designs, parlor suites were very much contemporary creations. Craftsmen's shops serving local and regional markets had largely disappeared. Furniture factories mass-produced parlor suites, and steam-powered vehicles carried them quickly to the outlets of a national marketplace. Technological innovation and new manufacturing methods made shopping by catalog more popular. Although Victorians chose furniture that depended on these technological developments, they expressed their sense of beauty and comfort in the styles of past times and places.

Wall decorations, including window hangings, paintings, portraits, and reproductions, added another source of visual and intellectual interest to parlors. Pictures of Victorian parlors show a profusion of objects; it is easy to conclude that most Victorians found accumulation irresistible. They liked to decorate, often in overabundance, with photographs of their families, reproductions of paintings or statues, items from the natural world, and souvenirs from their travels. Recognizing this predilection among their readers, many advice book authors cautioned that parlors could degenerate into scenes of "cheap and vulgar display."[5]

Because few people could afford original portraits, most families displayed photographic portraits of themselves, their official image for the world to see. Illustrating the qualities that Victorians respected and personalizing the parlor in a particular way, photographs gave their ideals a visual presence. For instance, the group pose confirmed family unity.

To modern observers, most of these photographs appear formal and stiff. Victorian seriousness worked against the candid, casual pose, and presnapshot technology required that subjects hold themselves still for long moments while negatives were exposed. To be photographed, usually in a studio, Victorians wore their best clothes. Portraits of individual family members focused attention on their particular characteristics, which were usually conventionally expressed. For instance, Victorian husbands were supposed to be dignified and prosperous, wives beautiful and pure, and babies innocent. Victorians prized an individuality that conformed to accepted ideals.

Other objects of parlor display suggest the harmony that Victorians thought existed in nature and between nature and civilization. On the shelves of étagères and on fireplace mantels, Victorians displayed seashells, mineral specimens, and fossils. Aquariums and terrariums also contained naturalistic displays. Frames of pine cones surrounded pictures, and arrangements of dried flowers and leaves adorned tables and shelves. Photographs show how people followed the advice of household advisers and arranged plants so that their vines wound around windows as a sort of natural drapery. The skillful use of natural objects was an economical way to decorate. The woman of the house could show skill in converting natural objects into household decoration. For the housewife of modest means, pine cone frames and plant draperies extended her decorating budget. If she was quite well off, natural objects showed that the main principle governing her decoration had its roots in morality, not the marketplace.

Although Victorians condemned the savagery of uncivilized peoples, they saw much that was worthy of emulation in the natural world and its plants and animals. Even after the publication of Charles Darwin's *On the Origin of Species* (1859), most Victorians still thought nature God's creation. Victorians associated parlor decor from the natural world with a larger world of meaning and believed that all elements of the temporal world suggested or stood before a larger moral and divine world of meaning. Therefore, according to *Cassell's Household Guide*, "The study of all animal and vegetable life presents to the mind a special and elevating influence in addition to the interest it excites."[6] Here, the word *interest* suggests that people looked at a natural object and associated it with something larger. The seashells, mineral specimens, and fossils of parlor displays recalled the larger, timeless order of the universe before humans were created. The "elevating" influence of these objects suggested that they were morally ennobling and related to a God-given standard of right.

The use of natural objects in parlor displays also reflected the harmony that Victorians believed existed between civilization and nature. By placing natural objects in their homes, they domesticated nature. Its beauty was present in family life and contributed to the home's influence on the moral development of its residents. Victorians presumed that nature shows God's benevolence in the way it provides for all the needs of its plants and animals. Similarly, they believed the parlor could meet all the intellectual and moral needs of its occupants.

Paintings, sculptures, and other artworks also filled parlors. Although few families could afford original paintings, most could purchase inexpensive reproductions selected from the huge number available in the marketplace. By the 1860s manufacturers had learned how to make high-quality color reproductions of paintings through a process known as chromolithography, and publishers were offering an incredible variety of art to the public at low prices. The 1868 catalog of Louis Prang, one of the most successful publishers in the United States, listed chromolithographic reproductions—chromos for short—of European and American paintings at prices ranging from $1.50 to $10.00. Catalogs included both timeless masterpieces and works that reflected the aesthetic of the Victorian period. Any art was acceptable in the parlor if it had a serious purpose. Prang's catalog included religious subjects, such as Correggio's *Magdalena*, American scenes by American artists, such as Albert Bierstadt's *Sunset* and two of the most popular chromos of the day—an image of several chickens at barnyard play, and Eastman Johnson's *The Barefooted Boy*, based on John Greenleaf Whittier's poem of the same name.

Prang's competitors offered a similar selection but often did not attract the best contemporary artists. Chromos in the Continental Publishing Company catalog of 1880 fall into several categories: American views of scenic rivers, such as the Miami in Ohio, and the Mississippi; rural scenes of farm animals or decaying bridges; European scenes, such as *The Alps in Twilight* or *Moonlight in Norway*; hunting scenes of fishing or duck shooting; still lifes of fruit; portraits of women admired for their devotion, such as Beatrice de Cenci, or the vestal virgins; pictures evoking the innocence of children; and Biblical scenes, such as the return of the Prodigal Son, or a woman clinging to the cross of Jesus. The catalog described these pictures as "rich in color" and "pleasing" and noted that some present a "natural appearance." Other advertising copy suggested that buyers may have wanted desirable artworks to act on their memories and to evoke associations. Catalogs touted some paintings as "historical," suggested that others might "recall pleasant memories," and remarked that still others were particularly "charming and instructive." The painting *Unconscious Sleeper*, which depicted a young boy sleeping in a chair, was described as "instructive as a work of art and an amusing copy from nature."

Portraits of famous contemporary and historical figures also had appeal. In some homes so many portraits looked out from shelves and walls that they must have outnumbered not only the pictures of family members but also those of all their friends. Some arbiters of taste condemned the display of portrait busts but most recommended that they be restricted to home libraries, where the display of busts would make it seem "as if poets and gods visibly haunted the place of thought."[7]

These portrait busts, photographs, and engravings, all available in a variety of sizes, usually represented men famous for their literary, musical, political, or military achievements. Some busts had a limited popularity. For example, a philosophy professor at Yale College put Kant in his study. Other images had a wider appeal. Shakespeare was by far the most popular literary figure, and his bust often presided over bookcases and desks. Catalogs offered portraits of prominent American authors such as William Cullen Bryant and Henry Wadsworth Longfellow, as well as English authors, including John Milton and John Ruskin.[8] Catalogs also listed portraits and sculptures of national political figures such as George Washington, Andrew Jackson, Daniel Webster, and Abraham Lincoln. Even during the Civil War, publishers offered portraits of a few prominent southerners, namely, the Confederate president, Jefferson Davis, and Gen. Robert E. Lee. Perhaps publishers thought some of their goods would reach the South. It is more likely, however, that they thought their lists would have as wide an appeal as possible in the North if they included some portraits that were attractive to southern sympathizers (known as Copperheads).

Catalogs also included portraits of women, though these numbered less than one-fifth the number of those of men. Portrait-worthy women were usually wives of famous men, Mary Todd Lincoln, for example. Women portrayed in portraits almost always had either achieved fame as actresses or singers or had an inherited position, Queen Victoria, for example.

When Victorians brought images of famous men and women into their parlors, they were bringing the influence of public figures into the private realm. There they served as models, especially to the young, and they represented yet another way to reconcile individualism with community values. Portraits and busts taught lessons of individual achievement. People admired George Washington's leadership skills as a president and an army commander, and they admired Jenny Lind for the sweetness of her voice. But they, like most of the great people the Victorians venerated, merited special reverence because they subordinated private interest to public service. George Washington left his family and Mt. Vernon to lead the nation in both war and peace. Jenny Lind gave to charity much of what she earned from her extremely lucrative singing tour of the United States.

As children grew up, the portraits of famous people in their parlors wordlessly reminded them of these conditions of true fame. Boys probably understood that they should be like Washington and serve their nation. In the words of a New York University commencement song of 1860:

> And we must be good citizens,
> And spout in Congress Halls,
> And we must be good citizens,
> Fight wrong—give right to all.[9]

The message for girls, however, was more complicated. Although public achievement had been possible for Jenny Lind and historical figures such as Joan of Arc, everyone knew that they were the exceptional few. Most Victorians expected girls to realize that the call to take responsibility for others did not require them to spout in Congress Halls but to participate in philanthropic and benevolent activities. And midcentury women did participate in many such activities. They provided relief and holiday meals to needy families, founded homes for orphans, and sewed for hospitals and Civil War soldiers. Moreover, in the late nineteenth and early twentieth centuries, many women who had grown up in midcentury parlors found new ways of serving the public in social service, government, and academic careers. Parlors and portraits had encouraged the serious-mindedness that led them to think of themselves as responsible members of communities.

It is possible to say that midcentury trade catalogs offered Victorian buyers no object that did not reinforce or at least fit into the serious purpose of the parlor. The trade catalogs of furniture manufacturers and chromolithograph publishers contained no furniture in the style of a period known for its immorality or irreligion, and no morally offensive artworks. Publishers did not offer portrait busts and photographs of notorious criminals, tyrants, or rulers—with the interesting exception of Napoleon I and the Empress Josephine.[10]

When Victorians looked at portraits of Napoleon and Josephine, they may not have learned exclusively undesirable lessons. Some may have been reminded of the Napoleonic code of laws which reformed the feudal legal systems of the countries that Napoleon conquered. Or Napoleon may have been admirable to Victorians because of his rise from obscurity to a position, for a brief time at least, as the most powerful man in the world. Their portraits may have brought to mind the elegance of Napoleon and Josephine's coronation, his great abilities as a military commander, or his conquest of Europe. Different associations with the life of Napoleon confirmed or subverted parlor lessons; as a whole, however, Napoleon's life seemed to caution schoolchildren that his ambition led to defeat in the snows of Russia and on the battlefield of Waterloo. His exile on Elba taught that a lonesome end awaited individuals with unrestrained ambition. Although the image of Napoleon put a potentially subversive presence in the parlor, it could also be taken as a warning against elevating personal ambition above the common good.

The decoration of the parlor set the scene for the intellectual life that Victorians actively pursued through their entertainments. Parlor tables held a display of books, Bibles, carte-de-visite albums, and stereoscopes. All these objects were for entertainment, but in the Victorian sense—entertainment always had a serious purpose.

Bibles, the most frequently displayed books on center tables, were often large and heavy. Elaborate, leather-tooled covers with religiously inspired gilt decoration were held closed by brass clasps and locks. By displaying these imposing volumes, families may have been showing that religion was integral to their lives, not something reserved for Sunday and formal church services. Still, some families were very religious, attended church once or twice on Sunday, and never read the Bible as a group. The real life of Victorian families often differed from the ideal life that they displayed. Thus, the presence of the Bible on the parlor table must be considered as a symbol of family religious life.

On parlor tables, the Bible held the central position. Its presence reinforced the religious meaning that most Victorians attributed to their homes. A young woman in Worthington, Ohio, looking forward to her own marriage and her own home, commented in her diary that a Christian home ought to be "a little heaven on earth."[11] This diary writer and many other Victorians believed that the family and the home were divinely ordained institutions. People chose architectural styles and home decorations that had religious connotations, and they created a home life that nurtured the Christian development of family members.

Ministers described the ideal form of family worship in advice books.

They recommended that time be set aside for worship in both the early morning and evening. On Sunday, besides attending a church service, the family would have a special hour for Bible reading. The mother would prepare for home worship by gathering the children and readying the Bible and prayer books. The father would conduct these worship services, for he was the minister in the home. He would read from the Bible and lead other members of his household in prayer.

This model of paternal leadership of home religious life looked to the past. In agricultural seventeenth-century New England, husbands, who usually worked where they lived, led family worship. Prayers and lectures were supposed to encourage children to be concerned about the destiny of their souls and to recognize God's direct effect on their lives. By the nineteenth century, however, because of the demands of fathers' work and schedules, most families no longer held morning and evening family devotions. By 1860, in towns and cities, most fathers left their houses early to work ten hours a day, six days a week.

The realities of the midcentury social world complemented general beliefs about women and their special natures in such a way as to support a more active role for mothers in their children's religious education. In fact, the elaboration of women's role in religion was general in all Christian denominations at midcentury. Catholics created a greater role for women as Mary, the Mother of Jesus, rose in importance as a figure of worship. In 1854 Pope Pius IX had announced the doctrine of the immaculate conception whereby Mary was the one human being to have ever been conceived without sin. Protestant ministers taught that women were especially pious because of their supposedly tender hearts. This piety combined with women's assumed innate ability to communicate with children to make them effective religious teachers.

In general, the more informal the religious practices of the home became, the more active a role women had. When women acquired the primary responsibility for domestic religious life, they enhanced its lessons through their choice of parlor decorations. And they led domestic religious life by singing hymns and popular songs and by reading religious books to their children.

In their parlors both Protestant and Catholic Victorian women created a world in which religious symbolism was omnipresent. Differences between the decorating practices of the two groups were slight. Catholic parlors sometimes contained a space designed to be a family altar or chapel; Protestant homes usually did not. In all Victorian homes, religious images appeared on the walls, whatnot stands, and mantels. In fact, religious display reached such an extreme in some Protestant parlors that one self-appointed arbiter of domestic taste was moved to say that parlors now seemed "more . . . a penitential chapel than . . . a place for cheerful repose."[12] The commentator, an extraordinarily pious Congregationalist, did not want homes to be less religious. Rather, he was objecting to a change in the practice of Protestantism.

From the Reformation of the seventeenth century until the middle of the nineteenth century, all Protestants, except high-church Episcopalians, had interpreted the Biblical injunction against worshiping images of the divine in a wide-reaching way. They suspected that religious imagery, whether displayed in church or at home, in statues, stained-glass windows, or religious paintings, distracted worshipers by placing a barrier between them and the word of God. By the 1860s, however, all but the most conservative Protestants had realized that visually appealing religious decoration could enrich worship by adding another dimension to it and appealing to people's sense of beauty. As the production of consumer goods increased after the Civil War, Protestants cast aside the restraint of their ancestors, ceased to look upon religious paintings and sculptures as graven images, and turned their parlors into multisensory religious experiences.

Domestic religious display taught both directly and indirectly. To children familiar with Bible stories, a chromolithograph of a scene from the Bible, such as the return of the Prodigal Son, sent a cautionary reassuring message. Although some children erred and left their father's houses, paternal love would greet them when they returned to beg forgiveness. The message conveyed by a reproduction of one of Raphael's Madonnas was more subtle. The Madonna could suggest merely a beautiful woman, or her beauty might remind children of their mother and of the divine source of their mother's household work.

Women also filled their parlors with religious objects that they made themselves. For example, women learned from magazines and books about hair art, a peculiar midcentury form of decoration. They braided and wove hair into religious symbols such as crosses and anchors that were then mounted, framed, and displayed. If the object was a mourning piece, the hair often was taken from the dead person and braided into the shape of an urn or a weeping willow. These objects were not only supposed to express grief but were intended to evoke thoughts of eternal life.

Domestic religious life included music, and during the midcentury years families purchased parlor organs to enhance home worship. A smaller, less expensive relative of church organs, the parlor organ was directly associated with the public culture of churches and revival meetings. Bringing the organ into the home strengthened the continuity between church-based and home-based religion. The largest piece of furniture in the parlor, the parlor organ had an imposing presence. Illustrations in trade catalogs and on the covers of sheet music showed customers that they could use their parlor organs to intensify and extend domestic religious experience. Their style was usually Gothic, which had strong religious associations with the cathedrals of the Middle Ages. Elaborately carved organ-cases contained shelves and nooks for the display of both religious and secular objects. But the objects, such as family photographs or statues, gained meaning from their places on these minialtars of the parlor.

During musical entertainments, families expressed their religious feelings and beliefs and celebrated the family as an institution. While enjoying themselves singing, families also learned both explicit and covert religious and moral lessons. In the image of the ideal home, musical entertainments united the family and gave women leadership roles. Wives and daughters played while sons and fathers listened or sang along. When her husband Rutherford was president, Lucy Hayes held Sunday evening hymn sings at the White House. Sometimes Secretary of the Interior Carl Schurz played while Mrs. Hayes led the hymn singing. In the homes of the famous as well as the not so famous, religious activities appealed to both head and heart, reason and emotion. In musical performances, mothers and daughters played to the emotions and a sense of beauty, while in prayers and Bible readings, fathers preached the word of God and addressed the intellect and reason.

Popular songs of the day often celebrated the home and anticipated togetherness in a divine destiny. Of the top twenty songs during the Civil War years judged by sales of sheet music, the first five had nothing to do with war and were composed in the prewar years. Like "Home Sweet Home" (1823), they evoked memories that served as touchstones of stability. These songs also evoked memories of wonderful bygone days—"The Last Rose of Summer" (1813) was the number-one song of the time—and expressed feelings of sadness and regret over families being separated. When the nation was severed into the North and the South and male relatives were absent on battlefields, the families at home thought about disunity and separation. "The Vacant Chair" (1863)—number 15 of the top 20—offered consolation over the loss of a son: "We shall meet but we shall miss him, / There will be one vacant chair; . . . / We shall linger to caress him, / While we breathe our evening prayer."[13] The themes of separation and reunion were also found in love songs—such as "Lorena" (1857), number one in the South and number five in the nation. A soldier laments to his lover his death and imminent departure:

> Our heads will soon lie low, Lorena,
> Life's blood is ebbing out so fast.
> There is a future. Oh, thank God!
> Of life this is so small a part!
> 'Tis dust to dust beneath the sod;
> But there, up there, 'tis heart to heart.[14]

Perhaps as northerners anticipated reunion with their loved ones, such a song also made them think of the reunion of the North and the South. And starting in 1863, perhaps southerners, anticipating defeat for the Confederacy, could gain consolation from such an image of eventual triumph.

Popular hymns also reveal how Victorians were interpreting the Bible. Unlike their ancestors of the seventeenth and eighteenth centuries, they did not sing about a strong and angry God the Father parting the Red Sea and punishing Pharaoh. They increasingly emphasized the New Testament and the Lord Jesus. By focusing on God the Son, Victorians were embracing a gentler god who entered unobtrusively into human life. As the hymn "O Little Town of Bethlehem" (1868) says, "No ear may hear His coming, but in the world of sin, / Where meek souls will receive Him, still the dear Christ enters in."

A few woman's rights activists asserted that God has both masculine and feminine attributes, but most believers still saw Him as masculine, though in a new way. Hymns described Him as a shepherd leading His lambs, and He was often pictured in a meadow filled with animals and "flowers in beauty blending." In God's company people were not filled with awe but were happy and delighted with His love. To be a Christian was to be like Jesus, to be more loving. "His love and light fill my soul tonight." Salvation was described as yielding to His embrace or leaning on His breast. Heaven became a place of comfort, a home: "Heaven, my home forevermore." This God was the special friend of the weak, who included children, women, and the virtuous poor. In a favorite chromolithograph, *To the Cross I Cling*, a woman gazes at the top of the cross of the crucifixion as her hands extend upwards to embrace it. [15]

Because Victorians associated softness and gentleness with women, these images seem to suggest that in the midcentury years religion was becoming more feminine and less masculine. But using the words *masculine* and *feminine* to describe nineteenth-century religion is misleading. The gentler God of the mid-nineteenth century was not for women exclusively; He appealed to men as well. College professors and preachers urged male students to find a role model in Christ, who led by His example and loving persuasion and offered forgiveness freely to all His children. As a well-known hymn suggests about the promise of redemption, "There's a Wideness in God's Mercy."

The image of the forgiving Christ began to form in the early nineteenth century. From then until the 1870s, definitions of acceptable authority were changing. Committed Protestants in Britain and America became humanitarian reformers, and the Victorian public in both countries supported their efforts. They organized movements to end public executions of criminals, corporal punishment of sailors and schoolchildren, and cruelty to animals. One of the horrors of slavery that people found most terrible was the brutal physical punishment that many African-Americans received. Disapproving of corporal punishment and authority based on physical coercion, Victorians urged that affection and noncoercive incentives be used to motivate proper behavior. Model schoolteachers appealed to students' consciences, college professors sought to lead students through the power of their presence, and custodians of the insane relied on drugs to contain the violent behavior of their charges. Humanitarian reformers looked for an end to absolute monarchies and lauded the democratic revolutions of the day. A God of storm clouds and thunderbolts would no longer do; He had become a shepherd whose lambs lovingly followed Him.

Although studies of hymns and sermons have yet to show exactly when the new image of God appeared in the nineteenth century, by the 1870s the change was complete. Victorians worshiped a Christ who ruled through the power of love and who led both men and women in their serious pursuits. Religious culture had indeed become less judgmental, but it was less masculine and more feminine only if hanging a criminal within prison walls is less masculine than a public flogging.

The Bible symbolized the religious activities and meaning of the parlor; the other objects on the parlor table were secular entertainments that reflected the seriousness Victorians brought to their entertainments. The stereoscope, for instance, a popular form of entertainment from the 1860s until the rise of films in the early twentieth century, resembles a modern-day viewmaster. It magnifies two side-by-side images of one view and merges them into one 3-dimensional image. Virtually all Victorian parlors had a stereoscope. People bought stereographs for 15–25¢ apiece from catalogs, at photographers' shops, from door-to-door salesmen, and on vacation trips. Tourists could choose one of many views of the same attraction. For example, stereographs pictured the peak of Mt. Washington in New Hampshire's White Mountains from every hotel in the area and in every season. Vacationers bought the stereographs that matched their own trip and personalized them by noting on the back the date of their visit and making comments such as "as seen," or, "a good meal."

Stereographs permitted viewers to take visual excursions at bargain prices to see people and places near and far from their parlors. Sometimes people simultaneously read from tour books and viewed stereographs. Popular scenes were of natural disasters, landscapes, historical ruins, the interiors of famous houses, the birthplaces of famous people, or even the viewer's own house. Stereographs reproduced scenes from U.S. cities both large and small, western attractions such as Yosemite, and eastern tourist spots such as Niagara Falls. Stereographs of cities show their public buildings, the houses of famous people, notable parks and cemeteries, and impressive public works. For example, some Philadelphia scenes depicted are Fairmont Park, Independence Hall, Laurel Hill Cemetery, and the city's waterworks.

Stereographs were also another way to look at art, such as antique statues from the Vatican museum or contemporary statues such as those executed by the commercially successful American artist John Rogers.

Stereograph viewers shared the interest that was propelling great numbers of prosperous Americans to visit Great Britain, the Continent, and the Near East. Interest in the Near East arose both because Muslim architecture and art were strange and exotic and because the region was the birthplace of Christianity and Judaism. The popularity of stereographs showing recent archaeological digs reflects the interest that Victorians took in questions of biblical history.

U.S. government expeditions through the American West hired photographers to accompany them. Commercial stereographs from these expeditions sold well. Presumably, they satisfied the public's curiosity about the western wilderness and its spectacular natural features. The creation of Yellowstone National Park in 1872 can partially be attributed to the public demand for the preservation of its unique features that stereographs had aroused.

Stereographs tell a great deal about what Victorians found interesting. They bought scenes of Civil War battles in great numbers. These scenes usually show the landscape where a battle occurred; taken some time after fighting, they show no soldiers and no military activity. People must have appreciated these stereographs because they showed the site of an important event in which a relative may have participated. Using their imaginations, viewers could fill in the empty landscape with information they remembered from the lengthy and detailed battle reports that newspapers had regularly carried.

Stereograph purchasers looked for vast, imposing natural features with a high degree of three-dimensionality. Successful photographers learned that piles of rocks and mountain gorges were especially popular subjects, particularly if a human figure or an object related to human life appeared in the foreground. Mediating between the viewer of the stereograph and the landscape, the human form hinted at the size of the natural feature and added a point of interest. Photographers often placed a rotting rowboat on the foreground side of a mountain lake. Viewers could then compare the impermanence of human creations to the enduring quality of nature.

When people viewed little-known peoples and places in their stereographs, they were learning about new subjects while confirming their preconceptions. Stereographs of the native peoples of the western states, Canada, and Mexico sold extremely well. The survey teams sponsored by the federal government to explore and chart the West included photographers who recorded the life of almost every Native American tribe. Sharing the attitudes and preconceptions of their eastern audience, photographers usually selected and composed images to satisfy the curiosity of that audience. Although stereographs show Native American dwellings, tools, and tribal rituals, Native Americans are not depicted as they actually lived. Photographers frequently posed women with papooses, and warriors on their horses in ceremonial dress, carrying both their traditional weapons and modern rifles and staring into the distance. In stereographs, Native Americans appeared either as noble savages, destined for extinction, or as a people whose parental affection confirmed the universality of Victorian values. As they appeared in stereographs, Native Americans did not threaten the parlor and its Victorian occupants.

Despite the multitude of stereograph images available at midcentury, some subjects were ignored. Few stereographs were taken of urban workers, and the few taken of rural workers are idealized. Farmers are shown doing simple and quaint rural tasks, such as maple sugaring; they are never shown performing exhausting tasks of drudgery. As in Victorian life, the erotic was a taboo subject. Erotic images appealed to the physical passions and did not educate the moral nature. No U.S. trade catalog offered suggestive or sexually teasing stereographs, but they were available on the street—most often imported from France and Germany for clandestine purchase.

During the Civil War and Reconstruction years, photographers made no stereographs of poorer urban districts and their people. To most Victorians, the poor, especially the urban poor, were "the dangerous classes," the title of a book by Charles Loring Brace published in 1873. Images of the poor might have raised disturbing questions: What if America contained too many people who would never have parlors? What would this democratic republic become if too many voters were not educated, thinking citizens who fulfilled their civic obligations? By choosing to live in neighborhoods of people like themselves, Victorians put actual distance between themselves and the poor. The nonexistence of stereographs of the poor shows that photographers, always attuned to public taste, helped to keep the poor out of sight.

While stereographs took Victorians far from their parlors, carte-de-viste albums more often celebrated the near and familiar. A sort of photograph album, the carte-de-viste album was named after the French term for "visiting cards," which happened to be the same size (2⅛-by-3½ inches) as the photographs known as "cartes," taken for these albums. Impressive in appearance, carte-de-visite albums displayed on parlor tables sometimes had brass clasps and locks and were bound in leather, velvet, or wood inlaid with mother-of-pearl. In the mid-1860s music-box albums became popular; some played "Home Sweet Home" when opened. A new album contained 20–50 blank pages onto which were glued precut frames for cartes. By the 1860s a carte could be purchased inexpensively for as little as 10¢. Maintaining an album, however, was expensive and a middle-class luxury. The cost, including the price of an album and a sufficient number of cartes for exchange, could exceed $100.

1.1   Front elevation. From George E. Woodward, "Design for a Compact Frame Cottage," in *Woodward's Cottage Home* (New York, 1865)

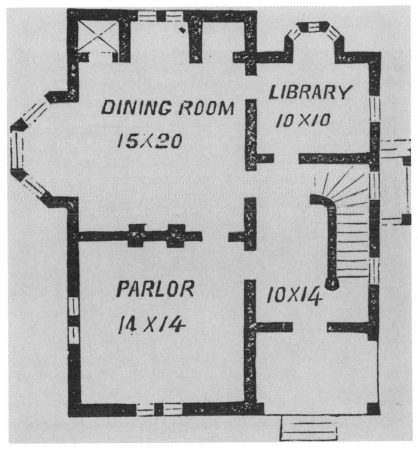

1.2 Plan of first floor. From George E. Woodward, "Design for a Compact Frame Cottage," in *Woodward's Cottage Home* (New York, 1865)

1.3 In this 1867 lithograph, *President Lincoln and Family Circle*, the chief executive reads as his wife, Mary Todd Lincoln, leans on his shoulder. The portrait of Washington, the sons in military dress, and the toddler's flag show the artist's intention to fuse parlor life with Union ideals. *Courtesy of the Lincoln Museum, Fort Wayne, Indiana, a part of Lincoln National Corporation*

1.4 The Bancrofts of Wilmington, Delaware, no doubt posed for this circa 1870 photograph, but this Quaker family's disdain for decorative excess is evident in the parlor's simplicity. There are no curtains on the windows, and the center table holds only a lamp, a few books, perhaps a Bible, and writing material. *Courtesy of the Historical Society of Delaware, Wilmington, Delaware*

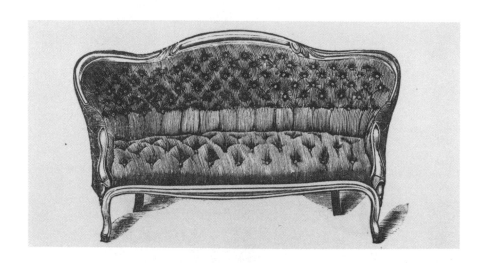

1.5 Advertisement for parlor furniture in the 1870 J. W. Hamburger & Co. catalog. *Courtesy of the Winterthur Library: Printed Book and Periodical Collection, Henry Francis du Pont Witherthur Museum, Winterthur, Delaware*

1.6 Trade card of Mason & Hamlin Organ & Piano Co. *Thelma Mendsen Collection. Courtesy of the Winterthur Library: Joseph Downs Collection of Manuscripts and Printed Ephemera, Henry Francis du Pont Witherthur Museum, Winterthur, Delaware*

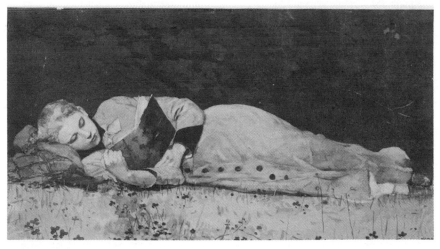

1.7 Winslow Homer, *The New Novel*, 1877, watercolor. *Courtesy of the Museum of Fine Arts, Springfield, Massachusetts*

The photographs of family members in a carte-de-visite album were some-times taken by a professional photographer and were also acquired through gift or exchange. A couple often had cartes made up several times during their marriage: just after their wedding ceremony, when their children were young, and when they were alone again in old age. Cartes also commemo-rated rites of passage, from the first portrait of an infant to the funeral dis-plays in the home parlor. Parents had their children photographed at regular intervals and added captions such as "first trousers." In an album that con-tained pictures of relatives, a particular family group was placed at the center of a larger network. Images of ancestors in an album suggested family per-manence and a respectable past. Carte-de-visite albums also depicted specific episodes in their owners' lives. Students attending academies or colleges often assembled albums during their senior year, when they requested cartes from classmates and teachers that were often personalized with autographs. Sometimes women continued their albums after graduation and noted under their friends' pictures the dates of their marriages. Capturing the years of transition from girlhood to womanhood, the albums begin with pictures of young girls and their parents and end with pictures of young women about to start their own families.

During the Civil War soldiers in both armies compiled albums to record the experience of their military units. They bought cartes of their brigades, generals and prominent officers, and scenes of battles in which they had participated. Every soldier's album contained the same purchased cartes, but exchanges with friends and the arrangement of the cartes made each album a personal creation.

Purchased cartes enhanced the meaning of albums. Commercially pre-pared cartes included views of landmark buildings, generic images of domes-tic animals, and portraits of famous people—royalty, religious and political leaders, actresses, society women, authors, and military heroes. An album owner with a cousin named Victoria, might include a carte of the queen. A wife might purchase a carte of her soldier husband's commanding general, say Stonewall Jackson or George McClellan. People also purchased cartes when they visited attractions. At Phineas T. Barnum's American Museum in New York City, midget Lavinia Warren sold $300 worth of her cartes per day when she was engaged to General Tom Thumb, another midget whom Barnum had made famous. Albums also displayed religious sentiment; own-ers could purchase cartes that illustrated "The Rock of Ages" or showed a decorated motto such as "Victory through Lord Jesus Christ."

Like stereographs and carte-de-visite albums, books were another form of serious entertainment. Victorians played parlor games such as charades and buzz and performed theatricals, but these activities were special, reserved for major occasions when guests visited and larger groups assembled. The main-stay of everyday parlor activity was reading.

A distinguishing characteristic of Victorian intellectual life was the social nature of reading. Letters, diaries, and memoirs reveal that people sat about their parlor tables and read. Sometimes reading and conversation intermingled when a reader told others about a book or newspaper article. Women and men enjoyed books with visitors, and they often discussed books in reading clubs that usually met in the members' parlors. Sometimes women knitted or did fancywork while others, often men, read to them. The images of reading found in chromolithographs and other popular sources always show men reading to women, never women reading to men, and therefore cannot be regarded as accurate depictions of everyday life. In fact, women sometimes read to men, adults read to children, and children looked at books together. Children used books as protective coloration to escape their parents' scrutiny and possible censure. When children sat apart from adults, they could pretend to be looking at an illustrated book and discussing its pictures when they might actually be enjoying themselves giggling about childish matters.

Almost every image of a Victorian parlor shows at least one book. Books appear on parlor tables and frequently on étagères and whatnots with other objects. Some parlors included either freestanding or built-in bookcases around a fireplace or window.

For Victorians, books had great symbolic importance and were a moral necessity. When people had their portraits taken at a photographer's studio, they frequently chose to pose holding books, although they could have selected any other object—for example, something connected with their work. By this choice, Victorians were saying that books held meaning for them in a way that mixing bowls and ledgers did not.

Books were pipelines to a world of meaning beyond the parlor. People had to leave their parlors to hear sermons and lectures; books brought learning home. Books aided men in getting ahead in the world and women in their domestic pursuits, and books were also morally and intellectually improving. They provided the reasoning that connected all the meanings implicit in parlors and their decorations. Books revealed why a seashell, a Bible, and a stereograph belonged to the same moral universe. Moreover, a display of books balanced the materiality of other parlor decorations, suggesting that their owners valued a world beyond the temporal one; book owners had spent some of their discretionary income on self-improvement rather than having devoted all of it to ephemeral entertainments. Books taught about the world and increased the power of the mind. Reading about human and natural history not only increased a person's knowledge but gave him or her a greater understanding of God's works. Most important, Victorians understood that desirable or moral books strengthened conceptions of good and bad. To one household adviser it seemed obvious that people reading in the parlor were filling their minds with the "beautiful, true, practical."[16] Implicit in this statement is the assumption that not all reading and not all books were beautiful, true, and practical. As we will learn in chapter 2, Victorians excluded some books from their parlors.

Furniture forms and decoration confirm that reading was an integral part of home life. Decorations on parlor bookcases and library furniture often had literary allusions. A portrait head of Shakespeare might be placed in the middle of a broken pediment over a bookcase or be applied to the middle of a library sofa-crest railing. A famous 1865 chromolithograph, *Our Great Authors: A Literary Party at the Home of Washington Irving*, showed Oliver Wendell Holmes, Sr., Ralph Waldo Emerson, James Russell Lowell, Bayard Taylor, Henry Wadsworth Longfellow, Washington Irving, William Cullen Bryant, James Fenimore Cooper, and John Greenleaf Whittier posed beneath a bust of Shakespeare. (Chapter 2 will discuss why this chromolithograph excluded women authors.) As mentioned above, a family that did not have a library room could buy a special reading chair in the same style as its parlor suite. Special stands were made to display especially large books, such as Bibles and folios of Shakespeare's plays. Some furniture companies made portable bookcases with removable shelves that were suitable for students or for families in small apartments. The 1876 Lockwood, Brooks, and Company catalog bragged that since the whole bookcase could "be taken apart in a moment," it was perfectly suited "for persons not permanently located."

Besides portraits of famous authors for display on their walls and in their albums and for viewing through stereoscopes, Victorians also decorated their parlors with ceramic plates and statues that recreated the heroes and heroines of fiction. Popular novels such as Elizabeth Stuart Phelps's *Gates Ajar* (1868) gave rise to mementos such as ceramic figurines, bookmarks, and lambrequins (decorative hangings for fireplaces and windows). British Staffordshire statues portrayed Uncle Tom with Little Eva from Harriet Beecher Stowe's *Uncle Tom's Cabin* (1852), and John Rogers created a sculpture group from the scene in Henry Wadsworth Longfellow's poem, *The Courtship of Miles Standish* (1858) in which John Alden talks to Priscilla at her spinning wheel.

Victorian books and diaries mention reading most often as a parlor activity. Probably little reading took place in bedrooms at night. Images of Victorian bedrooms almost never show lamps beside or directly over beds. Moreover, trade catalogs did not offer bedroom suites that included bedside tables.

Some fortunate Victorians could read in their libraries. Furniture catalogs confirm that libraries were for the rich and upper middle–class. Whereas catalogs advertised parlor suites in a price range within the means of almost every middle-class family, the price of library suites started at the high end of the parlor-suite range. People probably decorated library walls with the same excess of paintings, photographs, and chromos that characterized parlor decoration, for advisers recommended exclusion of artworks that could divert the imagination. Advisers thought libraries should display exclusively busts of poets and authors to remind readers of the human being behind the printed word. Unlike parlor sofas, which inclined their occupants toward one another, library sofas did not encourage conversation and ran straight across. Library bookcases, chairs, sofas, and desks were appropriately decorated. Needless to say, images of Shakespeare abounded; other decorative motifs were a globe, pen and paper, and a brush and palette.

Outside the home Victorians read whenever and wherever they had free time: in railroad waiting rooms, on trains, on benches and in gazebos in their backyards or in parks, and reclining on the grass or sitting on rocks during picnics. Still, reading outside the parlor was not necessarily an escape from the parlor's serious purpose. In *Little Women* (1868, 1869), Louisa May Alcott's best-selling novel, the young heroine chooses as her favorite daytime reading place an old three-legged sofa by a sunny window on an upper floor of her family's house. There she curls up in a comforter to read novels such as *The Heir of Redclyffe* (1853) by the British author Charlotte Yonge. Readers could draw a serious moral from Yonge's story of English family life in which the hero discovers the richness of ritual-filled religious worship. The lesson of Yonge's book fully reinforces the moral lessons that Alcott's heroine learns from her mother while she and her daughters are sitting in the parlor knitting and sewing.

Given the omnipresence of books, it is surprising that most Victorians rarely mention reading in their diaries and letters. Most men's diaries say little, and women's only slightly more, about what they read, where they read, and how they read. Diarists and letter writers usually mention reading only when a certain book has a special meaning for them. On first analysis, the absence of discussion of reading in these sources suggests that Victorians displayed books but rarely read them. The material evidence, however, suggests otherwise. Also, Victorians had a vast publishing industry and many reading clubs and lending libraries, and reading held a central place in their common school curricula. It is probable that Victorians thought reading so invaluable and read so much in their everyday lives that it resembled eating and sleeping: so accepted and regular an activity that it was taken for granted and rarely noticed.

Sitting around the Victorian parlor table, a person could be alone while being part of a group, at once an individual and a conforming member of a community. Nonetheless, during the period 1860–80 changes in thought and the material world were beginning to dilute the emulsifying power of seriousness. Opportunities arose for the fuller expression of individuality; more specifically, some people began to exclude the divine dimension from serious thought.

Some Victorians had always been dissatisfied with how others decorated their homes. They eschewed unqualified participation in the marketplace and expressed tastes that set them apart from the Joneses and the Smiths. In most societies there are always some who, because of their values, wealth, family ancestry, or social pretensions, seek to set themselves apart from the many.[17]

Not all Victorians, for instance, approved of all chromolithographs. Perhaps thinking of Prang's hens and chicks and the sleeping child in his chair, a critic warned in 1869 that "in strengthening or in forming the intellect, [chromolithographs] are of no more use than mothers' kisses or the smiling loveliness of a flower garden."[18] Such critics wanted art to do more than tug at the emotions. It should appeal, they thought, to the intellect and elevate the imagination by representing the highest achievements of civilization. Critics of chromos did not oppose inexpensive reproductions. They simply wanted people to appreciate a different kind of art, and most agreed that European art by the acknowledged masters was worthiest of attention. Harvard art professor Charles Eliot Norton endorsed the reproductions of the Soule Photographic Company of Boston. He praised the quality and diversity of its offerings, adding that the company had brought works of art "within the attainment of persons of moderate means." In its 1883 catalog, for instance, Soule offered reproductions of paintings from periods throughout the history of European art, including famous works by Van Eyck, Hals, Dürer, El Greco, Watteau, and Turner. It also offered photographic reproductions of sculpture from the ancient civilizations of Assyria and Greece, as well as contemporary works from Europe and the United States.

During the early 1870s writers on the home often spoke for those who disdained the decorating styles advertised in trade catalogs. They showed readers how they could disavow the popular taste. Such disaffection ran in two related directions: some advisers turned to contemporary aesthetic theories, especially those of the English designer Charles Eastlake, while others embraced the American colonial past and its designs. No matter what their recommendations, advisers expressed their dislike of the contemporary world by protesting both the products of modern manufacturing and the social world upon which it depended. One adviser complained that modern factories produced hundreds upon thousands of articles that turned parlors into shrines cluttered with "French and German miracles of ugliness," and he viewed with distaste immigration, which he saw as the "invasion of the Biddy tribe from the bogs of Ireland."[19]

The influential Eastlake, who recognized the merits of furniture from the past, was more concerned with aestheticism than with Victorian-style seriousness. He wanted to develop the artistic sense and so advised appreciation of the beautiful. He recommended that people look for quality objects in all lands. The display of an Indian ginger jar or a Japanese fan could educate the eye by showing "good design and skillful workmanship."[20] Eastlake never mentioned serious purpose; to him, an appreciation of art was good in itself.

The new emphasis on the aesthetic appeal of objects, on valuing them exclusively for their own sakes, meant that their moral and religious associations were becoming either irrelevant or taken for granted. In the early twentieth century the household decorators associated with the arts-and-crafts movement went even further by setting aside the decorative aspect of objects and emphasizing their function. To Eastlake's successors, furniture should be designed to function exclusively in the here and now, with no regard for the divine and eternal.

As the influence of Eastlake shows, not all Victorians agreed on how to fulfill their serious purposes. While many based their seriousness on an emotional religiosity, others, especially well-educated, religiously liberal Protestants, had more appreciation for the intellectual dimension of religion and viewed the former group as overly religious and sentimental. One significant difference between "emotional" and "intellectual" Victorians was the latter's preference for the piano instead of the parlor organ.

By purchasing pianos, families showed their status aspirations. When mass-production techniques reduced the price of pianos in the mid-nineteenth century, they stopped being the exclusive possession of the wealthy. Moderately priced pianos sold on installment plans became affordable pieces of furniture, even necessary ones, in many homes. In 1864 a New York City journalist observed what she called the prevailing piano "mania" and suggested that many a young girl was "predestined to sit and exact dreadful screechings and wailings from some unhappy instrument for at least ten years of her natural life."[21]

Unlike the parlor organ, the piano was historically linked to cosmopolitan European culture, which was supported by those highest in birth, rank, and wealth. The rectangular cases of home pianos had none of the strong religious associations of parlor organs. The music played on the piano had less to do with church services and more to do with European culture. Girls practiced the three Bs—Bach, Beethoven, and Brahms. Parents paid for piano lessons for their daughters who aspired to study music in Germany. In 1881 one young pianist, Amy Fay, published her recollections of 1869, when she studied music in Germany with Franz Lizst. Her enormously popular book, *Music-Study in Germany*, went through 20 editions by 1910.

The new preference for the piano over the parlor organ was a reflection of some Victorians becoming less religious and more secular than others. They reserved religious expression for Sunday church services and excluded it more and more from their everyday lives. The more secular Victorians were beginning to pursue culture as an end in itself rather than as a means to a serious moral world. Their numbers included followers of Eastlake and other advisers who eschewed popular taste. They thought cultural pursuits enhanced individuality, another end in itself.

Technological innovations and the development of new furniture forms also freed individuals to express themselves more fully. Thomas Edison's improvement of the electric light bulb in 1879 led to the most significant transformation of parlor life. Electric lighting freed people from the orbit of the parlor table and its hanging lamp, which had made reading after dark a social activity. With the development of the portable camera and George Eastman's introduction of roll film in 1885, amateur photography took off. Scrapbooks began to replace carte-de-visite albums as storehouses of family memories. More informal than carte-de-visite albums, scrapbooks were rarely locked shut, and photographs, newspaper clippings, and other mementos could be glued to their heavy paper pages. Photographs could show the informal side of life and capture the unique and transient. A family could take a camera on a picnic and return with an image of a child at a particularly joyful moment. In trade catalogs new furniture styles appeared that raised questions about people's seriousness. In the 1880s the Turkish or Moorish style, which evoked the exotic, often sensuous life of the Near East, became popular. Wealthy people created rooms where men could withdraw from parlor life. For instance, J. D. Rockefeller's mansion, built in 1884, had a Turkish smoking room.

Chairs designed for private reading also show that reading as a social activity was on the wane. The Marks company patented the adjustable reclining chair in 1876. In one of its late 1870s trade cards, the company boasted that its chair "combines in one a handsome Parlor, Library, Smoking and Reclining chair, a perfect Lounge and full length bed." Besides appealing to people who had limited space and needed furniture that served multiple purposes, the Marks chair also offered "Solid Comfort." Reclining in a Marks chair, people were freed from the parlor table orbit.

Comparing antebellum and postbellum pictures of people reading suggests, moreover, that some Victorians no longer feared that individual expression would threaten community. Many popular woodcut prints in books and magazines from the 1830s and 1840s had suggested unequivocally that reading was undesirable because it drew people, especially women, away from their family responsibilities. In one image, a woman reads while the baby screams, a dog nabs the ham off the kitchen table, and a husband protests. By 1870 images of reading had become much less negative. Winslow Homer's famous painting *The New Novel* (1877) shows a woman engrossed in her book while lying on a flower-speckled lawn. The dominance of the woman's physical form, which extends across the foreground of the painting, and her total absorption in the book raise questions. The picture shows no furniture and no home—merely the woman, her book, and grass and flowers. What social purpose does this woman's reading serve? Will she use her reading to support her home and its values, or will her novel subvert her home responsibilities? Homer did not answer these questions; some viewers could be reminded of their bookish unmarried aunt and would answer yes to the latter question, and others could recall a recently married, college-educated cousin and answer no. Homer himself merely painted an intriguing picture that remains neutral on these questions of individual expression.

By the 1880s it was clear that families of the future no longer would enjoy intellectual life around their parlor tables. New furniture forms, technological developments, and a more positive attitude toward individual expression made tension appear between the paired words that describe Victorian culture. In the early twentieth century the modern living room appeared in full form. The parlor had a central table as its focal point, whereas the living room had a fireplace. As Victorianism dimmed, the intellectual gravity of the parlor table was replaced by the magnetic pull of the fireplace. Families gathered around it, drawn to its warmth. In the home with a fireplace, comfort—a physical pleasure—replaced the intellectual and spiritual rewards of seriousness. As the nineteenth became the twentieth century, the parlor vanished, along with Victorian culture and its serious intellectual life.

two

Serious Reading and Reading Seriously

By 1860 almost all native-born American whites could read: more than 93 percent of men and 91 percent of women. Literacy rates were highest in the northeastern states, slightly lower in the western states, and lowest in the southern states. Most middle-class families owned books. Statistics for the Ohio frontier show that, in the antebellum period more than 50 percent of families above the median wealth level owned books, and at least 81 percent of these families owned three or more books. It can be assumed that book ownership and literacy rates were even higher for Victorian families, who belonged to the middle and upper classes, and for people living in the more prosperous urban areas.[1]

But statistics showing that literacy was almost universal and that book ownership was widespread describe the quantitative dimension of reading and say nothing about the nature of Victorian reading itself. What made reading the central activity of Victorian intellectual life, and what did Victorians hope to learn from books? In other words, what was serious reading, and how did people read seriously? The answers to these questions will reveal how Victorians came to terms with a literary marketplace that could teach very unserious lessons.

The people whom Victorians consulted about reading provide some answers to these questions. These authors, whom I will call "reading advisers," suggested how and what to read. Advice about reading appeared in household manuals written for women and in books exclusively about reading. Although there is no way of knowing whether readers followed their recommendations, advice books still reveal a great deal. First of all, advice book authors were students of the contemporary scene who observed people's actual behavior and then recommended changes. Second, advice book authors and their readers came from, or wanted to belong to, the same social and cultural group, namely, Victorian America. Third, advice books usually appear as a response to an unarticulated but real need. Far from being the off-beat ideas of a minority, they supply an actual demand. Finally, the observations of advice book authors can be compared with comments in diaries and letters to give a fuller picture of how Victorians were reading and what they preferred to read.

Reading advisers thought it necessary to describe proper ways of reading because they feared the influence of the burgeoning literary marketplace and because they perceived that their audience was hungry for this advice. Many advisers started their books with a description of olden times. Thirty years before they said, families had owned few books: a Bible, a devotional work or two, such as John Bunyan's *Pilgrim's Progress*, (1678) several standard histories, and three or four novels at most. A story entitled "Young Men a Generation Ago" in the *Phrenological Journal* for 1865 reiterated this view of a simpler past. Its author, a reader of the journal, suggested that young men of the previous generation, when not amusing themselves by attending barn raisings and apple-paring bees, read fewer books and magazines, and that what they did read consisted mainly of works of religion and American histories and biographies.

Although the past was not quite as simple as commentators imagined it, they accurately perceived that the present was more complex in at least two ways. First, reading in the rural, agricultural world of the past, where the workplace and home were one, was a social activity. Second, the abundance of the literary marketplace was a recent phenomenon, dating from the 1850s. Publishers were offering a great variety of books at low prices. Whereas in 1829 publishers thought an edition of 6,500 copies was large, by 1860 editions of 10,000 were common. And for readers who could not afford to pay between 75¢ and $1.50 for an inexpensively bound hardback book, there were story newspapers, which serialized novels and cost 5–6¢.

What commentators sensed but did not see was the changed relationship between books, their readers, and the marketplace. Before the mid-nineteenth century, reading and learning had taken place in a social world in which the male masters of the house provided intellectual leadership. As men in the antebellum period increasingly began to work at locations distant from their homes, mothers assumed responsibility for giving their children their first reading lessons. Further, the proliferation of books, magazines, and tracts gave women and children much easier access to opinions with which their husbands and fathers might disagree. Critics of what people were reading often complained about the availability of undesirable literature, pointing out that in cities and towns it could be purchased at newsstands, which were everywhere. Unlike the marketplace for furniture and home decorations, the literary marketplace was full of anything and everything that would sell.

In the antebellum years, people sometimes acted illegally to stop the distribution of offensive reading matter. Trying to block the flood of pamphlets from antislavery organizations, southerners in 1835 forced post offices to stop delivering them; in 1837 citizens of Alton, Illinois, murdered abolitionist editor Elijah Lovejoy and burned his printing press. Most citizens of course, eschewed violence and depended on readers to follow voluntarily the recommendations of older, established authorities, such as ministers, or the newer secular authorities, such as reading advisers. These advisers showed Victorians how to apply their ideals to the reality of the marketplace.

Readers consulted and presumably sometimes obeyed advisers because of the new kind of credentials they claimed. Title pages often noted that the author was a professor in a prestigious college and prefaces boasted that the book resulted, for instance, from "years of careful investigation, of actual experiences, and of a profound veneration for the Divinely instituted Home."[2] Neither inherited nor based on established social position, the authority of advice book authors was earned in a new-fashioned way: by reaching a respected position, perhaps as a professor of literature or a college president, or by showing that they had the practical experience and had done diligent research to buttress their pronouncements.

In some ways reading advisers liberated their readers; in other ways, they enforced Victorian conformity. They gave readers permission to set aside the rules of their childhood and youth and adopt new standards of behavior. With advice books in hand, people no longer had to seek guidance from elders, who frequently drew on their own outdated experience. Reading advisers made it possible to avoid asking another person for recommendations, thereby implying that that person's taste and knowledge were superior—a public show of deference was an embarrassing act in a democratic age. Buying and reading an advice book were impersonal, private acts, and nothing bound the reader to obey its words.

The popularity of advice books also shows that people wanted to conform. Readers wanted to know how books could help them be serious and Victorian. For some, advice on how to be Victorian was advice on how to get ahead. Advice books on how and what to read were a subgenre in an immense field of how-to books. The New York publisher S. R. Wells offered a series of "Works for Home Improvement," including Amelie V. Petit's *How to Read: Hints in Choosing the Best Book*, as well as *How to Write, How to Talk, How to Behave, How to Do Business, How to Sing, How to Conduct a Public Meeting, How to Paint, The Right Word in the Right Place, The Temperance Reformation, How to Raise Fruits, Thoughts for Young Men*, and *Aims and Aids for Girls*.

These titles suggest that buyers cared about more than how to get ahead materially. The final criterion of success in Victorian America was how you appeared to other people, on and off the job. Many of the titles in the above list suggest this concern. Reading was crucial in a twofold way: books could help you improve yourself morally and intellectually, and they reflected who you aspired to be.

But reading advisers were ambivalent toward books. Although they hoped that readers would use them as aids to moral and intellectual growth, they also worried that books would overpower readers and suppress such growth. Advisers frequently used food metaphors to express what a natural part of life they considered books and reading to be. Books, they suggested, could be nourishing but might be poisonous. Recommending a balanced diet of reading, advisers warned against addiction to one author. Gorging on one author's works might lead a reader to assume the characteristics of the author or his creations; the author's mental world would become the reader's real world. Some reading advisers warned that an immoral book was like a poison; they would cite the example of the eighteenth-century French philosopher Voltaire, who most Victorians considered an atheist, to prove that one book could ruin a life. Other advisers worried that readers would stuff themselves on the inexpensive abundance of the literary marketplace. Yale College president Noah Porter, one of the most enlightened critics on the subject of what to read, suggested that modern readers might develop "intellectual dyspepsia."[3] There was a danger that books would become mere articles of consumption. Advisers guided readers toward gaining moral and intellectual sustenance from reading.

Underlying the reading advisers' worries about whether books or readers would dominate the other was the Victorian concern over individual growth. In a serious world, books helped people develop their individuality. Advisers wanted readers to dominate their books, to take control of the reading process by choosing serious books and reading them seriously. All readers, advisers hoped, would share the intentions of a Pennsylvania woman who wrote in her diary, after receiving a packet of new books, "Now I shall have plenty of new matter to pry into. New & grand thoughts & theories to store up in my mind for present & future use."[4]

Besides contributing to personal growth, books also had a social purpose. Advisers recognized that the social necessities of parlor life should inform a reader's choice of reading matter; people had to be aware of the authors and books alluded to in polite conversation. In most families, reading provided some of the substance of everyday conversation. Family members read aloud jokes and articles from weeklies, and in the 1870s the parlor card game Authors was popular. Literature was often applied to the real world. As a young farm boy of the Midwest, Hamlin Garland was inspired by John Milton's *Paradise Lost.* Pretending to be Satan, he harangued his team of wagon horses so vigorously that they ran away. In an Iowa farm family that avidly read

Dickens's novels, a sister described a visitor as standing "with an old hood tipt on her head [and] an old coat of Mr. Smiths over her slim skirts reminding me of Davy Coperfields Aunt Betsy." A more educated letter writer, a major in the Union army, mentioned in a letter to his family in Delaware that he "might insert two lines of Ovid here to verify my feelings. I suppose you know them."[5] In other words, effective communication with friends and family drew on shared literary knowledge.

In the ideal parlor described by reading advisers, people discussed good books exclusively. These books followed nature's truth in their description of human affairs and character. They told about "good deeds, good men and noble thoughts."[6] Good books did not subvert the social or intellectual life of the parlor. For readers who did not know exactly what books to buy, advice books often listed recommended books. One advice book even described four different home library collections to fit budgets ranging from $25 to $100.

Reading advisers advocated active reading. When readers took the time to digest the meaning of books, they were nourished by them. Advisers urged readers to fix their attention on a book and to devote solid hours to reading. One or two evenings a week, they recommended, was minimal, and an efficient woman, should be able to spare two hours every morning. But if no regular time was available, it was important that people read whenever and wherever they could. Women were told to read between cooking chores and while rocking their babies, men during their leisure hours in the evening and on Sundays.

Readers were to draw meaning from books by comparing, criticizing, and generalizing from them. They were advised to read aloud to discover an author's style and to keep a blank book at hand to record significant passages or facts. Advisers told them how to create social situations that encouraged reading. A family could fill winter evenings by reading aloud a nonfiction best-seller like Elisha Kane's *Arctic Explorations* (1856). Geographies and maps could be used to illustrate and expand on the book. Then curiosity would suggest what other related books to borrow from a library. Friends could pursue a course of reading when visiting one another. Or people could form reading clubs and circles to bring together old and young, men and women, in a program of serious reading. Because advisers encouraged people to read more, they probably thought that people were not reading enough. Or perhaps they worried that people were too often reading merely for entertainment. The ideal reading practices they advocated reflect midcentury middle-class life: Victorians obviously had more leisure time and more entertainments tempting them away from serious occupations than did their grandparents.

Advisers agreed that history and biography should come first in any course of reading. These genres were based on facts which supplied the building stones for mental development. Young people could benefit from reading fictional works with morally upright characters drawn true to real life. Such books would stir young readers' interest and lure them into more serious reading. Travel books, geographical books, and works in natural science were also highly recommended because they increased general knowledge. Young readers, especially boys, might become interested in natural history. As collectors of fossils, shells, and other natural specimens such as Indian arrowheads, they would become more familiar with the order of nature and would have less time for less desirable pastimes.

Some advisers detailed the special nature of Sunday reading. Reading choices should be explicitly religious, in contrast to the implicitly religious teachings of everyday reading. On Sunday readers had an opportunity to gain "intellectual excitement and enlarged information upon religious themes."[7] Children could gain appreciation for religion by reading Biblical stories such as those of Jonah and the whale, Ruth, and Daniel in the lion's den. One adviser even went so far as to suggest that Saturday reading be restricted to ancient history and geographies of the Near East, which would increase knowledge of the Bible and its times.

These recommendations reveal that most books in the midcentury marketplace were not on religious topics and that explicitly religious reading was no longer an everyday affair. Although life in the parlor remained thoroughly religious in meaning, the many people who still practiced their religion at home increasingly were doing so only on Sundays. Before the rise of the novel in the mid-eighteenth century, all reading matter, for both Sundays and weekdays, had taught lessons that were religious in a broad sense.

During the nineteenth century the novel became the most popular genre of literature. Although most of the books that reading advisers condemned were novels, all but a few of the 45 or so books that were best-sellers between 1860 and 1880 were novels. Librarians found the public's demand for novels insatiable, and some complained that many borrowers thought nothing worth reading but novels. Wholesale condemnation of novels and novel reading came from religiously conservative people who feared that modern life prevented divine salvation. A Methodist preacher told his Arkansas lecture audience that novels contained the most "dark, filthy, fiendish, infernal, devilish babble ever lighted by the fire of hell." Yet most reading advisers, book critics, and librarians held more religiously liberal views. They helped people perceive the moral potential in contemporary life by explaining how some amusements could promote serious ends. While there was a danger that reading a novel might degrade a reader's taste or supplant his or her taste for "cultivating and instructive books," there was also a recognition that "a good well-written novel is one of the charms of life."[8] Leading authors whom the advisers recommended included the British writers Charlotte Brontë, Sir

Walter Scott (especially his Waverley novels), William M. Thackeray, Dinah Muloch, George Eliot, and Anthony Trollope, and the American writers Louisa May Alcott, Nathaniel Hawthorne, and Harriet Beecher Stowe.[9]

There was a universal concern about women's reading choices; it sometimes included an animus against a particular class of readers whom book critics and advisers pejoratively called "fashionable women." They were materialists who preferred the elegance of satin gowns adorned with bows to the everyday practicality of merino wool dresses. Such women valued the superficial, were captives of the marketplace and its fashions, and read for entirely the wrong reasons. Their choice of books led to "an utter waste and frivolity of thought." "Trashy" literature was "the cheap and vapid representative of their empty minds, their heartless affections, and their frivolous characters."[10]

By attacking "fashionable women" readers, advisers were acknowledging that middle-class women were the chief buyers and readers of books and that they were reading novels in great numbers. In *The Gilded Age* (1873), Mark Twain and Charles Dudley Warner created a fashionable reader. She consumed "romances and fictions which fed her imagination with the most exaggerated notions of life, and showed her men and women in a very false sort of heroism." Such books gave the heroine "an exaggerated notion of the influence, the wealth, the position a woman may attain who has beauty and talent and ambition and a little culture, and is not too scrupulous in the use of them."[11] Many reading advisers and other authors shared Twain and Warner's opinion that women readers had little will and could easily become the passive victims of wily novelists. The lessons of fiction would sway them because women supposedly had no experience in the real world with which to compare fictional stories.

Here reading advisers tripped over their own recommendations. Although they wanted women to lead domestic lives devoted to their families and to self-improvement, they feared that self-improvement wrongly undertaken would lead to disaster. History, biography, and poetry were acceptable avenues to self-improvement because they taught lessons about ideals or about real people and places. But novels could, "with deftly-concealed, yet poisoned threads," "entwine the soul in fatal meshes of false morality, or false views of life."[12]

Reading advisers were particularly criticizing those midcentury novels, especially those written by women, that permitted women to escape their parlors and domestic roles. In popular novels of the day—for example, Mrs. E. D. E. N. Southworth's *The Hidden Hand* (1859) and Augusta Jane Evans Wilson's *St. Elmo* (1867)—heroines have adventurous and powerful roles. Mrs. Southworth's heroines often disguise themselves as men, literally leaving their femininity behind to engage in duels and outwit villains. These heroines often scoff at or overcome traditional authorities such as ministers and wealthy men. Edna, the heroine of *St. Elmo*, rises from a penniless beginning as an orphan to become a wealthy author of best-sellers. Despite the strength of character implied by such success, in the end Edna swoons at the altar, falling into the arms of her husband, who has reformed his profligate and swashbuckling ways and entered the Christian ministry.

Focused as they were on the subversive potential of these novels, advisers were blinded to their twofold appeal. Readers could enjoy learning about the possibilities outside of domestic life; they could also have their domestic lives validated by the common ending to these novels: the heroine renounces her independence, discards her disguise, and marries. Perhaps the painter of the chromolithograph *Our Great Authors . . .* did not include fabulously successful women authors like Susan Warner, Harriet Beecher Stowe, and Mrs. Southworth because he wanted to depict only the authors that Victorians *should* be reading, not the authors they *actually* were reading.

Reading advisers were especially concerned about women's reading probably because of the central role that women had in domestic intellectual life. Men left home everyday for their workplaces while women stayed in the home to give children their early education. It was women's responsibility to fill their parlors with suitable reading that taught appropriate lessons. If women were reading about immoral fantasy worlds, what lessons would they teach their daughters, and what lessons would their sons carry into the world? From a Victorian perspective, the quality of women's reading was crucial: if mothers read immoral books, they would teach their children immoral lessons and ultimately jeopardize the future of society.

Advisers usually did not specify what books to avoid; they relied on a vocabulary of words like *vulgar, vicious, vapid,* and *flashy* to describe stories that were violent or superficial and materialistic. Many women heeded the advice; a mother of a Confederate soldier wrote her son asking him to "avoid a trashy book as you would a viper, for nothing saps the intellect more completely. I think a well-written history contributes as much toward expanding political genius as any sort of reading. Poor boy! I am talking to you about reading history and writing poetry, when . . . you may be engaged in a deadly conflict with the enemy."[13]

Some advisers insisted that young people avoid all novel reading until the teen years, by which time they believed the imagination had been formed. Religiously conservative advisers recommended avoiding books that refuted biblical teachings, but others were content to tell readers to read nothing that robbed them of their seriousness and purity, and to "never read what you do not wish to remember."[14]

Book critics and reading advisers believed that literature had great influence over the moral development of young people. They warned against unpersuasive, goody-goody books, which they called "moral dish-water trash." These stories told of "boys who went to a circus and thence by short and easy stages to the state-prison," and of heroines whose "patient sweetness won over wicked but dark-eyed and chivalrous young men to give up wickedness and painting and take holy orders, and the white-robed girl to wife."[15]

Although advisers doubted that such cloying stories would win over young people, they did warn that other books made no contribution to parlor discourse. Such discourse depended on the use of proper language and the ability to relate facts and experiences that strengthened moral and intellectual life. Unacceptable reading matter was not uplifting or ennobling, it did not convey facts that could be mentioned in parlor conversations, and it did not hold up great men and women for emulation. Most often advisers complained of story newspapers and dime novels that offered "blood-and-thunder tales."

Story papers contained five to eight stories and bits of humor, short sermons, fashion advice, and descriptions of oddities. Dime novels had brightly colored paper covers illustrated with an action scene. The first and most famous firm to issue pamphlet novels costing a dime was Beadle and Adams. From its founding in 1859 until 1864, the firm reportedly printed 5 million books, of which half were dime novels. The major audience for story papers and dime novels was working people—German and Irish immigrants who worked at manual occupations. Laborers read on streetcars going to and from work, during breaks and slack times on the job, and at home during their leisure time on Sundays and in the evenings. Sometimes literate children read to their illiterate elders. Advisers condemned this inexpensive, working people's literature as "sensational" because it featured fights, daring feats of manhood, and rescues of maidens from Indians. In a typical scene, the hero finds a young woman tied to a stake. Surrounded by "hideously painted savages" and their leader, "the fiend incarnate—sitting Bull," she has lost consciousness as blood drips from the wounds on her "snow-white back."[16]

Advisers, however were discriminating in their condemnation; there were degrees of undesirability. The more respectable story papers published stories and serialized novels by authors who also wrote acceptable parlor literature. And sensational stories confirmed Victorian values by rewarding virtue and punishing vice. Their working-class heroes and heroines were quite acceptable to readers, who believed that a virtuous American republic was founded on the honesty of its workingmen and the purity of its women. Vice and immorality were found in secondary characters exclusively. Gamblers, prostitutes, drunkards, and swindlers enter the story in sensational episodes that provide titillating diversion as the main plot moves predictably to a moral end. Victorian readers could put down these sensational stories assured that the values of their parlors were universal.

The word *sensational* also describes the language used in story papers and dime novels. Language was key to the Victorians' presentation of themselves, and their literature was supposed to reinforce its acceptable use. Writers trying to teach boys how to acquire Victorian respectability differentiated between the street language of the cities and parlor language. Such distinctions appear in the many novels that Horatio Alger published from the 1860s through the 1890s. Among them, *Ragged Dick*, a best-seller of 1867, was his most popular effort. Its hero, Dick, learns how to become the respectable Richard Hunter, and in the process he stops using expressions like "it's hunky" (meaning really good, possibly terrific). In other children's literature, the distinctions were often more finely drawn. Editors of children's literature ran into problems when readers became interested in the speech of rural folk. Mary Abigail Dodge, editor of *Our Young Folks*, a successful children's magazine, explained that she would allow a fisherman's son to use the phrase "alive and kicking" to describe fish in the bottom of a boat. But the "well-bred" boy in the story would not be allowed to say it. His use of such a phrase would merely show vulgarity and the author's "coarseness of mind or want of culture." Children's literature should present for emulation no "street and newspaper slang." Writers of sensational stories that violated the standards of respectability inflated "the English language till it almost bursts with the expansion."[17]

Critics found the characters in undesirable juvenile literature insufficiently real. Alger's heroes, for example, seemed too good, almost like Christians "of the first two centuries," and they often survived because of clever talents such as singing, dancing, or ventriloquism. Their prosperity came from lucky breaks, such as chance meetings with successful men who offered them jobs. Critics saw that Alger would never persuade working-class boys to take his books as practical guides; they would only hoot at his heroes' goodness and luck. But Alger created no role models for middle-class boys either; his stories taught that success came by chance, not by sustained hard work and intelligence.[18] On balance, critics and reading advisers found Alger's books harmless and possibly helpful. They hoped that if boys read Alger stories they would stay away from even more sensational stories. Despite their condemnation of story papers and dime novels, advisers believed that reading them was better than not reading at all. They predicted that boys would grow out of their taste for blood and thunder and, as young men, would appreciate more desirable literature.

Many boys did grow out of their taste for sensational literature, and for some young men this literature provided valuable building blocks. Some prominent authors of the late nineteenth and early twentieth centuries admitted to having been dime-novel readers in their youth. The young farm boy of the 1870s who drew on *Paradise Lost*, Hamlin Garland, read as many as 100 dime novels a winter. He loved encountering "Indians and wild horsemen and dukes and duchesses and men in iron masks, and serving girls who turned out to be daughters of nobility, and marvelous detectives who have charmed lives and always trapped the villains at the end of the story." Another author, Herbert Quick, credited dime novels and authors like Mrs. Southworth with helping him gain command of the language. In contrast to the vernacular speech of his prairie neighbors, fictional heroes used correct grammar and proper diction. The elevated prose, so false-sounding today, expanded the young Quick's vocabulary and gave him "a more complex intellectual life." In his real life he "picked the stubs of burned prairie from my bare feet," but in his dime novel–inspired world, he "stanched the wounds of Indian arrows or repelled boarders from the sinking frigate."[19]

Despite the preoccupation of book advisers and critics with novels and novel reading, other sources—library reports and records, book catalogs, and diaries and letters—confirm that Victorians' interests ranged beyond contemporary fiction. Library officials complained that two-thirds of their patrons borrowed novels, but statistics also show that 52 percent of patrons borrowed no novels or borrowed other books in addition to novels. Readers checked out histories and biographies and, increasingly, books about natural science. In 1872 the Astor Library in New York City reported that scientific books were being requested as often as books of more general literary interest. An Arkansas woman who enjoyed Gothic novels, such as *The Blockaders*, and Ann Radcliffe's *Mysteries of Udolpho* (1794), also read histories and biographies, such as James Parton's *Andrew Jackson* (1859–60) and William Prescott's *The Conquest of Mexico* (1843). Novels do not dominate publishers' announcements in the *American Publishers' Circular* for 1862; works in other genres outnumber them. In fact, a reader of these advertisements could easily conclude that sermon collections and other religious works composed the bulk of American reading matter. The lead offering in the 1877 holiday catalog of Claxton, Remsen and Haffelfinger, a Philadelphia bookseller—which offered "choice gift books, standard authors, and finely illustrated works"— was Dr. Henry Schliemann's *Discoveries and Researches on the Sites of Ancient Mycenae and Tiryns.* Along with the complete works of Shakespeare, the Scottish poet Robert Burns, and the American historian George Bancroft were collections by little-known women authors and nonfiction titles like *Muspratt's Chemistry* (1860). Borrowers at a small New Jersey town library found fictional works such as *St. Elmo*, James Fenimore Cooper's novels, and Charles Burdett's *Three Per Cent a Month: The Perils of Fast Living* (1856) and nonfiction titles such as I. E. Hachik, *The Sultan and His People* (1857), *Wood's Illustrated Natural History* (1867), and Henry Drummond Wolff, *The Island Empire: Scenes from the First Exile of the Emperor Napoleon* (1855). In its collection of about 200 books, this library had only a dozen or so published after 1865, the year of its founding. Whereas some books in its collection were enduring works such as *Robinson Crusoe* and Shakespeare's plays, others were novels by now forgotten authors, such as Fred Folio, Jeremiah Clemens, Marion Harland, and Mary Jane Holmes.[20]

Respectable magazines and journals did not advertise disreputable books and reading matter. The heroes and heroines in objectionable literature, the advisers explained, expressed themselves in unacceptable ways and had no aspirations to respectability. Lacking self-control, they screamed "out all the possible varieties of hysterical passion."[21] Immoral articles and stories appeared in papers like the *National Police Gazette*, an eight-page tabloid. Filled with reports of crimes and criminal trials, it gave readers all the facts, which often were bloody, violent, and suggestive. In immoral books and the fiction of pulp newspapers, major characters were often criminals—and sometimes were women, making these stories even more unacceptable because women were supposed to be "blameless," as one editor said. "Vicious" stories asked readers to suspend their moral judgment as they read about murderous deeds, robberies, and swindles. The villains in these stories enjoy themselves immensely as they plot crimes and engage in adultery. In the end, they do not always repent or die but they always earn readers' approval and complicity. These stories violated Victorian morality and even raised questions about its survival.

Given the presence of immoral literature in the marketplace, it may seem that advisers were overly optimistic when they unilaterally encouraged reading and trusted readers to discriminate between moral books and trash. Their advice, however, shows more than their optimism about reading as a morally therapeutic activity. The publishing revolution of the antebellum years had made immoral as well as moral books available in great quantities and at low cost. Advisers writing before 1873 were probably confident that moral individuals could successfully negotiate the hazards of the marketplace. Those writings after 1873 commonly believed that readers would graduate from trash to good literature because recently passed federal legislation had forcefully removed the most offensive trash from the marketplace. Worried about the impact that pornography would have on the nation, and in particular on its young people, Congress passed the Act for the Suppression of Trade in, and Circulation of, Obscene Literature and Articles of Immoral Use in 1873.

Commonly known as the Comstock Act, after Anthony Comstock, its author and promoter, the act banned pornography and contraceptive devices from the mails. The year after its passage, federal authorities seized 200,000 pictures and photographs, 100,000 copies of books, and 5,000 packs of illustrated playing cards, plus many contraceptive devices and aphrodisiacs. Both public opinion and educated opinion backed the passage of state antipornography laws in the 1860s and the Comstock Act in the 1870s; the vast majority of Americans thought that these laws did not violate the First Amendment. Ever since the antebellum period, local governments had been assumed to have the right to limit circulation of "whatever outrages decency and is injurious to public morals."[22]

41

As mentioned earlier, many middle-class families owned no books, and some owned as few as three. Evidence from diaries and letters, however, shows that book ownership did not correlate with the amount of reading going on in a household. Adult family members usually read daily, and their reading matter did not always come in book form.

Reading advisers had little to say, however, about magazine and newspaper reading—a surprising silence given that periodicals constituted the preponderance of many people's reading matter. A British observer of the American scene during the Civil War called newspapers the "People's press." He noted that everyone above the level of a casual laborer read a daily, and that papers expressed views and prejudices that readers often shared. The *Missouri Republican* did not support war against the South until the firing on Fort Sumter, the *Boston Herald* opposed emancipation, and the *New York Times* espoused a moderate Republican position on the war.[23] In the 1860s urban newspapers reached a mass readership. Hawked by newsboys throughout New York City for 2–5¢ (they kept the amount over the 1¢ cost to them), the *New York Herald* sold 100,000 copies daily. The *Boston Post, Philadelphia Enquirer, Cincinnati Gazette*, and *Louisville Journal* served the same great public in their respective cities.

Unlike big cities, which could support more than one daily, small towns usually had only one paper to report local and national news. In 1860 Texas had 89 newspapers with a total circulation of 108,300. While big-city papers contained only news, papers in towns and small cities printed stories, often in serial form, and poems, both of which were often contributed by readers. Many rural areas had no newspaper, but rural families were still newspaper readers. They eagerly anticipated the arrival of packets of newspapers mailed by friends and relatives who lived in cities.

Among periodicals, weeklies such as *Harper's Weekly* and *Frank Leslie's Illustrated Weekly* reached the widest audience. Their readership overlapped that of story papers, and they contained material of interest to both men and women. The biggest attractions of the weeklies were serialized novels, often by the most popular authors of the day, who usually were English. Weeklies also contained news on Washington D.C., foreign affairs, and New York City—the home of many readers—religious news, lists of recommended books, and humorous puns and jokes. For example, a *Harper's Weekly* humor column named new additions to the orchestra—"the man who blows his own horn," and "the man who fiddles with his watch chain." A typical issue of *Harper's Weekly* reported on the war in Cuba, spectrum analysis, the rescue role of St. Bernard dogs in the Alps, and the life of Sir Walter Scott. Readers also were able to continue Wilkie Collins's novel *Man and Wife*, (1869) and saw Thomas Nast's cartoons making fun of the Pope and the ecumenical council then meeting in Rome.[24]

The more popular women's magazines, *Godey's Lady's Book* and *Peterson's* magazine, carried stories of interest to women in their home lives. Both fiction and nonfiction informed women about proper behavior, home decoration, and current fashions. Children's magazines, such as *Our Young Folks*, contained stories by leading American authors and introduced young readers to world history, geography, and natural science. Articles and regular features also taught children parlor games and magic tricks, some of which were extremely complex. For instance, one article told young readers how to pretend to fire a gun at themselves without incurring harm.

Midcentury readers could choose from a wide variety of periodical literature. Magazines, weeklies, and journals were directed at different ages, sexes, and religions, and many families subscribed to more than one periodical. An avid and highly educated reader, the southern diarist Mary Chesnut, subscribed to nine newspapers and several magazines, including the *Atlantic Monthly* to keep abreast of developments in American literature, *DeBow's Review* for information on the southern economy, *Harper's Monthly* (a more literary and less newsy publication than the weekly) for lighter British and American literature, and *Blackwood's Edinburgh Magazine* and *Cornhill Magazine* to keep informed about British thought and opinion. An Iowa farm family that read mostly for entertainment often turned to *Frank Leslie's Illustrated Weekly*, *Godey's Lady's Book*, the *Eclectic Magazine of Foreign Literature*, and *Harper's Weekly*.[25] Many families also subscribed to a religious weekly or quarterly for news of missionary, temperance, moral reform, and benevolent societies and to read stories and other features with appropriate religious messages. They chose from the many newspapers representing various American churches: the *Independent* (Congregationalist and Presbyterian), the *Religious Banner* (United Brethren), the *German Reformed Messenger*, and the *Episcopal Recorder*. To keep abreast of European intellectual and religious life, northerners chose either the *North American Review* if they were Unitarians or the *New Englander* if they were Congregationalists or Presbyterians.

Because most books by reading advisers date from after the Civil War, historians have had to rely on other sources to discover the impact of the war on civilian reading habits. Except in the few areas the Confederates invaded, the daily lives of northern civilians went on very much as they had before the war. Publishers tell of their increasing prosperity during the war years, and some library officials noted an increase in patronage. Diaries and letters show that some families took a greater interest in public affairs and consulted newspapers regularly for national news, including war news. The many families that had a father, son, or other relative in uniform were obviously the most interested in war news and regularly bought newspapers to scan the casualty lists. Still, some people read papers for trivial reasons. Primarily a magazine reader, one young woman read the newspaper merely to scan the personal columns for the names of soldiers who wished to find correspondents.[26]

In the South the story was very different. Its invasion by the Union army, the blockade, and wartime inflation combined to make reading matter precious. The arrival of shipments of books at bookstores was an event that newspapers announced. As the war progressed, more and more bookstores had to close and more and more southern newspapers ceased publishing. Word of mouth became an even more important source of news. People who had seen a newspaper within the last few weeks or who had been near a combat area became valued sources of information. War pressures led to the suspension of publication of the distinguished southern journal *DeBow's Review* from 1862 to 1866. The *Memphis Appeal* was dubbed the "Moving Appeal" during the war as its editors moved the paper's presses and type from one location to another to stay ahead of the Union advance. Paper and ink became so expensive that papers and journals used smaller type, reduced the size of their pages, published less frequently, or had to cease publishing. To keep in business, one desperate publisher reportedly resorted to printing on used wallpaper. Paper was so dear that a few sheets of stationery were a valued gift. For her own writing, one woman used the blank endpapers from books.

During the war, southern reading preferences changed. Northern books and journals served the Union and would not do in the new Confederate nation. Some southerners terminated their subscriptions to periodicals like *Harper's Monthly* and *Atlantic Monthly*, and others agreed with Texan Kate Stone that novels by northerners were "unreadable trash."[27] During the long siege of Vicksburg in 1863, books were in tremendous demand. Still, Harriet Beecher Stowe's *Sunny Memories of Foreign Lands* (1854) found no readers and remained the last book for sale in a bookstore. Although southerners had relied on northern papers for their national news before the war, they now turned to them only when starved for any news whatsoever or when no Confederate ones were available. As the blockade closed in, British periodicals like *Blackwood's Edinburgh Magazine* and *Cornhill Magazine* also became unavailable.

Untouched by the war until 1864, and filled with refugees, Richmond, Virginia, the Confederate capital, became the new nation's publishing center. Publishers, writers, and editors took upon themselves the task of creating an identity for their country. The *Southern Literary Messenger*, which had been founded in 1834, came under the control of a new editor in 1860 and assumed a secessionist stance. It devoted itself to printing a "truly Southern literature" and did so until its printers had to leave their presses and help defend the city in 1864. *The Countryman*, published from 1862 to 1864 from a Georgia plantation, contained political essays, poetry, travel pieces, reports from the warfront and on northern opposition to the war, advice on how to cope with shortages, and humor. It also printed nationalistic poetry, songs, and the unofficial southern national anthem, "Away from Yankee Land" (1860). The high cost of these papers and their limited distribution networks prevented them from reaching many readers.

Of the entertainments that Union and Confederate soldiers took to war, reading was the most important. Soldiers wanted news of the war, news from home, and amusement. An officer in a Delaware regiment wrote that his soldiers would shoot their generals if newspapers did not arrive soon. Soldiers appealed "to those who are enjoying the blessings of home to write and write regularly to the brave soldier boys who are guarding them against their traitor foes." Settled into winter quarters and bivouacked between battles, soldiers were occupied only partially by picket duty, rifle practice, and drill. In February 1864 a member of the 16th Pennsylvania Cavalry noted "lots of reading going on in Camp." Because many soldiers in the Union army came from rural areas or were foreign-born, the illiteracy rate for soldiers was higher (21 percent) than that for the civilian male population (7 percent). Further, almost as many as one out of three Confederate soldiers may not have been able to read.[28]

Nevertheless, social reading exposed even nonreaders to books and compensated for the shortage of reading matter. In most camps, public reading was a regular evening event. Soldiers chose a comrade to read aloud newspapers or books of general interest, such as the *Life of George Washington*. Union soldiers had an easier time getting books. There were more publishers in the northern states, and transportation and mail lines were more fully developed and not severed by invading forces. Still, a Confederate officer of the Second Virginia Cavalry was able to read 200 books from 1862 to 1865 and wrote in his diary that he found his principal "pleasure in books which I have as yet always succeeded in getting a supply. God bless the man who first invented books, he was a great benefactor to the race."[29]

Soldiers published their own newspapers, though Union soldiers were far more likely to do so. Some papers were elaborate weeklies, and others were one-page issues; some papers were long-lived, and others lasted for only one or two numbers. The Literary Association of the First Delaware Regiment published a handwritten weekly, the *Regimental Enquirer*, during its 1863–64 winter encampment in Culpeper, Virginia. Like other soldiers' papers, the *Enquirer* was thoroughly patriotic; it promised to rebuke severely "every odious deed or utterance prejudicial to loyalty." Like their civilian counterparts, the paper's editors and writers promoted their readers' self-improvement. They urged productive use of the time available while in winter quarters. Readers should "select your star in the firmament of knowledge, let diligence and industry be your dependence, and your hopes will culminate in realizing a diadem more precious than the treasures of Golconda." Their high-minded purpose, however, did not keep the editors from including humor. While the drilling and obedience of army life molded men into a unified fighting force, the paper drew attention to individuals. For instance, a writer composed puns on the names of soldiers in the regiment. Readers were asked, "Why does Company H live well?" and told, "Because they always have (Grubb)." Or "Why is Company B like an ax? Because it has (Steele) in it."[30]

In both the North and the South religious societies viewed the prospect of thousands of men being removed from the moral discipline of home and community with alarm. Diaries and letters reveal that many soldiers felt the temptations of gambling, drinking, and prostitution, and that some yielded to them. In no sense were military camps extensions of the parlor, as Victorians hoped that they would be. Northern and southern voluntary societies mobilized to counter the temptations of a soldier's life. In 1864 alone, one northern organization distributed over 500,000 Bibles and over 4 million religious newspapers, magazines, and tracts to Union soldiers. The superior resources of the North allowed for the greater distribution of reading matter and the establishment of libraries. The United States Christian Commission, a YMCA outreach program to the northern troops, established reading rooms and hospital libraries. There soldiers could obtain pen and paper for writing letters and borrow from a modest collection of religious and moral books. Tracts available in reading rooms and handed out to the soldiers in camp included standard titles such as *On Swearing, Lives of the Clergy*, and *A Welcome to Jesus*, as well as others adapted to soldiers' interests: popular biographies of soldiers, such as Catherine Marsh, *The Memorials of Captain Hedley Vicars, Ninety-seventh Regiment of the British Army*, (1856), and new titles such as W. S. Sanford, *A Soldier's Welcome Home*.

Soldiers' reading tastes mirrored those of the larger population. Not unexpectedly, Confederate soldiers read more books by southerners and about the South, and Union soldiers read more books about the North. Otherwise, members of both armies preferred novels by English novelists—especially Scott, Bulwer-Lytton, and Dickens—story papers, and dime novels. In fact, the quick success of the Beadle and Adams publishing firm is attributed to the fabulous popularity of its dime novels among soldiers. Some cheap-book publishers initiated series addressed to soldiers. The "Books for the Camp Fire" series included Jonathan Swift's *Gulliver's Travels* (1726) and Louisa May Alcott's *On Picket Duty* (1864). Some soldiers read for more than amusement. A college-educated southern officer often meditated on philosophical problems. Some soldiers studied Latin, even Greek, and trigonometry. Because few officers had pursued formal military studies, they educated themselves by reading about military science and engineering.

Reading advisers probably would have told soldiers what they told civilian readers: avoid thoroughly vicious books and read as much as you can. The war effort did not exempt soldiers from the conventions of Victorian morality, including the expectation that even amusement would be pursued seriously. While Confederate and Union soldiers fought for freedom as defined by their two governments, no soldier fought for freedom as we so often understand it today—the freedom to do whatever one wishes. While Union soldiers helped to preserve the Union and to bring about the downfall of slavery, they also fought to preserve a Victorian society in which all would remain free to pursue moral development.

three

Beyond the Parlor: Cultural Institutions in Small Towns and Big Cities

For most Americans the public world was still a rural community or small town from 1860 to 1880, but for more and more it was a city. Towns and cities of all sizes grew rapidly at this time. Towns of 2,000 people located along railroad lines doubled in size. In the South the number of cities (population over 10,000) doubled, and the number of towns (fewer than 10,000 people) quadrupled. In the more populous Northeast states, the federal census shows that by 1875 more than half the population lived in cities. Large numbers of rural Americans moved to cities, and great numbers of immigrants from Ireland and Germany—and increasingly, Italy and southeastern Europe—joined them. By the last decades of the nineteenth century, native-born Americans were in the minority in many northeastern and midwestern cities, where as many as seven out of ten residents were foreigners or had foreign-born parents.

Urban growth implied more than increasing population and the arrival of European immigrants. Old friends and neighbors departed and new interests and allegiances arose among new friends and neighbors. As a result, the middle class in small towns and cities, if it ever had been unified, became even more fragmented along political, social, and religious lines. Cities and towns, for instance, had long been home to many religious denominations; as urban life developed, the "First Church" of a denomination was joined by the Second Church, which in turn was joined by the Third Church. As a founder of a women's club in Cedar Rapids, Iowa, recalled during the postwar years, "cliques, social, religious, and political," appeared and seemed to threaten "all possibilities of unity on a higher basis."[1]

Responding to changes in their cities and towns, many middle-class families moved to the new peripheral urban neighborhoods and suburbs that the recently constructed streetcar lines connected with city centers. Before the war, urban middle-class residential areas had been adjacent to commercial and manufacturing districts and working-class neighborhoods; now the middle and upper classes had their own kind for neighbors. In New York City middle- and upper-class families moved to the areas around Central Park; in other cities, including Boston, Cincinnati, and Nashville, they moved to the suburbs.

Although the postwar South suffered from a loss of manpower, capital, and property, the rest of the country, especially members of the middle and upper classes, enjoyed the fruits of increasing wealth. In New York City alone, from 1859 to 1879, the number of probated estates exceeding $50,000 increased almost threefold, and in 1863, 79 residents of the city had yearly incomes of $100,000 or more. During the 1860s and 1870s in the Northeast and Midwest (and in the 1880s in the South), private wealth supported the founding and maintenance of an array of cultural institutions. From their parlors, Victorians extended their interest in art, music, literature, and nature into public art museums, symphonies, libraries, and parks—in sum, the institutions that gave the late nineteenth century its distinctive public culture.

The movement to establish these institutions began with the founding of the Boston Public Library (1852) and the beginning of construction of Central Park (1857), followed by the founding of the Metropolitan Museum of Art in New York City (1870), the Museum of Fine Arts in Boston (1870), Golden Gate Park in San Francisco (1870), the Chicago Public Library (1873), and the Brooklyn park system (1874). Many smaller institutions, such as the Delanco Free Library Association (1865) in Delanco, New Jersey, and the Shedd Free Library (1867) in Washington, New Hampshire, were also established at this time. Although nationally insignificant, they were central to the intellectual lives of their communities. Large or small, these new institutions generally had a common purpose, organization, and management, and they set long-lasting precedents for public institutions. The establishment of these institutions gave Victorian ideas about public life tangible expression.

The new institutions presided over the network of voluntary associations that had constituted the organized public culture of both the antebellum and postbellum years. And they stood as alternatives to commercial entertainments that Victorians thought materialistic and immoral. The founding of these public institutions was part of an effort to reform urban cultural life, and even urban form itself.

Before the war there was no public organized cultural life in the United States that was open to all citizens at no cost. Until public libraries and museums were established, people had to pay to borrow books and to enjoy art and music. And opportunities to enjoy art, music, and theater varied tremendously between rural and urban places.

In rural areas of the South and the newer settled areas of the West and Midwest, cultural life centered on the churches and family occasions like weddings and funerals. In sparsely populated areas, communities sometimes had no churches and families worshiped either privately before home altars or with others at the schoolhouse. Limited opportunities for an organized cultural life prompted a mother living with her family on the Iowa frontier to lament the lack of "congenial friends and acquaintances," "good society music and graceful intelectual [*sic*] amusements."[2]

Even in small cities and towns, organized cultural life was very simple. Community chorales and church choruses put on musical entertainments, spelling bees were frequently held, and church societies sponsored public lectures. Often small communities had no special halls for these entertainments, and schoolhouses, churches, and libraries opened their doors to them.

In larger towns and cities, opportunities to enjoy art, theater, music, and literature abounded. Patrons expected to be entertained and to pay for their pleasure. The owners of museums, theaters, galleries, and private libraries often were entrepreneurs. Proprietary museums were among the most popular cultural institutions of the century and existed in most large cities. The most famous, the American Museum in New York City, was just one of the money-making schemes that made its owner, P. T. Barnum, an exceedingly wealthy man. Before fire closed his second museum after it had been open for only two and a half years, almost 4 million people passed through its doors. Comparing the U. S. population in the 1960s and 1970s with that of Barnum's time reveals that his museum proportionately sold more tickets than did Disneyland in California.[3]

Midcentury artists formed unions or cooperative associations to show, popularize, and sell their works. Boston, New York, and Pittsburgh, like other cities, had streets or sections filled with galleries. In New York, the city with the largest number of galleries, art shops on lower Broadway exhibited American artists and historical and scenic dioramas and panoramas. In Pittsburgh a display of the works of a painter of local scenes "attracted such crowds that one could hardly get along in the street."[4] For music, Pittsburghers attended outdoor band and fire company concerts, and during the summer months New Yorkers went to Central Park Garden to hear the Theodore Thomas Orchestra, which toured nationally the rest of the year.

More than any other entertainment, theater illustrates the spontaneous, bawdy, often raucous quality of antebellum cultural life. At the theater, eating, drinking, and conviviality continued during performances. Popular presentations included minstrel shows, comic operas, and particularly melodramas—adventures centering on the perils of a heroine and her eventual marriage to a hero. As in dime novels, the entertainment came not from the predictable outcome of the plot but from the cutthroat escapades of the villains and heroes, sensational occurrences such as railroad and steamboat collisions, and comic characters drawn from ethnic and racial stereotypes. More serious plays were preceded by and interspersed with farces and comedy routines in which largely male audiences actively participated with hoots, applause, and jeers. Audiences welcomed comic improvisations in a script and demanded that actors repeat favorite lines.

In general, public antebellum city life was unsafe for women. Studies of lower-class life show that men from all classes suspected women on the streets of selling their sexual favors and treated them accordingly. Lower-class domestic and public life was full of violence, and women and children were frequent victims. When middle-class men attended the theater, their wives stayed at home. Attendance at the theater or a park concert raised questions about a woman's sexual intentions. Theaters usually attracted prostitutes who sat in the third tiers or galleries, where they made arrangements during performances to meet clients later in the evening. Moreover, plays often contained sexual references that Victorian men thought no respectable woman should hear. During the Civil War a Richmond magazine editor complained that the mayor had had to assign police to the neighborhood of a new theater where saloons were flourishing "like rank dock weeds in the fetid soil."[5]

At midcentury the redefinition of urban form and Victorian morality solved the problem of public life for respectable women. Middle-class women lived and walked in their own urban and suburban neighborhoods, where they met gentlemen like their husbands and workingmen in their employ. When these women left their neighborhoods, they visited the commercial centers of downtown areas where hotels, department stores, ice cream parlors, banks, and art galleries were located. To attract respectable women as customers, many of these institutions provided separate entrances and even special ladies' parlors and restaurants. Respectable women never attended dance halls and saloons, institutions associated with the working class and its less restrictive sexual morality. Although charitable work gave Victorian women a legitimate reason for entering lower-class areas, women on benevolent missions still had to dress and act appropriately.

Commercial cultural institutions also reformed themselves in hopes of attracting and profiting from middle-class audiences. Music halls and theaters like the Astor Place Theater in New York City began to charge more for tickets than prostitutes could afford. The proprietors of the Grand Opera of New Orleans advertised it as "The Ladies Theater" of the city.[6] Proprietors of halls looking for an audience of more modest means followed strategies like Barnum's. He banned all alcoholic beverages from his museum and admitted no inebriated customers. Further, he transformed melodrama into family entertainment by editing profanity and vulgar gestures out of even the plays of Shakespeare.

As reformed by Victorians, public life lost some of its spontaneity and robustness but gained the participation of middle-class women. The Victorian assumption that women were sexually pure gave them an invisible shield against sexual harassment in public places. But the shield was perceived only by those who recognized its power. It had most power in middle-class neighborhoods, although sometimes even Victorian men failed to recognize its power.

In the antebellum period men did not have to choose between parlor life and rowdy urban entertainments. They could leave their wives and children at home to enjoy the company of their fellow male members of voluntary societies and associations. Societies and lodges such as the Odd Fellows prided themselves on cutting across class and ethnic lines, although such interclass fraternalism was becoming increasingly rare. By the 1870s, for instance, Episcopalian businessmen and professionals dominated the Society of the Sons of St. George in Philadelphia, but an old song recalled the times when the society had unified workingmen:

> At factory, forge, or bench,
> In store, or field, or trench,
> With Germans, Swedes, and French,
> We freely toil.[7]

Although many societies began to restrict their membership on the basis of race, ethnicity, and religion in the antebellum and midcentury years, such restrictions did not fragment communities because these societies all had similar or overlapping purposes. In Jacksonville, Illinois, for instance, native-born whites, white immigrants, and African-Americans all had their own voluntary societies to promote temperance, industry, independence, and thrift.

In the antebellum years workingmen joined societies for self-improvement, and not because they wanted to enter a higher social class. Apprentices' libraries, also known as mechanics' institutes, served artisans, achievement-oriented clerks, and other young men ambitious in their careers. These institutions lent books and organized lectures and classes. Workingmen saw themselves as essential members of society and as the class responsible for national prosperity. At the laying of the cornerstone of the New York Mechanics' Institute in 1822, its president proposed that "industry and enterprize belong to" workingmen. The institute would help them "assume that respectability and that influence which are due to their numbers, and to their wealth; the streams of knowledge and intelligence must be infused among them."[8]

Victorian businessmen and professionals furthered their intellectual interests through membership in literary societies and reading clubs. In the nineteenth century every city from San Francisco to Boston with a healthy intellectual life had clubs of like-minded gentlemen who met regularly to discuss current topics and books. Reading clubs in New Haven, Connecticut, Rochester, New York, and Springfield, Massachusetts, each called themselves simply "The Club," as if their prominence allowed them exclusive use of the generic name. Jacksonville, Florida, had three clubs: the Plato, the Clio, and the Literary Union. Although these clubs had an intellectual purpose, the social interaction that they fostered often encouraged their members to cooperate on other projects, such as the founding of public libraries, museums, and parks.

During and after the Civil War, upper middle- and upper-class women actively shaped a new institutional public life for themselves by founding study and reading clubs.[9] Although these groups had existed before the Civil War, in the postbellum period they gained momentum until interest and memberships had grown enough to support the founding in 1890 of a national organization, the General Federation of Women's Clubs. Although most study clubs were kept small—under 25 members—so that meetings could be held in a member's parlor, the movement included thousands of women. At least one study club existed in each town and city throughout New England and the Midwest; they were somewhat less common in the South.

Much as men's literary societies did, women's study clubs brought together middle- to upper middle–class women. Participation in a study club may have been the one extradomestic activity for some women; for others, it may have been one of many such commitments. Members often had previous experience in organizational work, perhaps in a church-related benevolent society or a women's auxiliary of a men's society. During the Civil War medical relief for soldiers depended largely on northern and southern women who raised funds and collected supplies. Among the founders of the Decatur, Illinois, study club were the wives of professional men, business owners, and three former mayors of the town. Although all club members did not belong to the same church, voluntary association, or neighborhood, members' interests, memberships, and family ties united them, much as they did in men's voluntary associations.[10] When a particular study club became exclusive, other groups of women could always form their own clubs. Having become disgruntled over a select group's monopolizing decisions, a member of the New England Woman's Club withdrew and with the assistance of her two daughters soon formed another club.[11]

Study clubs marked an advance in women's intellectual life. In the ante-bellum period women's associations had usually focused on reform or charity work. Study clubs gave women a place beyond their own parlors in which to pursue self-development. Compared to men's opportunities for intellectual pursuits outside of the home, however, women's study clubs were Janie-come-latelies. Men had been associating for intellectual purposes in all-male societies since Benjamin Franklin founded his "Junto" group (1726), which later became the American Philosophical Society (1743). In the 1860s both men's and women's clubs encouraged personal discipline, hard study, and self-improvement. But men's clubs were oriented toward public life, women's toward domestic life. Men most often discussed matters of interest to them as public citizens, their careers less often, and their roles as husbands and fathers almost never. In contrast, women almost always discussed their do-mestic lives and their public charitable responsibilities.

As quasi-public institutions, study clubs helped many women in their pri-vate lives as wives, mothers, and thinking individuals. In this way the growth of women's study clubs paralleled other developments of the day in women's higher education. By midcentury the women's academy movement was well established. Students in these institutions pursued studies in literature, art, and history that went beyond the basic education of common schools, much as the members of study clubs did. Study clubs allowed academy graduates to continue their intellectual pursuits.

The period 1860–80 was a time when young women gained many other opportunities for higher education. Vassar College (founded 1865) and Smith College (1875) were two of the earliest single-sex institutions, while Boston University, Cincinnati University, and the University of Wisconsin were among the first universities to open their classrooms to women coeds, in 1873, 1870, and 1867, respectively. (Chapter 5 discusses the founding of women's colleges and the coeducation movement.) But the new opportunities for collegiate and university study bypassed study club members, who were usually of an age, in their forties and fifties, when their child-rearing duties and responsibilities had diminished. Nonetheless, future historians may dis-cover that mothers who belonged to study clubs were more liable than non-members to send their daughters to college.

Study clubs usually met twice monthly for 10 months of the year. Most clubs studied literature, history, and art, though a few adopted more spe-cialized projects, such as the reading of Dickens's works. Study club pro-grams were a blend of parlor entertainment and public lecture. The club met in a member's parlor. The agenda, usually specified in great detail in a care-fully drawn constitution, included conversation, the presentation of a paper, and criticism of the paper's grammar and content and the speaker's pronun-ciation. The papers delivered in a particular period or year often formed a course of study covering a broad survey area, such as English monarchs or the history of art. Members were expected to research their papers to the full extent that a local library permitted. For most women, this presentation was probably the first time that they had spoken formally to a group.

Plenty of criticism greeted the founding of study clubs, and their members were sneeringly called "clubbers." Protesting the founding of a club in Indianapolis, one woman wrote that she took care of her daughters and did "not wish for other work." A few male reporters greeted club foundings with "cheap wit" and "scorn and sneers." The *Boston Transcript* announced that "homes will be ruined, children neglected, woman is straying from her sphere."[12] For some men, the problem was the word *club* and its implications. The word had always denoted a man's organization. But women adopted it, broke from the tradition of benevolent work for others, and organized themselves for self-improvement. Some organizations, such as the Fortnightly of Chicago, sidestepped the issue by simply omitting the word *club* from their names; others, such as the New England Woman's Club, intentionally included *club* in their name to signal that their members were participating in something different from charitable work. Other critics faulted the clubs for offering a superficial education, noting that a paper covering the history of art in the early Renaissance, for instance, might be based on information from an encyclopedia and one or two other books. Others suggested that some club members thought of culture as a commodity and collected bits of knowledge much as one collects art or antiques. Such women looked upon culture as something to pursue and possess through participation in the clubs, not as the foundation of the process of becoming a changed, well-rounded, growing self. Although some of these criticisms were probably true of some study club members, they also applied to the members of other clubs and cultural institutions. One sex never has had a monopoly on superficiality.

By the end of the century, club women were viewed more benignly, and the press was reporting their doings more favorably. Study clubs represented an undeniable change in women's intellectual lives. Their proliferation shows that the idea of even married women pursuing intellectual lives was becoming broadly accepted. Women who read books, studied literature, and found pleasure in intellectual discussions no longer thought of themselves as "bluestockings," a derogatory term for strong-minded women. Club members' intellectual lives had a bona fide status. As a reporter for the *Boston Transcript* explained, the time had passed when, to have a clear conscience, a woman attending a reading of Dante had to maintain a show of being useful by "having her fingers employed with needlework while her mind reached after ideas."[13] Although clubs were not colleges and members were not engaging in truly thorough studies of particular subjects, clubs did provide discipline and structure for women's intellectual lives. At club meetings sociability moved beyond talk of children and husbands. Although members used their new knowledge to enhance their domestic lives, their clubs opened non-domestic fields of study to them.

While the women's study club movement gained strength in the postwar years, lyceum-sponsored lectures went into decline as they devolved from an educational forum for self-improvement into a money-making platform for national celebrities. Although the Civil War caused the suspension or reduction in frequency of lecture programs, they were probably the favorite form of public entertainment among Victorian Americans from the 1840s through the 1860s. Most diarists and letter writers mention attendance at lectures, and almost every town of 1,000 people or more had at least one association that sponsored them. By the midcentury years lectures had more power than churches or political parties to unite a community. While party and church membership divided the middle class, nonpartisan and nonsectarian lectures could unite it. Among the middle class, however, lecture-going was not universal. Lectures had special appeal for the young and ambitious. Besides pursuing mental and moral self-improvement, male lecture-goers could further their careers by becoming known for their interest in the issues of the day.

Audiences heard the same lecture as speakers traveled from one town to the next and repeated their popular talks. In 1866, for instance, the Association of Western Literary Societies hired P. T. Barnum, the "museum man," as he liked to be called, to give his lecture "Success in Life" to "some sixty lyceums, Young Men's Christian Associations, and Literary Societies" in Pennsylvania, Ohio, Indiana, Illinois, Wisconsin, Missouri, and Iowa.[14] The publicity generated by lectures brought even stay-at-homes into the lecture public. Extensive newspaper reports of lectures and audiences' reaction to them, and often verbatim reprints of the lectures themselves, filled newspapers. Small-town papers even reprinted columns from big-city papers describing lectures.

Lectures were public entertainment in many senses. People did not go to lectures to acquire completely new knowledge; they had become familiar with the subjects of public speakers through parlor discussion or viewing stereographs. Books and articles in the weeklies frequently discussed natural history, history, world geography, and contemporary concerns. Also, many lecturers were well known to their audiences through their work as scientists, authors, editors, educators, or reformers. The more popular lecturers—Ralph Waldo Emerson, Bayard Taylor, J. G. Holland, Edward Youmans, and Henry Ward Beecher, to name only a few with star status—wrote prolifically and were written about.

Attending lectures built on the educational experiences of the home. Domestic reading and study were activities restricted to the family circle or shared with friends. By going to a lecture, people announced to others that they aspired to knowledge and self-improvement. When individuals came together as an audience, they confirmed that the value they placed on the pursuit of knowledge was shared by many others.

Lecture attendance was not only a cultural pursuit; it was a sign of "culture." Newspaper articles reflected the self-congratulations that audiences bestowed upon themselves. A Cincinnati reporter, for instance, praised an audience at a lecture by Ralph Waldo Emerson as one of "the most elegant assemblages." "The literary public of Cincinnati honored themselves" because they were honoring Emerson, "perhaps the finest scholar and most profound thinker of the country."[15] Afterward, the lecture and lecturer probably became subjects of discussion and further reading. No lecturers on the lyceum circuit secluded themselves in ivory towers to pursue rarefied research. Male lecturers usually belonged to professions devoted to the furthering of knowledge or the cultivation of intellect. Through the pipeline of the lecture, information flowed freely between public and domestic intellectual life.

Although a specific young men's association, lyceum, or library society often invited speakers, newspapers widely advertised lectures and anyone could attend for a small admission fee. Local organizations recognized that big names drew and preferred inviting national figures over speakers with merely local reputations. By the 1870s successful lecturers could make as much as the large sum of $20,000 a year. Because Victorians wanted to hear about the strange, foreign, and exotic, speakers chose topics that showed their special knowledge of subjects such as astronomy, foreign lands, and spiritualism.

Good lecturers understood that audiences expected both to acquire new knowledge and to learn how to apply that knowledge to their own lives. For example, Bayard Taylor, an author of popular travel books about Russia, the Near East, and Egypt, followed the conventional lecture format no matter what country he was discussing. In the first part of his lecture, he related his experiences in a foreign country. By describing people and places in great detail, he established himself as an authority. His choice of experiences to describe—say, being in a public bath—allowed his listeners to experience foreign travel vicariously. Although Taylor could engender appreciative responses to foreign countries from his audiences, he left them sure of his position and theirs as Victorian Americans. His lectures always contained comparative passages that assured audiences of the superiority of Western civilization. When discussing his travels in Egypt, for instance, he observed that peasants regularly deceived travelers. Because Egyptians lived under a government based on force, they could not develop the habits of truthfulness that life under a democratic government promoted.

Taylor and other lecturers had reform as their primary purpose, in its broadest Victorian sense. That is, they wanted their audiences to eschew certain values and to take others more seriously—to be less materialistic and more aware of their potential as moral individuals. For instance, Ralph Waldo Emerson—who, despite his advancing age, remained a strong attraction on the lecture circuit after the Civil War—lectured about cultural reform and focused on the individual. Other lecturers, such as Taylor, approached the subject of reform indirectly as they discussed their foreign travels, historical subjects, and literary topics.

Lecturers saw their audience as a unified public, not as one fragmented into men and women, young and old, Baptist and Presbyterian, more and less prosperous. The audience comprised citizens of Victorian America who shared one set of values and beliefs and hopes for the future. Popular lecturers chose topics with universal appeal to the Victorian public and understood that religious topics of sectarian import were taboo. The apparent exceptions to this rule were the few women lecturers, such as Anna Dickinson and Elizabeth Cady Stanton, who usually spoke about woman's rights. Nonetheless, even these lecturers assumed that they were addressing both sexes and that all their listeners had or would have a family. Righting a specific wrong—for instance, abolishing separate standards of sexuality morality for men and women—would improve family life in particular and American life in general. Like all Victorians, women lecturers believed that social improvement started with individual improvement.

During the Civil War years, the northern public demanded lectures on topics of national concern. The Cleveland Library Association reported in 1863 that lectures by "literary men seemed to be at a discount and political addresses demanded."[16] Popular speakers included Sen. Charles Sumner, Maj. Gen. Cassius M. Clay, editor Theodore Tilton of the *New York Independent*, and reformer Wendell Phillips. Northerners wanted to hear denunciations of the South, elucidations of Union war aims, and descriptions of the reforms that would follow Union victory. Thomas Wentworth Higginson, an officer commanding African-American soldiers during the war and a journalist after the war, observed that audiences wanted to see public men and reformers. A lecturer, he recommended, should not be colorless but appear "as if he was an Indian warrior in his war-paint. . . . He must bring tomahawk and scalping-knife every time."[17]

Wendell Phillips brought his war paint and weapons in March 1863 when he addressed an audience in Cincinnati, a center of antiwar sentiment and Democratic party strength. His lecture, "Slavery and War," had been well publicized in the newspaper, and Phillips found himself facing an audience of both friends and enemies—500 tickets had been distributed to toughs, some of whom were former Kentuckians. Speaking straight, Phillips insulted many in his audience by proclaiming, "The North represents a democracy, founded on industry, brains and money; the South an aristocracy, founded on slave labor—an aristocracy whose right hand is negro slavery, and whose left is the ignorant white man." After this remark, and another about "the poor, ignorant whites of the South [being] tools of the despotism that was warring upon the liberties of the Nation," rioters pelted him with rotten eggs, called for his lynching, and even hurled a paving stone onto the stage. Phillips escaped the mob and did not return to Cincinnati until after the war. His lecture then was less controversial and met no opposition. A local newspaper reported that "he favored sending capital, enterprise, spelling books, &c., to aid the South in regaining her former wealthy position, provided she accepted the institutions of the nineteenth century as promulgated through those agencies."[18]

The lecture system began to deteriorate in the early 1870s. With the end of the war and passage of the Fifteenth Amendment (1870), which removed obstacles to freedmen's voting, national reform efforts seemed to have culminated, and public attention turned from the issues that had reigned for 20 years. New issues of the early seventies, such as woman suffrage, had partisans and plenty of opponents but not a wide following. The lecture platform also suffered from a dearth of talent. Many veteran lecturers had moved on to other ventures or had grown old. Emerson, in his seventies and showing signs of senility, had been lecturing for 30 years, and his words had lost their novelty. Searching for fame and easy fortune, lecturers with little ability entered the field. A previously popular lecturer lamented the caliber of the newcomers: "Literary jesters and mountebanks, readers, singers, etc.,—men who, outside of a lecture course, would not draw auditors enough to pay for the rent of their audience rooms."[19]

By the 1880s lectures promoted self-improvement less and amusement more. Audiences wanted to laugh with Mark Twain and Josh Billings (Henry Wheeler Shaw). Twain lectured on the Sandwich Islands and offered to demonstrate their residents' appetite "if some woman present would kindly lend him her baby." Still, Twain was praised for "recognizing in his audience something higher than merely a desire to laugh." Josh Billings, whom audiences found less tasteful than Twain, often gave a lecture entitled "Milk" that was not "refined or elegant."[20] While circling a table on which a glass of milk stood, he gestured and made allusions to it in anecdotes and jokes that raised the audience's expectation that he surely would refer to the milk directly. But he never did.

At the same time that lectures were becoming commercial amusement, public art museums, libraries, and urban parks were being established. These cultural institutions that blossomed at midcentury had roots extending deep into Victorian life. In many ways they were specialized urban extensions of the parlor and its seriousness.

Before the founding of public museums, libraries, and parks, American cities had no noncommercial cultural districts. Victorians wondered whether their cities reflected their serious purposes at all. Expanding working-class areas filled with saloons and dance halls threatened Victorian respectability. With their burgeoning commercial centers full of financial institutions and department stores, cities seemed to reflect no higher purpose than the pursuit of the dollar. A group of well-educated, public-spirited Victorians—whom we will call reformers—sought to redirect urban growth along more desirable paths by establishing public libraries, museums, and parks.

Historians differ about the motivations of these reformers and institution founders. Some believe the Victorian gentry imposed its definitions of art, nature, and good literature on an unwitting public. Admittedly, the new institutions ignored the folk cultures of the United States and the peasant culture of recent Irish immigrants. (The great East European immigration was only just under way by 1880.) Also, art museum founders denigrated the artifacts of Pacific and sub-Saharan African civilizations as the work of savages. But most other Victorian Americans shared these views. The new public institutions did not impose alien beliefs on the Victorian public; to a large extent, they represented that public's aspirations and beliefs.

For example, the founding of public parks stemmed from Victorians' tremendous interest in nature and belief in its morally therapeutic effect. In addition to the geological specimens and vine draperies used in parlor decoration, yards around suburban homes were landscaped to complement natural parlor displays. Moreover, the mid-nineteenth century was the heyday of the great American landscape artists, including Frederic Church and Albert Bierstadt, who painted huge canvases of awe-inspiring mountains, soaring redwood trees, waterfalls, and icebergs. Throngs of people paid to see these paintings when they were exhibited on tour, and even more people bought chromolithographic reproductions of them for display in their homes. Victorians believed that contemplating nature, whether in chromos or in a landscaped backyard, brought viewers in closer contact with the divine, and that places of special natural beauty showed most graphically where God had touched the earth. In the 1860s more and more Victorians sought out opportunities to experience the wonders of nature directly. Trips to natural features, including Niagara Falls, the Hudson River valley, and the New England mountains and seacoast, became popular. Winslow Homer's painting *The Bridle Path, White Mountains* (1868) shows a woman in a broad-brimmed hat, long skirts, and chiffon scarves riding sidesaddle on the rocky trails of the White Mountains.

In the parlor, the proliferation of chromos, portrait busts, and reproductions of European paintings was but one reflection of a growing interest in art. The *Independent*, the northern weekly with the widest prewar circulation, regularly featured the comments of a well-known art critic. Exhibitions of works by local artists were also becoming more popular as early as the late 1850s. In major northern cities, art galleries attracted tourists and crowds.

Close to 7,000 people paid 25¢ each to view an exhibition in New Haven, Connecticut, in 1856; in New York in 1864, the Metropolitan Fair Picture Gallery, organized by the U.S. Sanitary Commission, drew large audiences. In the South, however war and the postwar poverty of the region disrupted museum-founding efforts. Even in Buffalo and Chicago, the founding of permanent institutions languished until civic leaders became involved. Eventually, the enthusiasm generated by the prewar exhibits flowered in the founding of the Buffalo Academy (1862), the Carolina Art Association (1879), and the Chicago Art Institute (1879).

In other ways, the new public institutions were more than extensions of the parlor. They were alternatives to both for-profit institutions and institutions serving specific interest groups. The new institutions could serve serious and elevating purposes based on ideals that all Victorians shared.

The new institutions created a democratic public culture in two ways. First, they were intended to serve a broad public, not special-interest groups such as particular political parties or religious denominations. For example, public libraries replaced the welter of libraries maintained in the antebellum years by school districts, Sunday schools, individual proprietors, voluntary associations, and library societies. The holdings of these various libraries reflected the interests of their sponsors; church libraries had sectarian literature, and for-profit lending libraries maintained a selection of popular books that did nothing for readers who wished to pursue topics in depth. Second, public institutions made available to all what most families could not afford for themselves. Municipal public libraries had books for all, required no fees, and had no membership tests. They loaned popular and specialized works to both pleasure readers and researchers. By the same token, urban parks were yards or trips to the country for families that could not afford suburban yards or vacation travel, and museums held a broader range of artwork than any parlor did.

In other ways the new public institutions counterbalanced the excesses of democratic culture; they attempted to correct and direct the development of popular taste by sorting out the jumble of cultural life. Both private parlors and commercial museums had randomly displayed natural history specimens alongside artworks. Barnum's museum exhibited stuffed animals and live whales in tanks of seawater, historical portraits and armor, historical objects such as a key to the Bastille in Paris, and curiosities such as a ball of hair found in the stomach of a sow. By contrast, the new public museums had specialized areas of concentration, generally art or natural history. They did not exhibit products of domestic manufacture like hair-art mourning pieces and curiosities like the ball of hair. Believing that ennobling art was moral art, museum managers also refused to collect the vicious and the vulgar. Explaining the goals of the museum and the rationale for its collecting policy, a founder of the Boston Museum of Fine Arts proposed in 1870 that the museum should be a "means of forming a standard of taste through knowledge of masterpieces of the past."[21]

In every city a group of energetic, public-spirited citizens founded the new institutions. Women stood behind the founding of many libraries, but men organized the first public parks and art museums. They were usually doctors, lawyers, college professors, journalists, and in lesser numbers, businessmen. Their public accomplishments as professionals had won them standing in their communities and brought them into elite and moneyed circles. Yet these men scorned those whom they called "mere capitalists"—those who, for example, had put personal financial gain ahead of the Union cause during the war years. Seeing themselves as the true aristocrats of America, they joined and founded associations and clubs, sometimes literary clubs, that brought like-minded men together socially, allowed them to recruit new colleagues, and helped to consolidate and develop their common interests and ideas. In New York City many of the founders of the Metropolitan Museum of Art belonged to the Union League Club and the Century Association. They read journals such as the *North American Review*, the *Atlantic Monthly*, and the *Nation*; in fact, their more outstanding members contributed to the pages of these journals. In New York and many midwestern cities, the institution founders were of New England ancestry. Yet they disdained narrow religious beliefs and dismissed the theological arguments and doctrinal disputes of the antebellum years as the work, in Frederick Law Olmsted's words, of "conceited, dogmatical, narrow minded, misanthropic, petty mind tyrants."[22] Their search for something other than religion upon which to base a unified moral society encouraged them to establish cultural institutions.[23]

Although most institution founders supported temperance, opposed slavery, and advocated a strict personal morality—including honesty, thrift, industry, premarital chastity, and marital fidelity—they had little faith that reform movements focusing on individuals would renovate society. Reform, they thought, had to have a firmer and more enduring foundation in permanent institutions that would educate individuals of both the present and future generations. The Civil War and the Thirteenth and Fourteenth amendments had created a moment of opportunity: a society of free men responsibly shaping their own destiny could be realized in the United States. The institution founders looked to England, France, and Germany as models; these older civilizations had museums and other public institutions to preserve their national heritages and enrich the leisure time of their citizens. In Europe, however, cultural institutions drew their support from ruling families and members of the aristocracy. Victorian Americans looked on European accomplishments as a challenge: Should not the United States be able to produce the same achievements? But given that the United States was a democratic republic, could it? Could Americans accomplish what European aristocrats and nobles had?

U.S. cultural institutions would have to grow from the aspirations, good-will, and philanthropy of a free citizenry. The construction of Central Park showed that this was possible. A supporter of the park and member of the founding group of the Metropolitan Museum of Art hailed the park as "a royal work, undertaken and achieved by the Democracy,—surprising equally themselves and their skeptical friends at home and abroad,—and develop-ing, both in its creation and growth, in its use and application, new and almost incredible tastes, aptitudes, capacities, and powers in the people themselves."[24]

Although profoundly committed to the idea of republicanism, and scorn-ful of those who disdained the American people, the institution founders distrusted just as profoundly universal suffrage and majority rule. Unlike P. T. Barnum and other proprietors of commercial institutions, the founders and managers of public institutions never assumed that whatever people want is good. Believing that majorities could err, they insulated public institutions from the influence of mass behaviors. Thus, the institutions were public in the sense that they served a public purpose and were open to the public, usually without charge; but they were not directly controlled by the public or its representatives, nor were they meant to be entirely responsive to public tastes.

Moreover, institution founders expected people to learn how to use public institutions so that their intended benefits would endure. Libraries fined patrons who soiled books, folded their pages, or otherwise damaged them. Patrons could borrow a limited number of books for a set time and were forbidden to lend a book "to any person not a member of the same house-hold." Specially trained forces patrolled parks and tried to protect them "from the shock of an untrained public," which might see shrubs and trees as po-tential firewood and open spaces as prospective garbage dumps. Other reg-ulations prohibited picking flowers, defacing benches, buildings, and bridges, annoying birds, throwing stones, shooting guns, racing carriages, climbing trees, and grazing animals.[25]

A board of directors or trustees usually oversaw the operations of the pub-lic institutions. Because boards either nominated their own new members or had members who were appointed by municipal governments, they did not have to please voters, and elected officials had little control over them. Di-rectors could do what they thought was right and ignore the *vox populi*, which might express fleeting whims and ignore its own long term self-interest. Di-rectors agreed that it would not do to have their institutions "subjected to the changing whims and the capricious actions of a popular majority or a city council sensitive to political currents and undercurrents."[26]

Most of the midcentury founders of cultural institutions were thoroughly disgusted with urban politics. Urban political organizations, or "machines," had secured the votes of immigrants and workingmen and entrenched themselves in office. Ignoring the long-term needs of poorer residents, they bought votes with jobs on city payrolls, holiday turkeys, Fourth of July picnics, and drinks on election day. Political machines enriched their own members with payoffs for city contracts and kickbacks from the construction of public works. In one instance of gross corruption, William Marcy Tweed's ring was accused of allowing a contractor to charge New York City the outrageous price of $12,000 for an ordinary doorknob on a municipal building. One cultural leader, newspaper editor and poet William Cullen Bryant, denounced elected officials as "bungling" and "utterly incompetent for the task" of managing cultural institutions.[27]

Men who wanted to reform urban life had no electoral following of sufficient numbers to elect them to public office; they gained power in their cities instead through their technical expertise. Boards entrusted their new institutions to managers with demonstrated competence. At a time when graduate schools did not exist for professions other than the ministry, law, medicine, and college teaching, these managers had acquired their expertise on the job. The landscape architect of Central Park, Frederick Law Olmsted, had managed a farm, traveled in Europe and studied its parks, and covered urban problems as a journalist. The librarians who founded the American Library Association in 1876 had diverse origins. Some came from wealthy families; others were the sons of farmers, artisans, and other self-employed men. College graduates were often able to use their B.A. degrees as a sufficient qualification for library work; nongraduates relied on their practical experience. The head of a public library in Hartford, for example, apprenticed at the Boston Athenaeum, an outstanding private library.

The managers of the new public institutions were members of a new middle class. They were not owners, but employees who split their loyalty between their boards of directors and their professions. For instance, librarians responded to the directives of their boards but also tried to instruct them about correct library practice, which they were learning about from reading the *Library Journal* and participating in their professional association.

These institutions reflected the new meaning that Victorians were giving to the word *culture*. *Culture* no longer signified naturally occurring growth, as it had in the earlier agricultural and commercial society (1800–1860). The 1841 edition of Webster's dictionary, for example, defined *culture* first as an "act of tilling," then as the "application of labor to improve good qualities," and finally as "any labor or means employed for improvement." By the 1869 edition, "tilling" had become the third meaning. *Culture's* new first meaning was "labor that improves," and its new second meaning was "the state of being cultivated," or, "enlightenment and discipline acquired by mental training." Founders intended the new cultural institutions to discipline and enlighten their patrons' intellects.

They looked with disdain on much of the actual world of 1860–80: the seemingly uncivilized nature of immigrants' lives, the immorality of city streets, the corruption of urban politics, and the muddle of the marketplace. They believed that institutions had to screen out the popular to promote cultivation in their patrons. Certain books and artworks, for instance, could enlighten people and encourage self-discipline. With increased understanding, and their selfish impulses held in check, people would develop their better natures and become broader or more liberal in their sympathies.

To pursue the mission of cultivation, managers of cultural institutions tried to establish an ideal; they eschewed mere representations of real life. Parks were landscaped—not left as simple open spaces—art museums did not collect all artworks, and library collections did not mirror the publishing marketplace. None of the new institutions chose to include art or literature that represented American working-class life, although libraries and museums did continue the tradition of mechanics' institutes in a limited way by promoting knowledge of crafts. The founders of the Metropolitan Museum of Art said that the museum should not merely "instruct and entertain" the leisure classes but should also offer artisans the "high and acknowledged standards of the past." The trustees of Boston's Museum of Fine Arts collected and displayed medieval armor as well as ceramics and textiles from the Mideast and East Asia in the hope of educating craftsmen. In 1876 they appropriated funds for the purchase of "Asian bronzes, Japanese and Tangiers leathers and Moorish textiles, pottery and tiles," which, they hoped, would "improve artistic design in the industries of Massachusetts."[28]

Nor did museum collections mirror middle-class life exactly. In their early years museums did resemble parlors with their exhibitions of photographs, plaster casts of antique Greek and Roman statues, and even chromolithographs. But their managers excluded original and reproduced art with sentimental subjects—chickens, barefoot boys, and John Rogers's statues of courting at the town pump. Although museum-goers could view portrait busts of Roman senators and Greek statesmen, they did not see representations of contemporary American war heroes, presidents, politicians, or other public figures. Whereas museums bought works of American artists from the late eighteenth century to the present, they were more interested, as were commercial art galleries, in works by European artists—either ones of the present day or those of the past whose reputation had increased over time.

As the young American museums raised endowments, they came to resemble their European ancestors. Among museum directors and managers, a consensus gradually formed: art that disciplined and enlightened was most likely to be found among the time-tested masterpieces of the Old World. Like other Victorians, midcentury museum directors and managers believed that future works of art, architecture, literature, and industrial design would be based on the works of the past. It was the task of their institutions to make these works available and thus to ensure the smooth, continuous flow of history from the past to the present, and on to the future.

Library policies show what forces Victorians identified as potentially divisive. Most library charters ruled that, in the words of one library, "no book that is sectarian in religion or partisan in politics shall have a place upon the shelves." Moreover, many library buildings were closed to political and religious meetings, and membership on library governing boards was frequently closed to members of the clergy. The ban against polemical religious works extended to books by those who argued against Christianity, such as Voltaire, Rousseau, and Marx. Library directors and managers also agreed that libraries should collect no thoroughly "vicious" books, such as *Rookwood* (1834), a British novel that glamorizes its hero, the robber Dick Turpin. Libraries discouraged young people and other casual readers from borrowing books on immoral subjects. Catalog cards noted that borrowers needed written permission to borrow the novels of the eighteenth-century English authors Tobias Smollett and Henry Fielding. Foreign novels that challenged Victorian ideals about marriage, like those by Gustave Flaubert and Théophile Gautier, often were not available in translation on the theory that "students of French literature and most other persons who ought to be allowed to read them find them accessible in the original."

Even with all these regulations, many users welcomed the opportunities for reading and sociability that the new libraries offered. In Delanco, New Jersey, Martha Fletcher visited her new town library weekly and commented after one visit that she had "had a great deal of fun."[29] And despite their policies limiting access to immoral books and excluding immoral art, managers and directors of midcentury cultural institutions were committed to the educational purpose of their institutions. Museums issued comprehensive and affordable guides to their collections, published annual bulletins, planned lecture tours, and established their own libraries and art schools. The first annual report of the Chicago Public Library stated that "every person in the community, however humble, or lacking in literary culture, has a right to be supplied with books adapted to his taste and mental capacity."[30]

Librarians hoped that their collecting policies would teach readers that popular books often did not promote cultivation. Libraries furthered the cause of truth by making works available that expressed currently unpopular opinions. On library shelves readers could find alternatives to the self-serving rhetoric of politicians and the sensational stories of the daily press. Librarians also believed that they could help readers develop "a more elevated taste." Hoping that readers would move onward and upward from reading novels like those by the fabulously popular Mrs. Southworth to books that deserved to be called literature, librarians purchased best-selling novels, though in limited quantities. In general, library directors and managers wanted their institutions to help form an "instructed common sense."[31]

Park planners exercised just as much discrimination in their approach to nature. Frederick Law Olmsted transformed the natural features of Manhattan's Central Park into an alternative to the surrounding city. To create a

3.1 This 1864 Currier and Ives lithograph of Central Park—Frederick Law Olmstead's ideal landscape—depicts the Victorian vision of proper entertainment in public places. *Courtesy of the Library of Congress*

pastoral landscape, he installed 60 miles of drainage pipes, moved nearly 5 million cubic yards of soil, blasted rock formations with 260 tons of gunpowder, and planted thousands of trees and shrubs. This monumental effort created a park with a picturesque landscape filled with meadows, tranquil ponds, and walking paths running along hillside contours. The gently rolling topography and scenic vistas offered calm. Open spaces for parade grounds, malls, and playgrounds allowed families to enjoy the park as they promenaded, picnicked, boated, and skated. Rows of tall trees around the park's periphery screened out the noise and commercial bustle of the city streets. The contrived, "natural" landscape of the park was meant to lure city residents away from the materialistic pull of window-shopping. Besides shaping the landscape, Olmsted also wanted to shape park-goers' behavior. To make sure the park had a morally therapeutic effect, park regulations banned "manly and blood tingling recreations."[32] Immigrants and workingmen visiting the park had to leave competitive, violent pastimes like boxing and cockfighting behind in their neighborhoods.

Although directors and managers sought to protect their institutions from popular opinion and politicians, they never could do so entirely. Museum of Fine Arts trustees, worried that the physical explicitness of some of its antique statues would provoke criticism from pious viewers, ordered the strategic installation of fig leaves. Demands from the public for more amusements—for instance, merry-go-rounds—and from politicians for more patronage from their supporters compromised Olmsted's vision of Central Park. Preferring that their creations be for "the comparatively few" who "really want seclusion and the beauty of nature," nineteenth-century park planners had scorned the many who "can only enjoy solitude in crowds."[33] Nevertheless, public pressure had the democratizing effect of forcing the planners to compromise with the public: they built most urban parks with spaces for both solitary moments with nature and promenades in the company of others who enjoyed seeing and being seen. Not daring to ignore the public's preferences entirely, librarians purchased books that they hoped borrowers would not read. Museum directors learned that the public could not patronize free days during the week, so they moved them to weekends, when workers had leisure time. The managers of the Metropolitan Museum of Art yielded to public demand in 1891 and opened the museum on Sundays. In short, a limited dialectic existed between urban residents and their public institutions. Although Victorian institution founders had wanted to reform urban life completely, their plans did not entirely prevail.

The records of these institutions show that the public supported them in great numbers, though not every urban dweller patronized them. Only certain members of the middle and working classes wanted to view art, walk in the park, or borrow books. In 1877 the Museum of Fine Arts attracted over

158,000 visitors, of which only one-tenth paid admission. The rest visited for free on weekends—as many as 3,000 per weekend—or were professional artists or students at Boston-area art and architecture schools, who always enjoyed free admission.[34] Of the half million people who visited Golden Gate Park in 1879, many were repeat visitors; San Francisco had a population of only 234,000. Central Park in New York City quickly became a favorite urban excursion and a tourist attraction. A guidebook noted that the park was filled with "a brilliant and ever-changing pageant," and a writer in the *Phrenological Journal* praised the park for being a pleasant resort that "inculcates order and control."[35]

After 1880 cultural institutions matured; the idealism of the early years dissipated, endowments increased, and professional staffs developed methods of classification and display. By the opening of the twentieth century, museums had departed from their earlier unsystematic practices, what one eminent historian has called their "tobacconist's window" approach to display.[36] That is, they stopped trying to display everything in their collections, and began to select their better, often more popular objects and arrange them in a purposeful manner. Museums also used their increasing resources to purchase original works of art. They departed from their use of reproductions and began to be repositories and storehouses for the best original artifacts and artwork.

Professional librarians Melvil Dewey and Charles Cutter developed schemes of classification for libraries to replace the shelving of books by date of acquisition or publication or other random schemes. Simultaneously, however, some librarians became less committed to public access. They began to devote more resources to the needs of patrons pursuing research and fewer resources to pleasure readers. Libraries reduced their hours and instituted other changes that made borrowing less convenient for working people. As the midcentury years faded, the imperatives of a democratic culture began to suggest priorities other than the education and uplift of individual citizens.

By 1880 Victorian institution founders and urban reformers had accomplished a great deal. Most cities and towns of any size had a public library, museum, or park. These institutions most certainly were not what all citizens wanted. Not imagining that they should, Victorian institution founders never had consulted all citizens. They assumed that they were acting in the interest of all by promoting cultivation and discipline. Even so, their new institutions did transform urban life. By creating areas beyond the parlor where Victorian rules of decorum and behavior could prevail, they created family entertainment and opened urban public life to respectable women from all classes. As the middle and upper classes retreated to their own neighborhoods and members of all classes and ethnic groups established their own voluntary associations, the new cultural institutions became the public meeting ground for all members of society. By founding and supporting these institutions, Victorian Americans gave their serious ideals about public life tangible expression. And through their physical presence and location on central squares and great boulevards, midcentury cultural institutions made it clear that Victorianism had become the official culture of nineteenth-century America.

four

_____

Preparing for Parlor Life

To prepare for parlor life, Victorian children had to learn certain essential skills and information. Homes first taught them some of these lessons, and friends, neighbors, ministers' sermons, stories, and plays imparted others. By the time children entered school, they most likely knew that the word *family* meant a husband, wife, and children. Because school lessons built upon elementary lessons such as this, they reveal only the more advanced cultural and intellectual knowledge necessary for parlor life.

Fortunately, it is easy to discover the cultural knowledge that Victorian Americans thought fundamental in Civil War and postwar sources. After secession, southerners published Confederate textbooks in the belief that the South should free itself from dependence on textbooks written by "people invading our country with fire and blood and remorseless cruelty, who deny to us the right to govern ourselves, to cherish and defend our own institutions and even *to think for ourselves.*"[1] Also, the war and emancipation of the slaves motivated northerners to launch an educational program for freed men and women who, they assumed, had never had families to teach them. Comparing these educational endeavors to the lessons given in northern common schools reveals the knowledge that Victorians took for granted.

On 3 March 1865 Congress passed legislation establishing the Freedmen's Bureau, which sponsored schools in the South. Freedmen's school teachers assumed that living in slavery had not given their pupils any desirable fundamental knowledge. The teachers wanted to wipe out the old ways—to start with a blank slate—and ready their pupils to lead lives of respectability. John Alvord, inspector of schools for the bureau, explained that teachers of freed men and women could not follow the precise routine of culture given to white children. The point from which the latter start, and the influences along their whole career—early precepts from intelligent parents, stimulus from mutual contact and example, helps and aids on every side, each increasing daily as these favored children rise to maturity—are not the heritage of the colored child. Nor has he usually, in morals, any good pattern to imitate.

In fact we are dealing with a people to be *untaught* in habits of thinking, feeling, and acting. A new foundation, mainly with new material, is to be laid, and upon it a superstructure reared and adapted to the coming time of these freedmen.[2]

As Alvord's proposal suggests, northern teachers wanted to teach freed men and women formally the lessons that proper Victorian homes transmitted informally. Before comparing freedmen's and common schools, however, a caution is warranted. The lessons that northern teachers took to freedmen can reveal the fundamental cultural knowledge of their world. We know very little, however, about the intellectual life of the ex-slaves, which is a story awaiting an author.

By the 1860s schools for young people in the Northeast and Midwest were "common schools." "Common" means general, or belonging to the community at large: all the children of an area could attend a common school, and a committee of elected citizens supervised its operation and hired its teacher. In an age when state standards for entry and exit varied widely, if they existed at all, common school students were as young as three or four and as old as twenty. The length of the school year also varied according to the needs and desires of a community.

The word *common* in the term "common schools" describes the hopes of common school supporters more accurately than the reality of common school enrollment. About 50 percent of school-age children attended common schools outside the South, although upwards of 90 percent of children from ages seven to fourteen attended in some areas of the Midwest and New England. Enrollment rates were low for children from poorer families, farming regions, the South, and certain religious groups. In the farm country of Pennsylvania, Mennonites kept their children out of the common schools, and in the major eastern cities Irish Catholics were laying the foundations for the parochial school systems that would develop in the last decades of the century. Farming families and poorer urban families often considered the immediate wages from the labor of their children more valuable than the long-term promise of education. Because most white southerners opposed tax-supported plans for school systems and sent their children instead to subscription schools, private academies, and church-supported institutions, merely four southern states and a few counties and cities elsewhere in the South had established common school systems for white pupils by 1860.

Common schools were the nineteenth-century equivalent of our public schools. Still, common schools were not always free; parents sometimes had to pay modest fees. During the antebellum years educators such as Henry Barnard in Connecticut and Horace Mann in Massachusetts led movements to establish statewide common school systems in the hope that, regardless of income level, all Americans would be able to enjoy a common education. To include all American children, state-supported and -directed schools not only had to appeal to the great middle class but had to replace both charity schools and private institutions, where the well-to-do preferred to send their children.

Besides confirming and extending lessons in values and behaviors that the home should have introduced children to in their first years, textbooks, teachers, and common school teaching practices imparted the skills necessary for participation in Victorian life. Children learned the basic skills of reading, writing, and arithmetic, as well as essential facts about the world and American history that would help them to be good citizens.

When children entered common schools at age four or five, they began reading and writing lessons. At the ages of seven or eight, addition and subtraction lessons started. Students who attended school for at least 170 days a year were able to read *McGuffey's Third Eclectic Reader* by age eleven or twelve. That is, a child could understand a three-page story composed of three- or four-sentence paragraphs. Words of up to four syllables were used in sentences that often were complex in structure and sometimes contained conversation. Students who continued in school for two or three more years and completed their common school education were able to perform the four basic arithmetic functions, compute columns of sums orally, write a friendly or formal letter in a neat, regular cursive hand, speak or read in public with standardized, acceptable pronunciation and fluency, and read *McGuffey's Fifth Reader*. Some could read the *Sixth*.[3] The readers contained selections from the writings of well-known British and American authors who had attained either classic status, such as William Shakespeare, John Dryden, Thomas Jefferson, and Benjamin Franklin, or popularity in the nineteenth century, such as John Greenleaf Whittier, Mrs. A. D. T. Whitney, Elizabeth Barrett Browning, and Sir Walter Scott.

Because schoolbooks were in short supply in the postwar South, freedmen's schools relied on donations from the North or used whatever books were at hand. Teachers adapted the stories and lessons of common school texts such as *McGuffey's Eclectic Readers*, *Goodrich's Pictorial History of the United States*, and *Fetter's Primary Arithmetic* to the perceived needs and interests of their students. The publishing house of the Congregationalist American Tract Society in Boston, however, issued a primer, or speller, and a pair of readers in 1865 especially for freedmen. Like other series, the primer presented the core lessons that the companion readers extended and elaborated. Published as they were by a religious organization, the *Freedman's Readers* contained denominationally specific lessons, but their prices were sufficiently low so that they were widely used in the freedmen's schools. In addition to material written specifically for the freedmen—for instance, biographies of famous African-Americans—the readers contained popular selections borrowed from other schoolbooks, such as a story about a chimney sweep. Besides teaching Congregationalist doctrine, the texts offered basic religious, political, economic, and social lessons for Victorian life adapted to the perceived situation of the freedmen. Following the most advanced pedagogical practice of the day, the lessons were connected to practical subjects, namely, "domestic life, civil institutions, morals, education, and natural science."[4]

Because of the barriers that slavery had erected against the acquisition of literacy, on the eve of the Civil War no more than 5 percent of slaves could read. As the Civil War progressed and Union troops occupied more and more southern territory, former slaves used their freedom to found schools and introduce their people to literacy. When the Union army occupied an area in the South, commanders often mandated the establishment of schools for freed men and women or permitted northern missionary associations to establish schools. From 1865 to 1870 the Freedmen's Bureau coordinated the educational efforts of northern missionary and benevolent associations and the freed slaves themselves. As southern states reentered the Union, their new constitutions contained provisions for the establishment of state-supported and -directed school systems. In most southern states it was unclear whether African-American students would be admitted to the public schools or separate schools would be established for them, and whether separate schools would receive their fair share of state funds for education. From 1860 to 1880 the number of institutions for the education of African-Americans steadily increased. In 1870 Georgia had 233 schools for African-Americans, enrolling 5 percent of that population, and in 1880 there were 1,688 schools, enrolling 40 percent of African-Americans in Georgia.[5]

The education that northern educators made available to freed men and women drew heavily on a heritage of republican thought dating back to the eighteenth century. Their ideas of freedom grew from an understanding of the word *slavery* as the antithesis of freedom and independence. To be a slave was to be dependent on others in a political, economic, intellectual, and social sense. Men who were slaves were not citizens and could not vote, their work benefited others, they could express none of their own ideas, and they could not form and protect their own families. To be a slave was to be less than a man, so many northerners referred to freedmen's education as "manhood" education. After ratification of the Thirteenth, Fourteenth, and Fifteenth amendments, slavery was ended, freedmen were citizens, and African-American men could vote, but many northerners thought that, in the words of John Alvord, the freedmen still had "to be educated *as men* for manly positions."[6]

74

The words *slavery* and *independent* with reference to women had other meanings for republican thinkers, who believed that mothers were the first teachers of future citizens. Revolutionary-era educators had stressed women's responsibility for educating virtuous citizens, but the domestically minded Victorians also stressed women's responsibility for creating homes. They looked to homes for the security of civilization. "Mothers, sisters, daughters—chaste and refined—must circle round happy firesides, filling the abode with those elements of civilization peculiar to the family institution." Education would help an African-American woman overcome the crushing effects of slavery under which "every surrounding influence forced her back to the stupor and brutality of the savage state. There was no binding matrimony, no family sacredness, nothing which could be called *home* in slavery."[7]

In the postwar South, freedmen's schools were not common schools in any sense. Besides being opposed to education for African-Americans and to public, centralized education, white southerners also held that African-Americans were their intellectual inferiors and were incapable of any intellectual advancement whatsoever. When the Union army and then the Freedmen's Bureau started to educate freed men and women, southerners met their efforts with hostility. Disregarding the freedmen's enthusiasm and support for education, southerners perceived these schools as northern creations, staffed by northerners who proselytized northern ideas. Whites not only refused to support them but would often not rent rooms to the teachers or buildings for the schools. Harassment of teachers and burning of school buildings were frequent events in all the southern states; reports of major incidents appeared regularly in the semiannual reports of the Freedmen's Bureau. In North Carolina in one year, white arsonists destroyed seven school buildings and one church. Teachers were persecuted and their lives were threatened; they had to renounce any friendships or ties in the white community and could not count on the protection of law. In one incident, an intruder with a knife entered the house of a white man inquiring for "that d——d nigger teacher." Upon appealing to the authorities, the victim "was informed by certain parties that if he persisted in his designs he would be compelled to leave the city." The climate of opinion permitted students of Washington College (later Washington and Lee University) in Virginia to terrify a teacher of freedmen by surrounding her house and creating a deafening din. A writer for the *Charlottesville Chronicle* explained that he and other whites suspected that the freedmen's school teachers were preparing their charges for citizenship, or "[for] something more than the communication of ordinary knowledge implied in teaching them to read, write, cipher, etc. The idea prevails that you instruct them in politics and sociology; that you come among us not merely as an ordinary school teacher but as a political missionary; that you communicate to the colored people ideas of social equality with whites."[8]

Unlike common school teachers, teachers in freedmen's schools were to some extent free from community control. Because the defeat of the Confederate nation also implied the defeat of Confederate thought, freedmen's teachers felt it was right to draw on northern values and antislavery ideas and offer what they perceived as a national education. On the Georgia Sea Islands in 1862, a school was named for William Lloyd Garrison, the abolitionist who before the Civil War had denounced the Constitution as a proslavery document and called for northern secession from a morally tainted union. Students often sang John Greenleaf Whittier's poems composed for the freed people:

> Oh! none in all the world before
>   Were ever glad as we:
> We're free on Carolina's shore;
>   We're all at home and free.

Commenting on the singing, a teacher wrote Garrison that the teachers wanted "Southern ears trained to appreciate the music of *good names*!!" Teachers in other freedmen's schools taught their students "national airs" such as "Hail Columbia," "The Star-Spangled Banner," and "Yankee Doodle" and popular songs of the war years such as "Just Come Home from Battle." To white southerners this music was not national but political, and it was banned when local school boards took control of the freedmen's schools.[9]

African-Americans had started to value literacy during their years in slavery. After suffering legal prohibitions against their learning to read and write, slaves had concluded that literacy was very powerful and desirable. When northern missionaries and schoolteachers arrived in occupied areas, the ex-slaves enthusiastically supported their educational efforts. The third semi-annual report of the Freedmen's Bureau reveals that freedmen supported one-third of the 1,200 schools reporting to the bureau, and almost half of the 972 teachers in these schools were African-Americans. Freedmen owned almost 300 school buildings, and the bureau merely 200. In 1865–66 John Alvord investigated the new schools and was struck by the tremendous drive of the students to achieve literacy. He observed that "throughout the entire South an effort is being made by the colored people to educate themselves." The educational institutions created by former slaves, which he called "native schools," appeared "often rude and very imperfect, but *there they are*, a group, perhaps of all ages, *trying to learn*. Some young man, some woman or old preacher, in cellar, or shed, or corner of a negro meeting-house, with the alphabet in hand, or a torn spelling-book is their teacher. All are full of enthusiasm with the new knowledge THE BOOK is imparting to them" (emphasis as in original).[10]

Although freedmen's schools and common schools were different in many ways, they shared some fundamental similarities. Both African-American and white children received an education primarily in reading and writing; schools rarely taught natural science, and those that did reserved the subject for advanced classes. Schoolbooks reflected the great value that Americans placed on literacy. In *McGuffey's Eclectic Readers* characters seemed to spend much of their time reading; in the *First Reader* more than 10 percent of the illustrations show people engaged in reading or writing. The *Freedman's Readers* also showed people excelling who had become literate. Biographical selections on notable African-Americans, such as authors Phillis Wheatley and Frederick Douglass, emphasized that their subjects were literate.

The teaching strategies of the *Freedman's Readers* and *McGuffey's Readers* were identical, and both were based on the definition of intelligence that prevailed in the 1860s and 1870s. Victorians believed that the Bible and the natural world revealed God's plan for the universe as well as the outlines of the natural, human, and divine universe. They expected that scientific discoveries would merely add to their understanding of the divine creation. A penmanship book expressed the hope that "the paths of Science may lead you reverently to the foot of Him whose works she delights to unfold." To explain how scientific investigation led to knowledge of the divine, a preeminent scholar of the day, Noah Porter, compared the universe to a mountain with its top veiled by clouds and its base buried in the earth. Because scholars could accurately measure and describe the accessible parts of the mountain, Porter did not believe "that what we shall hereafter discover will belie what we already know."[11]

The questions posed by schoolbooks were consistent with the prevailing Victorian concept of a known universe. Reading selections always stated rhetorically the answers to the questions that followed them. If a question seemed to imply that its answer might vary according to point of view, the story made it clear which point of view should prevail. For example, after a story about boys who have had great fun spooking the horse of an old man in a sleigh, the question was, "Is thoughtlessness any excuse for rudeness or unkindness?" The last paragraph of the story contains the correct response: "The boys perceived how rude and unkind their conduct appeared."[12]

Holding to absolute standards of right and wrong, Victorians insisted that their way of seeing the world was right; they did not entertain the possibility of multiple viewpoints or of relative degrees of rightness. Victorians assumed that mastery of concrete facts was the foundation upon which understanding rested. For example, history students learned a chronological sequence of events and the relationship of dates to people and places. A scholar in an Iowa common school of the late 1870s tells of a typical lesson. The teacher assigned a chapter that students read two or three times. In class she asked students to recite the chapter from memory. She let children who could not repeat the chapter verbatim on the first try proceed at their own rate. The Iowa scholar recalls, perhaps too generously, that no matter what their ability, each student "eventually got something out of the effort."[13]

Teaching strategies in other subjects developed intellectual ability in similar ways. Developing spelling skill was a matter of mastering everyday words and the intricacies of the language. Mastery of elementary mathematics was aimed at being able to compute sums mentally and swiftly. Students developed their mental capacity through memorization and repetitition. In the classroom these skills allowed for play and fun when they were practiced and rewarded through competitions. And when students left school, they had the practical skills necessary for participation in the intellectual and economic life of the midcentury world.

The midcentury economic and social world also required facility in the public presentation of self. Students had to know how to put themselves forward as speakers and as writers. Because the typewriter and the telephone were not invented until 1867 and 1876—and did not enter into general use until the last two decades of the century—handwritten communications were vital in both private and public life. In a world where few had academic or professional degrees and résumés, personal presentation mattered, not just clothes but also voice and handwriting. As an author of a penmanship book explained, letters had to be legible and pleasing, much as "the writer should be decently and becomingly clothed."[14]

Reading aloud was a necessary form of social expression for men, and to a lesser extent for women. As Lincoln did in his famous debates with Stephen A. Douglas in 1858, politicians won support and sometimes fame by how well they spoke before live audiences. Writers and poets, including James Russell Lowell and Emerson, composed many of their great works for public presentation at special events or on the lyceum circuit. (The reclusive but prolific poet Emily Dickinson, who did not publish more than seven of her poems in her lifetime, was a lonely exception.) Victorians assumed that the ability to make public presentations led to personal advancement. In the freedmen's schools, students were often called upon to orate before visiting committees of prominent whites. In all schools the culminating event of the year was a public exhibition before parents and community leaders that always included star students' declamations of famous essays and original compositions. In 1868, perhaps recalling the antidraft riots of the war years, an Ohio girl gave the following salutatory address before her school: "To promote the cause of liberty, we must promote the cause of intelligence. Let those, then, who mourn over the popular commotions which sometimes agitate our country, do everything in their power to lengthen the cords and strengthen the power of the common school."[15]

A story in *McGuffey's Fifth Reader*, "The Good Reader," predicted the rewards that those who made oral presentations would receive. In the story, Frederick the Great, king of Prussia, suffers a momentary inability to read and calls on one of his pages. The boy, a son of a nobleman, could not read well: "He did not articulate distinctly. He huddled his words together in the utterance, as if they were syllables of one long word, which he must get through with as speedily as possible. His pronunciation was bad, and he did not modulate his voice so as to bring out the meaning of what he read. Every sentence was uttered with a dismal monotony of voice, as if it did not differ in any respect from that which preceded it." The king then asked a second page, who was conceited, to read the petition. "He commenced reading slowly and with great formality, emphasizing every word, and prolonging the articulation of every syllable." Then the king summoned a little girl whom he had seen sitting by a fountain in his garden. Although she was the gardener's daughter, she had received a good education in the free schools of her country. Her reading of the petition impressed the king. First, she had glanced at the document to get an impression of what she was to say. Then she "told her story in a simple, concise manner, that carried to the heart a belief of its truth; and [she] read with so much feeling, and with an articulation so just, in tones so pure and distinct," that the king was moved. He granted the petition and dismissed his two pages for one year with the advice that they learn to read aloud. In the end, the king paid for the girl's further education, her father became chief gardener, and the former pages studied and rose "to distinction," one as a lawyer, the other as a statesman.[16]

"The Good Reader" is just one example of how Victorian values were supported in midcentury schools. No one thought that lessons should be "value-free." Instead, as soon as they started learning to read, students also learned that to do well in school and in adult life they had to follow school lessons. Because many stories were set in human or natural history, they seemed universal, not the social creations of a particular group. Schoolchildren believed that they were learning the way things were, not simply the way that their parents and teachers wanted them to be.

McGuffey's Readers and the *Freedman's Readers* introduced students to reading and the natural world in a similar way. In the 1879 edition of *McGuffey's First Eclectic Reader*, the first sentence is, "The dog. The dog ran," accompanied by an illustration of a running dog. As the sentences get longer, the stories and illustrations fill out the picture of a benevolent world. Nature offers a bounty of food, beauty, and opportunities for play. Everyone, including the cartman and a poor family, knows one another and is friendly. There is no evil except that embodied in a rat who lives in the barn, and it meets a fitting fate.

In both series of schoolbooks students learn about the social and intellectual differences between the sexes. Although they read as much as men, mothers and daughters read in woodland settings and relaxing in their parlors; men read sitting more formally at desks and tables. Men ride horses and their sons go fishing; mothers go marketing and daughters build sandcastles. Such lessons were sufficiently persuasive to one woman student who in a school debate affirmed the proposition that "the mind of woman is inferior to that of man." Writing in the 1870s, she found that women "have not ac-

4.1 From *McGuffey's New Second Eclectic Reader* (Cincinnati, 1865), p. 30

4.2 From *McGuffey's New Second Eclectic Reader* (Cincinnati, 1865), p.44

LESSON XV.

cock	wash	pig	too
crows	dawn	dig	two
food	bound	hoe	scrub
wake	clean	plow	bake
home	know	noise	eyes
cheer	knives	kneel	school

What letter is silent in hoe? in clean? Say just, not *jist* catch, not *cotch;* sit, not *set;* father, not *fader.*

THE FREEDMAN'S HOME.

SEE this home! How neat, how warm, how full of cheer, it looks! It seems as if the sun shone in there all the day long. But it takes more than the light of the sun to make a home bright all the time. Do you know what it is? It is love.

4.3 From *The Freedman's Second Reader* (Boston, 1865) p. 35. *Courtesy of Yale University Library, New Haven, Connecticut* complished anything great, nothing worth mentioning." Evidently, school lessons had not taught the young woman about theorists like Mary Wollstonecraft or bestowed the crown of greatness on any famous women, say, Margaret Fuller or Harriet Beecher Stowe.[17]

Schools also taught children that love and concern for others should motivate conduct. They learned to be polite to one another, to respect older people, and to be charitable to those in need. A boy in *McGuffey's First Reader* does as his grandmother bids because "she takes such good care of me that I like to do what she tells me," and a girl's mother gives a lame orphan boy a daily "basket with bread and meat and a little tea for his grandmother." Students also learned kindness to animals, who usually are loyal, obedient, and capable of saving their young friends from drowning. Children never bother birds in their nests, boys never whip their horses and always give them hay or corn when they finish riding, and girls "do not like to see even a rat suffer pain," even if they are not very sorry when a cat kills the rat. Work always precedes play, and there is a distinct time for each. Rewards at both home and school go to children who are industrious and persevere. Above all, God—beneficent, wise, all-knowing, and attentive—rules the universe. "When to Him you tell your woes, / Know the Lord will hear."[18]

Much more fully than *McGuffey's Readers*, the *Freedman's Readers* developed the Victorian definition of home. Assuming that freedmen's children had never experienced a proper home, the authors of the *Freedman's Spelling-Book* defined the home precisely: "Home and family have duties which should be understood and performed. When this is done, home becomes the happiest place on earth." The *Freedman's Second Reader* continued this domestic lesson: in an illustration an African-American husband and wife sit around a parlor table. She sews while her daughter kneels by her side assisting her; the son listens to his father read. The text exclaims, "How neat, how warm, how full of cheer" this home looks. Then it cautions that "it takes more than the light of the sun to make a home bright all the time," for a home needs love.

Students learned that to fill their homes with love their days must follow a certain routine. They must rise at cock's crow, straighten their rooms, and "wash and dress with care." Having set the table and said grace over their food, families breakfast while observing good manners. Children eat slowly, and not "with a noise like the pigs." After the meal, fathers read from the Bible, and if time permits, all sing hymns and pray together. The work of the day follows. Offering more advanced information, the *Freedman's Third Reader* explains that God has ordained marriage and "made it sacred and binding." A most terrible effect of slavery, according to the text, was that it encouraged, even forced, the slaves to violate the "divine law of marriage."

Like *McGuffey's Readers*, the *Freedman's Readers* assigned primary responsibility for the home to mothers. Freedmen's school students learned that poverty was no barrier to their keeping a home so clean and tidy that it would impress visitors. A mother's work is blessed by God, and angels watch her all day;

> Toiling at morn like the busy bee;
> Teaching the little ones A, B, C;
> Hearing the older ones read and spell;
> Smiling and praising when all goes well;
> Washing and brushing, 'twixt work and play,—
> Such is my mother's work, day by day.[20]

Whereas morality in *McGuffey's Readers* and the common schools seemed to be rooted in general assumptions about rightness, the *Freedman's Readers* presented the Bible as the basis of all knowledge, including knowledge about right behavior. To teach "the first principles of morals and religion," every lesson in the speller included at least one appropriate extract from the Bible. Following definitions of weights and measures is a passage from the Gospel of Matthew: "With what judgment ye judge ye shall be judged; and with what measure ye mete it shall be measured to you again." In addition, the readers included as lessons the essential stories from the Old and New Testaments: Adam and Eve, Noah and the flood, the annunciation, the miracles of Jesus, and the resurrection, among others. Freedmen's school teachers also had their students learn the Ten Commandments, the Lord's Prayer, and the Beatitudes. A state school superintendent considered this religious teaching as routine as teaching children "to name all the States and Territories in the United States, and their capitals; the principal rivers and mountains; to bound the United States and many of the States, and to recite items of history connected with the early settlement of the country."[21]

Biblical lessons supplied the foundation for other social and moral lessons in the *Freedman's Readers*—mostly in poems and stories about children, animals, and famous people—as well as the particular doctrinal emphases of the Boston Congregationalists who sponsored the textbooks. While *McGuffey's Readers* presented the religious doctrines of midcentury liberal Protestantism, the *Freedman's Readers* taught the doctrine of religious conservatives, insisting on the existence of innate human sinfulness. Lessons in the *Freedman's Readers* frequently mentioned that children need God's saving grace. In an early lesson in the speller, a bad boy is caught in a web of sin where "no one but God can aid him." A child laments, "Each word I speak with sin is marred, / And every thing I do"; he asks God to

> wash my soul in thine own blood;
>   From every sin set free:
> Renew my heart, and make it good;
>   Then I can live to thee."

83

The corollary of the doctrine of original sin proposed that freedom entails duties, and the *Freedman's Readers* explained how freed men and women could apply this concept. All people had the religious duty to "yield to Christ's yoke," but freed men and women had to realize that "the abolition of slavery has made an alteration in the condition of the freedmen, and laid upon them corresponding duties." The ex-slaves no longer had earthly masters to spell out their duties because the duties of all free people were God-given. The readers minimized the difference between slavery and freedom; whether enslaved or free, no one ever was completely free. Previously physical coercion had made slaves obey their masters; now love of God motivated free people to do His bidding. In a free society, divine duty disciplined and ensured social order.

Promoting such disciplined individualism, lessons in the readers taught freed men and women how to behave as individuals and as members of an orderly society. Significantly, social lessons preceded economic and political ones, and lessons about individual behavior preceded those about behavior as a member of society. An individual's first duty was to recognize that God has provided for everyone and decreed that love is the guiding principle of life. Specifically, the *Freedman's Readers* told ex-slaves to forgive their former masters.

The remainder of the lessons condemned specific behaviors, such as smoking and drinking, and promoted others—honesty, perseverance, kindness, obedience to parents, observance of the Sabbath, respect for the elderly, and benevolence toward others. In a poem, a child resolves:

> I never will do a thing that's wrong,
> Though Satan may tempt me hard and long;
> I never will shun the thing that's right
> And holy and just in God's pure sight:
> I never will; I never will;
> By God's good help, I never will.[23]

Almost all northern teachers were unprepared for their southern assignments. Never having seen an African-American, they went south with preconceptions about the ex-slaves derived from antebellum antislavery debates, the popular press, and especially *Uncle Tom's Cabin*. Assuming that slavery had stunted their capacity for self-control, the teachers believed that the ex-slaves would tend to passionate and immoral behavior. These assumptions conditioned their judgment of the freed people's lives. The emotionalism of African-American religion, with its responsive preaching and physical demonstrations of anguish and joy, struck them as "absurd." Frequent use of tobacco and liquor, especially among young people, appalled the northerners. They complained that the ex-slaves had no concept of an enduring marriage;

men would desert one wife for another. They generalized from incidents of stealing and dishonesty, assuming that they reflected the lack of moral character of an entire people. Still, freedmen's school teachers could appreciate some of the differences between their charges and northern students, and they recognized that their students had had no training in the orderly, self-contained behavior that sitting at school desks required. But northern teachers did not perceive the irony in their stressing individual achievement to a people whose survival as slaves had depended on mutual assistance and complicity.

Even so, the profound religious conviction of most teachers moved them to view freed men and women with sympathy and some understanding. Northerners went south driven by a vision of doing God's work. Educating the freed people was winning souls for Christ. As millennialists, teachers believed that their good work would help prepare the United States and the world for the day when God came to judge the world's people. Deeply feeling the differences between herself and an illiterate ex-slave family living in an agricultural world, a well-educated missionary from comparatively cosmopolitan New England found a common subject in Jesus. "Our hearts were drawn together in the love of a mutual friend." She trusted that an all-knowing God had provided for the ex-slaves' religious practices, such as the "protracted meetings and conversions" that she was inclined to criticize.

Imbued with antislavery convictions, most teachers believed that all are equal before God and condemned slavery for preventing people from achieving full moral growth. Observing dishonesty and thieving among the ex-slaves, teachers attributed their so-called "wrong ideas" to the experience of slavery and maintained their faith in education to bring forth the freedmen's moral potential. Teachers often questioned their own assumptions about race, including the prevalent notion that whites, whom they referred to as Anglo-Saxons, had the greatest intelligence of all the races. A Quaker teacher on the Sea Islands wrote a friend that her experience contradicted the "common knowledge" that superior intelligence among African-Americans belonged to those with the lightest skin. In her experience, "the *blackest* are the *smartest*."[24]

Freedmen's school teachers observed that lessons had to stress "moral culture," which alone would "neutralize the corrupt influences of slavery still remaining." John Alvord advised giving everyday lessons, for "children and adult freedmen have been wronged out of the knowledge of the most common, and to us, familiar things." He believed that drill "in mere technical scholarship" should take second place to the rounding of "every point of character" and lessons in "the minutest habits which perfect the well-trained child."[25]

Superintendents of freedmen's schools told teachers to insist that their students' language and behavior be free "from all offensive and vulgar habits."

Students learned rules of politeness, "Good morals and Gentle manners," as well as promptness, industry, thrift, and as one teacher said, "some grains of yankee energy and ingenuity."[26] In one model school, a teacher made sure that her pupils knew what it was to be clean and neat. She supplied needle and thread to mend torn clothes and soap, towels, and a wash basin for students "in an unwashed condition" to use before taking their places. When they could, teachers tried to mold behavior outside the classroom. Distributing books and clothes donated by sympathetic northerners, teachers in the Sea Islands sought to cultivate the character traits they considered essential in a free society. For their impoverished students they developed a system of exchange: grits could be traded for a petticoat, a chicken for a dress, a dozen eggs for baby clothes, and a half-peck of sweet potatoes for a shirt. Teachers wanted the freed people to learn self-respect and self-reliance and to realize that the government in Washington could not "do as much for them as they could do for *themselves.*"[27]

Common schools also sought to instill habits of neatness, industry, thrift, self-reliance, and politeness, but their lessons were not so elementary. Penmanship drills often required the repetition of phrases such as "Nothing is profitable which is dishonest," "Peace is the glory of a nation," "Aim to reach perfection," and "Youth is the time to learn."[28] Teachers awarded printed cards, called "rewards of merit," for "Industry, Punctuality, and Good Conduct." A reward card was decorated or illustrated, had a student's name filled in on a blank line, and was signed by the teacher. Typical illustrations were scenes of children playing at school, reading in a woodland niche, or having their mother read to them. Some illustrations related to the nation's politics and economy—for example, an eagle superimposed over a view of the Capitol, or a railroad scene with passenger trains going west and freight trains going east. Cards often had captions affirming the behavior for which they were awarded. For instance:

> Oh tis a lovely thing for youth
> To walk betimes in Wisdom's way.
> To fear a lie, to speak the truth,
> That we may trust all they say.

One card counsels its recipient to follow the Golden Rule; another advises:

> When you are told, "Do this or that,"
> Say not "What for," or "Why."
> You'd be a better child by far
> If you should say "I'll try."[29]

Besides encouraging proper behavior through the distribution of reward cards, teachers promoted classroom order by the judicious use of punish-

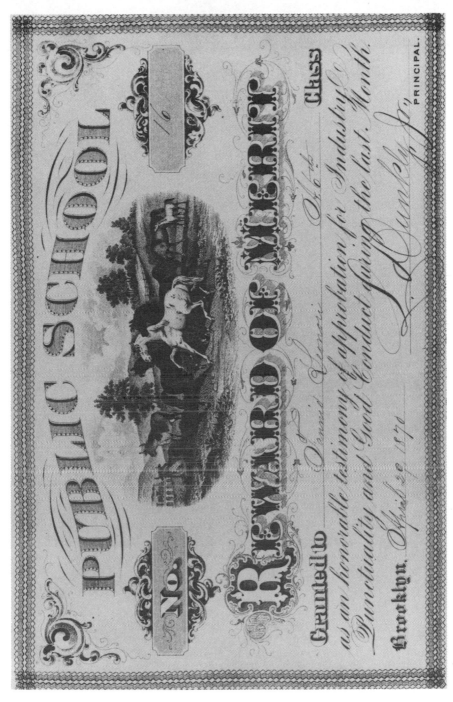

4.4 A Brooklyn, New York, public school merit award, 29 April 1870. *Thelma Mendsen Collection. Courtesy of the Winterthur Library: Joseph Downs Collection of Manuscripts and Printed Ephemera, Henry Francis du Pont Winterthur Museum, Winterthur, Delaware*

ment. In the period 1860–80 state education journals and summer teachers' institutes were discouraging corporal punishment and promoting new methods that motivated obedience by developing students' loyalty and affection for their teachers. Moral suasion thus replaced physical coercion. When students disobeyed, teachers appealed to their consciences and attempted to invoke guilty feelings in them. The last story in *McGuffey's First Reader* tells children that if they are good and try to learn, "your teacher will love you, and you will please your parents."[30] In the common schools the new methods did not immediately take hold; many teachers continued to use physical discipline and humiliation to punish inattention and breaches of order. Unruly students had their knuckles rapped with a ruler or were required to stand for an afternoon on a stool. In the freedmen's schools teachers found that physical punishment was less effective than guilt, for slavery had taught their students to withstand all but the most brutal treatment. Freedmen's school teachers, however, did resort to physical punishment when other measures failed. A teacher in North Carolina observed that, to some students, "the rod is a more potent incentive to duty than any appeal to the affections or reason."[31]

But the stick of discipline, whether physical or mental, usually was accompanied by a carrot. Students were rewarded by being chosen to participate in the public exhibitions of declamation and oration. Especially in rural areas, a standard entertainment was the spelling bee. Students competed against one another, and sometimes against the teacher, to show their mastery of the language. Those who could spell words such as *incomprehensibility, daguerreotype*, and *theodolite* triumphed.[32]

Public exhibitions, spelling bees, and reward cards all had meanings beyond academic success in the schoolroom. They established a different standard of behavior and achievement from what probably prevailed on the street or on school grounds where children played pom-pom-pullaway, needle's eye, ante over, fox and geese, and dummy on a rock. Spelling bees and exhibitions created opportunities for distinction that depended on neither a student's strength and prowess nor a family's economic and social status, and reward cards allowed a child who might never excel at academics to earn commendation.

Nonacademic school lessons were vital for success in the larger world. Encouragement to try and try again not only helped students to succeed in school but also helped them learn how to achieve in a society where little was fixed or permanent. In public exhibitions and oral contests, students practiced the self-presentation skills that would make them successful in everyday life when they had to win mates or talk their way into first jobs. Above all, school competitions permitted self-assertive individualism within the context of community solidarity. The exemplary performance of a few students at a public exhibition was a favorable comment on the accomplishments of their classmates. The triumph of one reflected the high standard of accomplishment in which they all proudly participated.

The economic lessons of the *Freedman's Readers* are much more complete than those of *McGuffey's Readers*, which merely hinted at the middle-class status of their main characters by the location of their homes in the suburbs or rural communities. If students from another planet read only *McGuffey's Readers*, they would wonder what adults did to support their children and provide them with comfortable homes and fashionable, but not ostentatious clothing. While the texts show mothers performing domestic chores, they leave the fathers' daytime whereabouts a mystery. Obviously, students were supposed to know the basics of family economy from their own experience. The *Freedman's Readers* made no such assumptions.

The *Freedman's Spelling-Book* began its elementary economic lesson with the statement, "Labor is man's chief business on earth. He was made to labor with his hands or his mind." In *McGuffey's Readers* agriculture is mentioned less and less frequently in editions issued after 1865; in the *Freedman's Spelling-Book*, however, agriculture is given premier treatment as "the most ancient employment of man," complemented by discussion of other artisan trades such as printing, shoemaking, painting, carpentry, and shipbuilding.[33]

More advanced lessons showed students the place of their labor in macroeconomic systems. To explain how manufacturing adds value to raw materials, a lesson explained the various stages involved in making a pocketknife, from mining the raw material to assembly of the finished product. Another selection explained the mutual dependence of laborers and employers and suggested that they should be friends, even though in the past they often did not understand their mutual dependence and "pulled different ways." Without saying whether labor or capital should take the reins, the reader quoted the proverb that when two ride together one has to ride behind.[34] But the readers' general emphasis on duty probably suggested whom the freedmen were meant to assume rode behind. When the readers addressed current issues, they showed their editors' political allegiances. In good Victorian fashion, selections condemned the importation of luxuries such as laces, silks, and jewelry, and in good Republican fashion, they advocated taxation to pay off the war debts of the Union.

Editions of *McGuffey's Readers* up to 1879 assumed familiarity with the many sides of urban life, for they include words and terms associated with working-class life, such as *foundling* and *public house*. In stories about working-class figures, moral lessons were more important than economic information. The stories were usually about boys who work hard and face some sort of trial. In a very popular story, a young chimneysweep overcomes the temptation to go after easy but dishonest gains. Working in a rich woman's house, he sees a gold watch and considers swiping it. But he thinks, "If I take it I shall be a thief—and yet no body sees me. No body! Does not God see me?

Could I ever again be good? Could I then ever say my prayers again to God? And what should I do when I come to die?" After watching the boy decide not to take the watch, the rich woman rewards him by giving him a home in her house and sending him to school.[35] Another story, new in the 1879 edition, described the success of a bootblack who is so honest, industrious, and polite that many gentlemen patronize him. Success for him means that he earns enough money to support his widowed mother and toddler sister. In *McGuffey's Readers*, individual success is always justified by and subordinated to service to others.

Englishman Thomas Hood's powerful poem "The Song of the Shirt," which appeared in editions from 1857 on, revealed the hardship of working people's lives and suggested that membership in a family brought security. A seamstress, "With fingers weary and worn, / With eyelids heavy and red," dressed "in unwomanly rags" and suffering "in poverty, hunger, and dirt," laments having to work hours so long that "the brain begins to swim" and "the eyes are heavy and dim." She compares herself to a slave working for meager wages:

> . . . a bed of straw,
> A crust of bread—and rags,
> That shattered roof—and this naked floor—
> A table—a broken chair—
> And a wall so blank, my shadow I thank
> For sometimes falling there.

She wonders if hers can be called "Christian work" and calls on fathers, brothers, and sons to realize that, "It is not linen you're wearing out, / But human creatures' lives," for she is "sewing at once, with a double thread, / A shroud as well as a shirt."[36]

Editors meant this poem to establish the family as the foundation of social security rather than to indict employers and expose the awful conditions under which many toiled. By focusing on a working woman, the poem leaves open the possibility that a laboring man could support himself and his family without having to work at such drudgery. Lamenting the loss of a home, the seamstress calls on the benevolence of fathers, sons, and husbands—not employers—to save daughters, mothers, and wives from a life such as hers.

The *Freedman's Readers* and *McGuffey's Readers* took opposite approaches to the great event of the 1860s—the Civil War. Published in the months after the Union victory, by an organization with antislavery views, and for an audience of ex-slaves, the *Freedman's Readers* reflected clearly the impact of the Civil War and the influence of antislavery thought. *McGuffey's Readers*, however, did not. Their editors always sought the largest audience for their books and knew that inclusion of strong antislavery, prowar statements probably would have reduced readership in northern areas of anti-war Copperhead strength.

The *Freedman's Readers* contained selections offensive to southerners but of interest to freed men and women, including the Emancipation Proclamation, the Gettysburg Address, and the full text of Whittier's poem about freedom coming to the Carolinas, "The Free Children." The readers stated clearly that the Civil War was about slavery, and they celebrated the role of African-American soldiers. They included selections about wartime heroes, such as the soldier who kept the U.S. flag aloft during the bloody Union attack on Fort Wagner, in which the 54th Massachusetts Infantry participated. The stirring poem, "No Slave beneath the Flag," extolled the contributions of African-American soldiers to the Union cause.

> No slave beneath that starry flag,
> The emblem of the free!
> No fettered hand shall wield the brand
> That smites for Liberty!
> No tramp of servile armies
> Shall shame Columbia's shore;
> For he who fights for Freedom's rights
> Is free for evermore!
> . . . .
> No slave beneath the grand old flag!
> For ever let it fly,
> With lightning rolled in every fold,
> And flashing victory!
> God's blessing breathe around it;
> And, when all strife is done,
> May Freedom's light that knows no night,
> Make every star a sun!

The *Freedman's Readers* suggested that, for African-Americans and whites with abolitionist sentiments, the war had purged some racist theories from intellectual discourse. Poems and prose selections explicitly refuted antebellum racist theories. Contradicting the southern evangelical belief that heaven is segregated, a poem claimed that both races go to the same heaven, and that this great and "glorious news is true." And countering the teaching of many prominent northern and southern scientists that God created the two races separately, one selection asserted that "we are all created by God, and of one blood; therefore we are brethren. Our first duty, then, towards every human being, is to love them. No one, however far away from us, however different in customs or features, though poorer, or more unfortunate, or more sinful, than we are, must be denied our kind regard, as bound to us by this tie of universal brotherhood."[37]

Selections also taught African-American students about their heritage and in the process transmitted Victorian values. For example, students learned that trade with money is superior to barter and that for money African tribes had used shells. In minibiographies of African-Americans, students found role models who were admirable for their literacy, honesty, modesty in manners and dress, and devotion to a larger cause. Complementing these biographies was one of Abraham Lincoln.

Although George Washington was mentioned in a few selections, Lincoln was the one white to receive a full biographical treatment, and he was presented as the paragon of American virtues. The readers include stories of his early life—mentioning the value that he placed on his first earned dollar—and they contain his most important writings of the war years—the Emancipation Proclamation, the Gettysburg Address, and the Second Inaugural Address. Lincoln's biography taught, on the one hand, about the power of the individual—to educate himself, to value modest achievement, and to rise above menial labor—and on the other hand, about the duty to do good for others. Victorian Americans understood that individual achievement by their self-made heroes and heroines contributed to the welfare of all. Although they recognized that African-American students needed a different pantheon of heroes and heroines, Victorians hoped that ultimately all would share Victorian values.

In response to the Civil War, the *McGuffey's Readers'* revised editions of 1862 and 1866 included war stories and poems, but never important war documents like the Emancipation Proclamation, condemnations of slavery, or justifications of the Union cause. Instead, stories and poems in these editions evoke the horror of war and its effect on loved ones, issues upon which Republicans and Copperhead Democrats could agree. Then, from the 1879 revised edition on, all selections about war deaths and the experience of battle were cut as were selections about the impact of the Civil War on personal lives in the North. For example, a portion of a longer work about the Revolutionary War, "The Brave at Home" by Thomas Buchanan Read, which evoked sentiments of loss that both northerners and southerners could share and had entered the *Sixth Reader* in 1862, survived the 1879 cut. It portrayed the bravery and self-denial of the sweethearts, mothers, and wives who send their men to war:

> The wife who girds her husband's sword,
> 'Mid little ones who weep and wonder,
> And bravely speaks the cheering word,
> What though her heart be rent asunder.[38]

On the other hand, "The Picket" by Ethel Lynn Beers, a poem commonly associated with the Union cause because of the first line of the first and last stanzas, was omitted from the 1879 edition. Beers described the solitary vigil of a picket in front of the Union lines and the effect of the decisive single shot that makes the night totally quiet:

> There is only the sound of the lone sentry's tread,
>   As he tramps from the rock to the fountain,
> And thinks of the two in the low trundle-bed,
>   Far away in the cot on the mountain.
> . . . .
> "All quiet along the Potomac to-night',"
>   No sound save the rush of the river;
> While soft fall the dew on the face of the dead:
>   The picket's off duty forever![39]

Even with all explicit references to the Civil War and the northern cause removed, *McGuffey's Readers* after the 1879 revision still fall short of being national readers. African-Americans, like ethnic groups whose members belonged primarily to the lower classes, appeared in no illustrations and were not principal characters in any stories.

Still, the 1879 edition did try to be national in one respect: the editors added a few more selections by southern authors, selected and edited to convey national or nonpolitical themes. For example, Robert Haynes's speech on the tariff controversy of 1830 was one of the few southern documents included before 1879. Read in its entirety, the speech is a sectional statement, but the *McGuffey's* version omitted his description of South Carolina's particular economic interests. The resulting extract evoked national unity by presenting Haynes's historical account of his state's loyalty to the national cause in the Revolution. Haynes's speech complements Daniel Webster's famous statement of the northern Whig position in the tariff controversy, which concludes, "Liberty and Union, now and forever: one and inseparable!" In 1879 the *McGuffey's* editors added "A Common Thought," a poem about death by South Carolinian Henry Timrod, and an extract from President Thomas Jefferson's first inaugural address (1801), which the editors entitled "Political Toleration." Although it was originally directed at the political controversy in the election of 1800, the editors obviously hoped that it would instruct citizens in both the North and the South after the bitter and contested election of 1876 between Rutherford B. Hayes and Samuel J. Tilden, which Hayes won by one electoral college vote. The edited selection begins: "During the contest of opinion through which we have passed, the animation of discussions and of exertions has sometimes worn an aspect which might impose on strangers, unused to think freely and to speak and to write what they think; but this now decided by the voice of the nation, announced according to the rules of the constitution, all will, of course, arrange themselves under the will of the law, and unite in common efforts for the common good."[40]

While the *McGuffey's* editors were sidestepping many of the controversial issues raised in the North by the Civil War, textbooks from the South reflect more clearly the impact of the war on southern education. Much fundamental knowledge changed with the founding of the Confederacy, for Southerners had to define the meaning of their own nation. During the war they issued schoolbooks, including arithmetics, spellers, readers, histories, grammars, and geographies; children learned to spell from the *Texas Primer* and read in *The First Reader, for Southern Schools*. These texts taught children specifically southern ways of thinking and how to expunge "Yankee degeneracies" from their speech. For example, *The First Reader* told students that "God wills that some men should be slaves, and some masters." An arithmetic text published in 1864 asked how many Confederates it would take to kill 49 Yankees if one Confederate could kill seven Yankees. Readers of the *Geographical Reader for Dixie Children* (1863) learned that the southern states seceded because "Abraham Lincoln was a weak man, and the South believed he would allow laws to be made which would deprive them of their rights." Besides such lessons in national politics, the texts also bore witness to the horrors of battle. Elementary students read: "That man's arm has been cut off. It was shot off by a gun. Oh! What a sad thing war is."[41] Even after the Civil War teachers tried to maintain the intellectual foundations of southern distinctiveness. When using readers published in the North that referred unflatteringly to the South, such as John C. Ridpath's *History of the United States* (1876), some teachers instructed their students to pin together the pages containing the offensive remarks.

After the war, southern textbook authors continued to defend the South. History texts, with their discussions of political issues, show Southern loyalties most clearly. Southern histories disputed the idea that the American republic owed its origins to the Puritan settlers of New England and that the Civil War resulted from southern violations of federal law. *A Southern School History of the United States of America* (1869) emphasized the contributions of Virginia to the growth of the American republic. It traced American "principles of liberty" back through the settlers of Virginia to England and its Glorious Revolution of 1688. The text cited the irreconcilable differences in politics, society, and commercial interests between the North and the South as the cause of the Civil War. Fanatics (abolitionists) supposedly had aggravated these differences by urging violation of the Fugitive Slave Law, encouraging violence in Kansas, and fomenting rebellion among the slaves. Abraham Lincoln was ultimately responsible for the war, however, because he had commanded the provisioning of Fort Sumter and then proclaimed war in response to its bombardment. During the war the Confederacy had been unified even though southerners experienced severe suffering, while the North had been the scene of "the wildest anarchy," such as the New York City draft riots of 1863. Finally, might had prevailed; the North had won the war because of its superior numbers.[42]

Despite their differences, northern and southern school histories shared an intellectual world founded on the premise that truth is divine and absolute. To both northerners and southerners, history was a narrative focusing on the political growth of the nation, with an emphasis on wars, especially the Revolutionary War. Even a writer who introduced his book by saying that he wanted to emphasize peacetime, for "the true glory of a nation lies, after all, in orderly progress," devoted 18 percent of his book to the Revolutionary War and the events leading up to it. It was an appealing period to authors: they could spin tales about the American people's supposedly innate commitment to liberty. According to one writer, a British officer whose troops had been snowballed by Boston boys purportedly exclaimed, "The very children draw in a love of liberty with the air they breathe."[43]

In all schoolbooks Native Americans were presented as an uncivilized and savage people. Without discriminating among the various tribes, authors claimed that all Indians had a passion for war and practiced the warfare techniques of ambush and massacre. They were barbarians in art, their houses were hovels, and their writing resembled "half-intelligible hieroglyphics." Native Americans supposedly had a shallow intellectual life, for their language appeared to be incapable of expressing abstract thought. Except for the tribes of the southeastern United States, which had acquired some civilization, all tribes were heading for extinction. Textbook authors never mentioned that diseases imported from Europe and American colonists' settlement of Indian lands were hastening this supposedly natural process.[44]

In the postwar years northern history writers attempted to put regional disputes behind them and to write for the nation. One author said his purpose was to write "free from partisan bias of sectionalism, politics, or religion"; he wanted his tone to be "as completely as possible *American*."[45] To balance their treatment, historians discussed both the good and bad aspects of New England and southern colonial history and devoted roughly the same number of pages to each region. For New England, they mentioned the advocates of "free opinion," such as Anne Hutchinson and Roger Williams, as well as the Salem witch trials. For the South, they balanced the persecution of Baptists and Quakers in Virginia with the democratic sentiments implicit in Bacon's Rebellion. When they reached the difficult issue of the Civil War, many authors followed the lead of former Confederate vice president Alexander H. Stephens, whose *A Constitutional View of the Late War* (1870) blamed the war on opposing constitutional interpretations. Although he was a Confederate partisan, Stephens showed the way to sectional reconciliation by elevating the constitutional issue and minimizing the idea of the war as a conflict over slavery.

Gradually, northern authors reduced the importance of the slavery issue; they referred to slavery indirectly as a labor system and noted it as only one of many secondary causes which included the regions' isolation from each other and the heated feelings stirred up by demagogues and sectional literature. Although by 1880 no northern text contained any remark about slavery that could be offensive to former Confederates, there were still many pages in northern texts that southern teachers told their students to pin together. Northern authors did not compromise their treatment of Lincoln, whom they considered an exemplary man and leader: "prudent far-sighted, and resolute; thoughtful, calm, and just; patient, tender-hearted, and great." Most northern writers blamed the South for starting the war.[46]

Not all changes in Victorian education from 1860 to 1880 can be traced through study of the freedmen's schools because after 1870 they were replaced by state-supported school systems. The relief agencies committed to freedmen's education transferred their efforts to higher education (a subject of chapter 5). The revised editions of *McGuffey's Readers* published in these two decades are a more revealing source. They reveal that the most significant intellectual change arose neither from the experiences of Civil War and the reincorporation of a conquered people into the Union nor from the impact of Charles Darwin's *On the Origin of Species*. In *McGuffey's Readers* Darwin's theory of evolution prompted only minor editing; it did not crack the certainty and orderliness of the Victorian intellectual world. In a selection first included in the 1836 edition, it was asserted that the earth began exactly 6,000 years ago; this statement was lightly edited in the 1865 edition to "many thousands of years ago." The most significant intellectual changes were in the religious content of schoolbooks; they became less evangelically Protestant and more nondenominationally Christian.

Since the founding of the common schools in the 1830s, there had been many objections to the lessons about Protestantism in the textbooks they used. Antebellum editions referred to the pope negatively and sought to teach evangelical Protestant doctrine. But driven by their desire to embrace the widest possible market for textbook sales and to make the common schools a truly common experience, textbook writers from 1850 to 1880 tried to eliminate the sectarianism of their lessons and reach the largest audience. Editions of the 1860s and 1870s were not militantly Protestant, nor were they critical of Catholics and Jews. Although *McGuffey's Readers* contained many selections from the Bible, most came from the Old Testament, particularly the Psalms. Selections from the New Testament were often general teachings, such as the Sermon on the Mount, rather than descriptions of the life of Jesus. The strident evangelical literature that associated the cruxificion of Jesus with the sins of the Jews disappeared, but the famous scene from Shakespeare's *The Merchant of Venice*, in which the Jew Shylock demands his pound of flesh, stayed. By the 1860s *McGuffey's Readers* had omitted all anti-Catholic references. Intemperate men who lose their jobs and end up in prison had inoffensive names like Tom Smith rather than Irish names. *McGuffey's Readers* did not expose students to the explicit anti-immigrant slurs that could be found elsewhere, such as in trade catalogs and stereographs.

By the 1870s the evangelicalism and sectarian religious doctrine of the antebellum years had disappeared from common school textbooks. In penmanship drills children of the 1870s copied "Fortune favors the brave," and, "Command all excellence," while children of the 1850s had written, "Fear God and keep all his Commandments," and, "No man may put off the knowledge of God."[47] As the century progressed, God became less judgmental and more benevolent. The chimney sweep story, in which fear of God's wrath inspires right behavior, was cut from the 1879 edition of *McGuffey's Readers* (although protests from students and teachers brought it back in 1885). The emphasis on original sin vanished, and children were presented more often as innately good. Reminders that even children should prepare for God's judgment and the next life disappeared as death ceased to be a recurring subject. And believing that students had the capacity to act correctly, common school teachers turned in their switches and tuned in to students' consciences.

Despite the changed relationship to religion in the common schools of the 1870s, Americans were just as religious in 1870 as they had been in 1850. Outside the schools doctrinal controversy still troubled the churches. As the 1879 *McGuffey's* revision was being prepared, Dwight Moody and Ira Sankey were conducting their wildly popular revival campaign and filling auditoriums in major cities with 10,000–20,000 people, huge crowds for the day. And the Young Men's Christian Association was just beginning to attract college men for missionary service in the cities. But all this was happening outside the common schools. Although their curricula included prayers, hymn singing, and Bible stories, their moral lessons were now primarily nondenominational. Most Protestants could agree with common school lessons about the importance of the individual and the rightness of hard work, thrift, honesty, and perseverance. Further, Catholics and Jews could adapt these lessons to their own religious and ethnic traditions because they did not include explicitly Protestant teachings. Common schools of the 1870s taught American values, not Protestant doctrine.

The largest question that Victorians of the 1860s and 1870s faced was how African-Americans would fit into American life. *McGuffey's Readers* do not show us how they answered this question. Their stories contained no racist slurs or statements because none mentioned African-Americans. Information about the place that Victorians gave African-Americans in American life must come from the *Freedman's Readers*.

The *Freedman's Readers* encouraged African-Americans to take their place in the world as independent men and women employed in the artisan trades and agriculture. In the 1860s and 1870s this vision was realistic, for the South was an agricultural region, 75 percent of Americans still lived in rural areas, and even in northern cities factories with owners and laborers had not yet totally replaced artisan shops and become the dominant institutions of industry. According to republican thought, once the former slaves became self-supporting farmers and artisans skilled in their callings, they would be able to support their families and be materially independent. As a freedmen's school teacher explained, they would "possess comfortable homes, land, and means to improve it; be skilled in labor; be a producing class, acting both independently and in combination; able to cope with all other men in any department of human achievement."[48]

Freedmen's school teachers also hoped that their students would realize their intellectual potential and become well-rounded and cultured people. Selections in the *Freedman's Readers* discuss art and music and mention noteworthy African-American ministers, teachers, and writers. Perhaps some teachers drew out the implications of these biographies for their students, as John Alvord did. "Why if thus trained, should not many of them be foremost at length in the great interest of agriculture, manufactures, and commerce? Why not wield capital and have the influence of it? . . . From such a stage of advancement the "American of African descent" would doubtless go forward into aesthetic attainment, furnishing, for aught we can see, his quota of the statesmen, poets, divines, artists, and philosophers of the day."[49]

Although the Civil War held out the promise of self-development to the few African-Americans fortunate enough to study in the freedmen's schools, it held slight promise for their integration into American society. The *Freedman's Readers* demonstrate that even white supporters of freedmen's education had no vision of freed men and women entering society as full equals. Alvord urged African-Americans to develop their own leaders but did not suggest that they would lead whites or that they and whites together would lead America. Rather, Alvord and most white Americans seem to have imagined that their society would dominate African-American society by existing parallel to it but above and separate from it. When in *Plessy* vs. *Ferguson* (1896) the Supreme Court upheld a Louisiana law and ruled that African-Americans had a right to separate but equal access to state-supported or -regulated facilities, it gave the highest legal sanction to the ways of thinking that had prevailed since immediately after the Civil War, even among the more enlightened northerners.

The illustrations and stories in the *Freedman's Readers* confirm that whites did not anticipate racial integration. Even though written for a readership of freed men and women, the readers contain few illustrations of African-Americans; pictures of white children predominate. In one story in which African-Americans and whites interact, "Tidy Learning to Read," whites play the active role. The servant Tidy carries the books of two white girls, whom she calls Miss Susie and Miss Amelia. Tidy expresses an interest in learning to read; the white girls start to teach her but when the school bell rings they leave to go to class. Tidy sits outside learning by herself. Here is a story of an African-American who even though she is becoming literate, is still dependent on whites and is excluded from the institutions of American life.

Compared to contemporary periodicals, stereographs, and advertisements, however, the racism of the *Freedman's Readers* is mild. Magazines popular among Victorian Americans and advertising literature for middle-class goods reveal that virulent racial prejudices permeated postwar society. While northerners sat in their parlors and read glowing accounts in *Harper's Weekly* of the achievements of the students in the freedmen's schools, they also were looking at illustrations in the same periodical that questioned African-Americans' potential for intellectual growth. Cartoons typically showed them at play. They jump in glee, wear oversized smiles, and get involved in situations that make them look foolish. Their physical portrayal—large eyes, big lips, and sloping foreheads—would have prompted readers versed in the latest phrenological thought to question their brain power. A typical cartoon appeared in the 8 December 1877 issue and was entitled "Return of the First Born from College." The son is dressed ostentatiously; he sports an umbrella, spats, a cigarette, and a handkerchief in his pocket. Surrounded by five children, his mother exclaims, "Bress his heart! Don't he look edgecated." White readers probably noted her language, surmised that the presence of five children meant that she had little self-control, and wondered if African-American colleges taught their students anything besides expensive self-indulgence. For long after the Civil War, most white Americans continued to think of African-Americans as inferiors. Most former slaves held menial positions, and their language, as rendered in popular literature, indicated that they could do no better. In an 1879 ad for a clothes wringer, a white woman asks, "What Dinah! Finished washing so soon?" The servant replies, "Hi Golly! Mistis, been done dese two hour. Dis chile hab no more trouble, since you done got dis wringer. Neber tear de clothes needer."[50]

Such caricatures suggest that a majority of Americans did not share the hopes of white freedmen's school teachers, however limited and racist those hopes were. The prejudice reflected in school readers may not have been the worst to confront African-Americans. By not opposing racism, however, schools let white children learn prejudice from the popular media, as well as from family and friends. When the subject was racism, schools did not teach—but also did not counter—the taken-for-granted lessons of postwar America.

Although education could not open doors for African-Americans into the white social world, social change was occurring, even in the South. In the North the Pennsylvania Supreme Court awarded damages in 1881 to a middle-class Philadelphia couple who had been refused admission on the basis of their race from a theater benefit for the 1876 International Centennial Exhibition. In the South progress took another route. Before the war even

free African-Americans had been excluded from all private and public institutions; after the war they began to be admitted to public institutions, including streetcars, restaurants, theaters, and schools. But admission came at
a price: legally mandated segregation within these institutions. In 1877 the
North and the South were politically unified; African-Americans had entered public life, on restrictive terms, but they never entered the parlors of
white Americans as equals.

five

Leaders for Parlor and Public Life

Few Americans pursued higher education in the 1860s and 1870s: merely 1.28 percent in 1870 and 1.38 percent in 1880 of white men and women between the ages of 20 and 24 enrolled in college and university undergraduate programs. But these few held important positions. Although nearly 1.5 percent of the American work force in 1860 was made up of doctors, ministers, and lawyers, about 70 percent of men college graduates entered these professions. After 1860 certain fields—publishing, for instance—began to require a college degree, as did new pursuits such as civil engineering. Although most high-status professions included only tiny numbers of women— they numbered fewer than 1 percent of lawyers in 1880—women college graduates were far more likely than women nongraduates to work at some point in their lives and to work as professionals. About 70 percent of women who graduated from college between 1869 and 1910 worked as teachers or college educators at some time in their lives.[1]

Despite the small percentage of young people attending college, the developments of 1860–80 suggest a consensus among Victorians that college education was necessary for individual advancement and for the improvement of American society. During these two decades, higher education was opened to new populations. Victorians founded colleges and universities for African-Americans, started women's colleges, and opened up state-supported and private universities to women. During the 1860s college enrollments of men increased 26 percent, and during the 1870s enrollments of men and women increased 28 percent.[2] It was also at this time that educational leaders introduced the reforms that would make college education a typical experience for middle-class youth by the mid-twentieth century.

Several interrelated ideas lay behind the expansion of American higher education. Victorians drew from republican thought the belief that the welfare, survival, and prosperity of the nation depended on an educated citizenry. Sons learned from mothers the principles of good citizenship. As patriotic citizens, they were to set aside self-interest for the civic good, much as George Washington did when he left his farm to lead the country. Virtuous daughters were supposed to recognize their duty to the republic, learn its fundamental principles during their school years, and dedicate themselves to passing those principles along to the next generation. Most educators agreed with Matthew Vassar, the founder of the college that bears his name, that women college graduates "will become the mothers of men who will hold in their hands the destinies of this nation."[3]

Victorians modified the republican thought of the new nation by emphasizing that individuals should develop all aspects of their being—aesthetic, moral, and intellectual—to become whole and they understood that self-development, or culture, had different meanings for white men, women, and African-Americans. Almost no white anticipated an integrated society. Whites hoped that African-American men would lead their own communities and that white men would lead their communities and the nation toward its destiny, which was usually described in Christian millennial terms. Women, too, could contribute to this future. In the postwar years, however, it was unclear whether higher education was intended to help women extend their influence into public life or to enhance their indirect influence through private life. This chapter will examine the different meanings of higher education for white men, African-Americans, and women.

To college students, professors, and presidents, it seemed logical that, as institutions of mental and moral culture, colleges should supply the nation's leaders. To understand the role of colleges and universities in the 1860s and 1870s, we need to understand the Victorian definition of intellectual leadership. In these years, that definition was changing. Since the Revolutionary era, only men had been intellectual leaders in public life. Although many men became leaders because of their practical accomplishments, Victorians usually recognized those who had become influential in their communities by dint of general knowledge and character. College education was no prerequisite for leadership, even though many leaders had attended college. Men like Abraham Lincoln, John Gough, and Elihu Burritt became leaders after following a program of self-education that complemented their moral character. Fluidity characterized many of these men's careers. Lawyers entered politics, theology school graduates became journalists and college professors or presidents, and journalists became landscape architects and city planners. In the cities, educated men formed clubs to read and discuss books of current interest. Doctors, lawyers, ministers, merchants, journalists, and men of leisure were expected to have informed opinions and to be able to speak knowledgeably and with authority on a variety of issues germane to not only their professions but also contemporary politics, morality, and public life. In northern and western communities, these men were the ones who shaped public opinion on common schools and public libraries, parks, and museums.

A new kind of leader began to appear in the midcentury years and overlapped for a time the old style. Victorians began to expect their intellectual leaders to be experts—that is, to have acquired specialized knowledge through an appropriate course of study in an institution of higher education. Equipped with academic degrees as credentials, experts owed their primary loyalty to a community not of place but of fellow experts. Lawyers established their first national association in 1878, librarians in 1876, and social workers in 1874. In the older professions that already had associations, the subgroups representing new specialties multiplied. Between 1864 and 1880 physicians founded 10 subsocieties, such as groups of neurologists and surgeons. The new leaders believed that those without similar credentials were amateurs—or worse, charlatans and quacks—and tried to minimize their public influence.

In the period of transition—from the 1850s to the 1890s—men often had old-style preparation for new-style leadership. For instance, through self-education, including travel, reading, and journalistic writing, Frederick Law Olmsted developed enough expertise on landscape architecture and city planning that he was selected to prepare plans for Central Park in New York City. In the 1860s and 1870s college presidents and city officials across the United States called upon him as an expert to advise them in developing their campuses and urban park systems.

At this time professional associations had many members with old-style educations. The founding of many associations preceded the development of formal professional training; for a while, their leaders continued to consider diligent, self-directed preparation a sufficient qualification for membership. In the 1870s most members of the American Library Association had acquired their education on the job and some had not even attended college. Further, associations often had members who merely had an interest in the organization's purpose. One of the more important organizations of the transition period was the American Social Science Association (ASSA), founded in 1865. It promoted the collection of the statistics necessary for formulating social reform programs, and its members were college professors, journalists, and supporters of reform causes.

But the commitment of social scientists to broad-gauge reform was transitory. Discipline-specific social science organizations began to appear in the 1880s, including the American Historical Association (1884) and the American Economic Association (1885). They appealed more and more exclusively to academics and included fewer and fewer supporters of general reform causes. Many professional organizations also began to restrict their leadership positions to members employed in the profession. In other words, professional organizations were no longer for amateurs. And starting in the late 1880s, academics who wished to advance in their own institutions and in their professional organizations had to eschew reform and pursue discipline-specific research problems. As the nineteenth century ended, informally educated experts like Olmsted had become an endangered species. Not surprisingly, the new leaders needed a specific sort of college preparation, and they found it in the reformed liberal arts colleges, state universities and newly founded research universities.

Founded on the principle that college students were youths in need of disciplined guidance, the liberal arts college had required all students to follow the same curriculum. For example, starting in 1875 Yale College freshmen and sophomores studied Greek, Latin, mathematics, and rhetoric—which was divided into declamation and composition—and one trimester each of hygiene and Roman history. Juniors studied logic, physics, astronomy, and a modern language. Seniors continued their study of rhetoric and the natural sciences with courses in chemistry and geology, and they could elect either astronomy or German. The remaining senior-year courses supposedly familiarized students with the principles and general knowledge that they would need to participate in the public life of their communities. They studied mental philosophy (psychology), moral philosophy, the history of philosophy, political science (politics, economics, and international law), and history (European, English, and American constitutional). As the Williams College catalog explained, "The work . . . is so arranged that the principal studies of senior year relate to man himself as physical, intellectual, moral and religious being."[4] Devoting 60 percent of their time to the study of languages and mathematics, 20 percent to natural science, and 12 percent to social sciences, University of North Carolina students followed a similar curriculum until 1875.

The term "old-time college," usually found in the speeches of proponents of educational reform, suggests that colleges had not changed much over the course of the century. That was partly true. The mandatory Latin, Greek, mathematics, mental and moral philosophy, and rhetoric courses of 1875 had been required since the early years of the century. Only natural science, political science, and history courses had been added to the standard curriculum during the antebellum period. Even so, the content of liberal arts curricula had been changing substantially. In 1875 professors taught courses differently from their precursors. Negatively influenced by the excesses of evangelical religion in the antebellum period, and attracted by the promise of romantic thought in religion and education, professors were reconceptualizing education as a means of cultivating the whole individual rather than merely disciplining the mental faculties. This new thinking affected some colleges profoundly, but others remained almost untouched. Throughout the 1870s the professor of classical languages at the University of Virginia continued to teach Greek and Latin grammar as a mental discipline.

In the 1860s and 1870s Yale College epitomized the effect of educational reform on the liberal arts college. Its professors modified the teaching practices of the old-time college, and through other means they extended their influence beyond their New Haven classrooms. Yale graduates who became college professors carried their teachers' ideas throughout the East and Midwest, and Yale professors' popular college textbooks in mental and moral philosophy, political science, international law, history, and natural sciences disseminated their ideas to a national audience.

Mental philosophy was a key course in the liberal arts college because it explained the intellectual premises of its teachings. From the preeminent mental philosopher of the 1860s and 1870s, Professor Noah Porter, Yale students learned that knowing was possible because "the *rational methods of the divine and human intellect* are similar" (emphasis in original).[5] Porter taught that the human mind acts creatively to see the facts found in natural science and in human life and history as part of a divine universe. Like most other Victorians, he assumed that God was beneficent and that He had arranged human and natural life according to certain uniform principles. Divine in origin, the world possesses an essential orderliness based on harmony, beauty, and grace. On the one hand, Porter sidestepped issues of Biblical accuracy by deriving from the Bible only the moral view that allowed him to interpret the world as a divine creation. On the other hand, he rejected the gloomy implication of Charles Darwin's *On the Origin of Species*: that natural progress is random, wasteful, and savage. For Porter, his colleagues, and the readers of their texts, facts in the natural world expressed "truth." Transcendent in meaning, truth suggested that this world stands before a divine reality. For example, students were taught to locate a fact—which might be a geological specimen or a literary text—ascertain its situation in time and place, and then associate it with the divine order. Reading the introduction to James Dwight Dana's *Manual of Mineralogy* (1849), a widely used college text throughout the nineteenth century, students learned that rocks could exhibit divine truth: "We are no longer dealing with pebbles of pretty shapes and tints, but with objects modeled by a Divine hand; and every additional fact becomes a new revelation of his wisdom."[6]

All Yale courses imparted both information and moral lessons. The study of history and the Greek and Latin languages provided students with models for public life and cautionary tales about pride, materialism, and hedonism. Students learned that individuals had largely determined the course of history. Their studies focused on ancient heroes, kings, statesmen, and religious leaders. Texts described how events flowed along until a moment of choice for such an individual appeared. Then, if he was in harmony with his times, he could rally people behind him to follow his course of action. Because successful individuals always drew upon the past, their actions contributed to continuous and seamless historical progress, which resulted from human action. Since historical progress was a matter of individual and national self-development, history and political science courses warned students, away from certain "false" theories, especially the social contract theory of government associated with the French Revolution, and the idea of *vox populi, vox dei* (the voice of the people is the voice of God) associated with Jacksonian democracy. Students were taught that such false theories had blocked national moral development: their proponents assumed that government had limited responsibility and could not promote moral development, or they recognized no higher law governing national policy.

Students in liberal arts colleges learned these lessons from professors who used the recitation method of instruction. Students came to class prepared to answer questions about the assigned reading from the night before. Some teachers, as has ever been the case, were boring and uninspired. Critics of the recitation method objected to knowledge being reduced to memorization of the assigned text. But a skilled teacher, a recitation advocate suggested, could touch "the inner life of the pupil by what he says and does, as no other person can." One former student praised his professor of moral philosophy for teaching more than facts: "He taught men how to think." In the late 1870s, when some professors at New York University began to adopt the lecture method of instruction, editorials appeared in the student newspaper objecting to the "merely mechanical work" of copying and memorizing lecture notes.[7] Through the recitation method, students learned to respect their teachers' minds; teachers could become for them the role model of the cultured man devoted to serving a nonworldly pursuit. Students' affection for their professors then replaced fear of punishment as the engine of college discipline.

An extensive system of rules and punishments had governed colleges until the decade or so before the Civil War, when many college faculties turned from a system of demerits to new disciplinary methods. Much like common school teachers, professors began to emphasize the development of loyalty between themselves and their students. Supposedly, affection would make students responsive to college rules and would govern their behavior. If this system of voluntary discipline did not work, academic performance kept students in line. Once his or her grades fell below a minimum level, a student could be suspended or dismissed. Even at reformed colleges in the 1860s and 1870s, requirements included class attendance, as well as attendance at daily, sometimes twice daily, chapel services and Sunday church services. And the new discipline based on affection did not penetrate all colleges. Vanderbilt University, which opened in 1875 as a university in name but an old-time liberal arts college in form, had extensive rules prohibiting students from forming secret societies, playing billiards, and attending horse races, theaters, saloons, and other "places of dissipation" (brothels).

Christian belief permeated liberal arts colleges, for they were thoroughly Christian institutions. Daily chapel services and Sunday worship were the formal manifestations of the faith that ideally united professors and students, as well as academic and extracurricular life. College was a way of extending Christian nurture from the family to the higher intellectual life. Even secular subjects revealed how divine law and truth pervaded human creations and the natural world. All college studies were part of a unified program of Christian education; one college president, Yale's Porter, compared the collegiate experience of Christian culture to a "fusing crucible." Students submitted their traditional beliefs to its heat, in which they were blended with ideas from the fields of history, philosophy, literature, and science. Combined with these new elements and purged of impurities, students' religious beliefs appeared "in purer metal and brighter luster."[8] With this fortified Christian faith, students could live in the world as Christian men confident that no new invention or discovery would overturn the basis of their belief.

Students' extracurricular life largely complemented official college activities. Most colleges had literary societies, which had been the mainstay of collegiate extracurricular life since the eighteenth century. The societies almost always took names derived from classical sources, such as the Cliosophic and the Philomathean, and most colleges had two rival societies to which most of the student body belonged. Recognizing their educational benefits, colleges sanctioned literary societies. At New York University societies enjoyed the use of rooms in the college building, while fraternities, which were unsanctioned, had no permanent meeting place and met wherever they could. The architecture and placement of the buildings of the Diagnothean and Goethean literary societies at Franklin and Marshall College in Lancaster, Pennsylvania, demonstrate the integral connection between the societies and the college. Students raised funds for these two impressive Gothic-revival structures, which were completed in 1857 and situated on either side of Main building. The literary society buildings complemented its design and with it formed the college row facing a city avenue. After leaving Main, which housed classrooms, chapel, and college offices, students entered their literary society buildings to participate in their self-governed societies. Leaving Main did not mean leaving one intellectual world and entering another. Just as the three campus buildings formed a visual whole, so the intellectual content of college studies and literary society activities were interrelated.

Most literary societies met twice weekly, once for debate and once for disciplinary proceedings, when a disciplinary board levied fines and punishments for absences and indecorous behavior during debates. At the debate meeting, members heard an original composition and engaged in formal debate on a prepared topic, and sometimes in impromptu debate on a nonsense topic ("Should the pig have gone to market"). In 1860 and 1866 students at the University of North Carolina orated on standard topics such as "The Washington Monument," "The Sublime and the Beautiful," and "The Destruction of Jerusalem," as well as on timely concerns such as "The Results of Abolition Teachings," "A Plea for Union," and "The Confederate Dead."[9] Students prepared their debates and compositions by consulting the libraries of their literary societies, which often were more extensive than college libraries. Literary society work directly complemented the work in the required rhetoric classes helping students prepare for the declamations and original compositions that some colleges required them to present at chapel services and assemblies. Oral presentations were also the featured parts of annual class exhibitions and commencement ceremonies. After college students used their oratorical skills—acquired through both college work and their literary society activities—to excel in the public presentations of mid-century life.

In their oral presentations students drew on the strategies and techniques peculiar to their day. Their orations and debates were set within a framework of moral absolutes derived from Christian teaching. To explain their present, they drew on the past, especially the histories of ancient Greece and Rome and modern Europe and America. Napoleon was a popular topic; his rise to power fascinated Victorians, and his fate warned that selfish ambition would eventually be thwarted. Modern debaters persuade by accumulating fact and evidence; by contrast, mid-nineteenth-century orators tried to impress with a rhetoric that combined ideas and feelings. Classical and historical references showed that speakers had a broad grasp of affairs. A rhetoric teacher advised speakers to choose forceful words that "suggest more than they express" and to be aware that "a simple and barren assertion seldom has anything interesting in it."[10] After leaving their literary societies and liberal arts colleges, many students hoped to enter public life. Seniors at New York University composed a commencement song expressing their intentions: "To breast the waves of life; / I'm going to serve my country, / And sport a pretty wife."[11]

Presidents and professors at liberal arts colleges shared their students' hopes for their careers and used a term, "the whole man," to describe the graduate who would serve his community. As the president of Williams College explained in 1868, the whole man had a liberal education, "which has for its object the symmetrical expansion, and the discipline of the human powers,—the cultivation of man as man."[12] A liberal education developed the human personality to a stage of completeness. By definition, whole men were not one-sided and susceptible to the narrow influences of political partisanship, religious sectarianism, or devotion to luxury. A liberal education was more than a job ticket or preparation for a profession. Professionals, liberal arts professors suspected, often deferred "to mere technicality and unintelligent tradition." College lessons gave students instead large views and broad sympathies. In American life, educators expected, college graduates would join the elite group of leaders who knew what was desirable in a moral universe. They would "soften our controversies and dignify our discussions, refine upon our vulgarities and introduce amenities into our social life."[13] The college was aristocratic in the sense that it was for the few, but democratic in the sense that it served the interests of all by promoting a moral universe.

Liberal arts colleges were institutions of men: they had men presidents, professors, and student bodies. At a more fundamental level, the curricula were designed for men. In the introduction to *Introduction to the Study of International Law* (1860), a widely used text in international law, Theodore Dwight Woolsey expressed his hope that readers would be "young men of liberal culture, in preparation for any profession or employment, who need the enlarging influence of a study like this; who in a republic like ours are in a degree responsible for the measures of government."[14] Literature and history courses in particular gave students the opportunity to study the example of other men and how they brought about change. College courses taught that real, lasting, determining power did not depend on the moral influence of women, the aristocrat's skill in battle and ability to win a throne, or the demagogue's ability to rouse a people. Real power belonged to men of culture—college graduates who led public lives.

Although college educators advocating the whole man expected their graduates to have a uniform intelligence and outlook, educational reformers of the 1860s and 1870s had different expections. A leading proponent of educational reform, Charles W. Eliot, who became president of Harvard College in 1869, criticized the concept of the whole man and drew upon a contrasting set of images to define intelligence. He argued that the concept of the whole man obscured the individuality of students, who each possessed particular talents and aptitudes. Believing that roundness did not accurately describe the mind, Eliot used words like *drill* and *auger* to suggest that it was a sharp, penetrating, cutting tool. The minds of college men should be "well-stored," he argued, and trained "to see, compare, reason, and decide."[15] Eliot's metaphors from the workaday world show that he intended education to be practical. Although he did not expect Harvard men to become artisans and mechanics, he wanted college to prepare them to enter business or any other profession. Eliot predicted that Harvard men would bring to their communities "a rich return of learning, poetry, and piety. Secondly [Harvard] will foster the sense of public duty—that great virtue which makes republics possible." Unlike the advocates of the whole man, who wanted college graduates to participate in the public life of their communities, Eliot wanted graduates to follow their public duty by serving in public office—specifically, and exclusively, national offices, namely, those in the Senate, Cabinet, diplomatic service, army, and navy. Eliot advocated the new leadership style and wanted his college to provide education for future leaders.[16]

Other factors besides the reformers' criticism that liberal arts education was undemocratic and unpractical encouraged revision of the liberal arts curriculum. In 1862 a Republican Congress passed the Land-Grant Act, also known as the Morrill Act, which awarded land grants to the states. From sales of the grants, states were to establish funds for the support of colleges where agriculture and the mechanical arts would be taught. The belief that artisans and farmers should be well educated was an idea rooted in the Revolutionary period. Influenced by his study at the University of Edinburgh, Benjamin Rush, a Philadelphia physician and signer of the Declaration of Independence, had wanted to establish colleges in Pennsylvania with a curriculum of practical studies including modern languages and agriculture and excluding Latin and Greek. In the 1830s workingmen and their supporters among reformers and journalists criticized colleges for being aristocratic institutions with classical curricula that in no way gave systematic and scientific expression to the intellectual needs of the artisan classes. In many cities in the 1830s and 1840s, these workingmen founded mechanics' institutes, which held courses of lectures and established lending libraries for artisans and young clerks. The Republican party, founded in the mid-1850s, joined the interests of artisans and farmers through a platform of "free land, free labor, free men." Hoping to appeal to farmers of the West and workingmen of the East, Republicans supported the Morrill Act, which promised federal aid "to promote the liberal and practical education of the industrial classes in the several pursuits and professions in life."[17] When the bill's authors used the term "industrial classes," they were thinking of artisans, who as craftsmen owning their own manufacturing shops were industrialists and small businessmen.

In the Republican slogan, the term "free man" referred to a freedom greater than that of merely being free from physical restraint. Free men were also independent men. Education would enhance the independence of farmers and mechanics by teaching them the fundamental knowledge and underlying principles of their professions. Colleges would free these men from traditional ways of pursuing their occupations and give them the independence of mind to draw on the best knowledge of their times. Although he believed that a classical education could not meet the needs of the contemporary world of work, the regent of Illinois Industrial University, John M. Gregory, did want his institution to "demonstrate that the highest culture is compatible with the active pursuit of industry."[18]

Southerners had their own reasons for advocating modification of the liberal arts curriculum. The Civil War had devastated most Southern colleges; they had lost their students and many professors to the army and had had to close down. In war zones college buildings had frequently been burned and libraries ransacked. Most southern colleges faced an impoverished future. Graduates and supporters had little money to replenish endowments that had been invested in now valueless Confederate securities. Assessing the reasons for the southern defeat and thinking about how to rebuild the region, Maj. Gen. Daniel Harvey Hill, in an 1871 commencement address, called for "a radical change in our system of education." Colleges had to abandon "the aesthetic and the ornamental for the practical and the useful. . . . Agriculture must be studied as a science, with all its coordinate branches. . . . We want . . . a comprehensive plan of instruction, which will embrace the useful rather than the profound, the practical rather than the theoretic."[19]

To introduce more practical programs, colleges pursued various reform strategies. Wishing to retain their classical curricula, Bucknell University in western Pennsylvania and the College of New Jersey (Princeton) adopted a reform strategy based on those of Yale and Harvard, both of which in the 1840s had established separate scientific schools with programs leading to the bachelor of science degree. For the B.S. degree, the study of modern languages, natural sciences, and mathematics replaced the study of Latin and Greek, and frequently only three years of study were required. Professors and students in the classical curriculum leading to the B.A. degree, however, viewed the B.S. degrees earned in parallel practical programs as inferior. Because attainment of a B.A. degree required a familiarity with the general principles of knowledge and included the study of Latin and Greek, it continued to be more desirable than the B.S. degree. The word *science* in the term "bachelor of science" connoted merely objective and practical knowledge.

To overcome the prejudiced perception that a B.S. degree was second-rate, most colleges and universities reformed their curricula in the 1860s and 1870s by reconceiving the relationship between the classical languages and the natural sciences. At Cornell University (1865), the first president, Andrew Dickson White, confronted the bias against natural science study by insisting that all studies had equal value in the Cornell curriculum. Scientific studies were just as liberal as Latin and Greek studies. A member of the board of trustees of the University of North Carolina said in 1875 that the university was not intended "for the manufacture of mere classical scholars" but would encourage "all useful learning." The universities of Virginia, North Carolina, and Illinois and other institutions with reformed curricula organized various schools or colleges. The University of Carolina, which had been closed down by the war, received land-grant funds and reopened in 1875 with departments of agriculture, engineering and the mechanic arts natural sciences, literature, mathematics, and philosophy. The University of Illinois began instruction in 1870 with courses in agriculture, chemistry, military science, and natural science, polytechnic courses in civil engineering, mining and metallurgy, architecture and fine arts, mechanical science and art, trade and commerce departments, and a department of general science and literature.

Although administrators nationwide hoped to attract students by offering curricula that prepared them for certain careers, the introduction of such practical curricula did little to enhance enrollments. In the 1880s and 1890s a majority of students enrolled in baccalaureate programs, which required at least one classical language, and less than 20 percent enrolled in B.S. degree programs. Even with a relatively low tuition, a scholarship program for needy students, and new degrees in vocational areas, enrollments at the University of Virginia continued to decline. Male students also were not attracted to the agricultural programs promoted by the Morrill Act. At the University of Illinois enrollment in the school of agriculture declined from 21 percent to 7 percent of students during the 1870s, and the program at the universities of Michigan and Wisconsin showed equally dramatic declines.

Against the wishes of reformers, enrollments were on the upswing in the liberal arts, and especially in the study of English literature, largely because of the introduction of coeducation and the resulting influx of women students. During the 1870s the number of women in institutions of higher education increased by one-half until in 1880 33.4 percent of all college students were women. College reformers often did not recognize that students matriculating in B.A. degree programs and studying literature were making a sound vocational choice. By the 1890s, 45 percent of graduates from the typical state university became teachers or college educators, and about 25 percent of graduates from all private colleges entered the teaching profession. Literary study had prepared these students for the rapidly increasing number of positions opening in common schools and newly founded high schools.[20]

Revision of the classical curriculum also sometimes entailed the modification of admissions requirements and the introduction of the elective principle of course selection. The organizers of Illinois Industrial University expected successful applicants to pass examinations in subjects commonly taught at "the better class of public schools": grammar, geography, arithmetic, algebra, geometry, U.S. history, human physiology, and Latin.[21] Like many reformed institutions of the day, Illinois Industrial did not require Greek. Its Latin and mathematics requirements were less demanding than those of New England liberal arts colleges, which required students to have read Latin texts associated with more than three years of study and to have mastered more advanced algebra and mathematics. Harvard's Eliot, the most eloquent opponent of the Greek admission requirement, did not succeed in abolishing it until 1886. Advocates believed that a knowledge of Greek impeded the creeping influence of materialism and superficiality in American life. But Eliot thought that without the Greek requirement, colleges could reach out to young men from public high schools who might be the sons of "professional men of small income" or "farmers, mechanics, operatives, clerks, [and] tradesmen." In his opinion, "the opportunity of education was the most precious of all" freedoms.[22]

The new view that natural sciences contributed to a liberal arts education gave students greater freedom in their choice of programs and courses. At some universities, students chose the school or department they wanted to study in and then followed its curriculum. At Cornell, students in the B.A. program selected a program of studies from several established curricula of required courses. At other colleges electives were introduced on a limited basis. Swarthmore juniors and seniors could elect two-thirds of their courses. By 1876 even Yale had modified its curriculum so that upperclassmen could choose a few of their courses from a specified list of optional courses.

Electives were introduced most extensively at Harvard under Eliot, who saw choice as a vital principle in the reformed university. Building on past changes, he expanded electives in a curriculum that already permitted considerable choice. In 1868 Harvard sophomores, juniors, and seniors elected about half of their courses from lists for each class. In 1872 Harvard abolished class-specific courses; any student could take any course for which he could persuade the instructor that he was prepared. By 1884 most freshmen requirements had been abolished and all Harvard students were free to exercise, in Eliot's words, "their spontaneous diversity of choice." He believed that the elective system arose from "the spirit of political liberty."[23]

In the reformed liberal arts college and university, curriculum changes paralleled less heralded changes in extracurricular activities. In the postwar years literary societies ceased to dominate student life and, with only a few exceptions, became extinct by the last years of the century. Fraternities and debating clubs replaced them, along with a host of other activities, including baseball and football. Fraternities gained strength in the postwar years, often attracting as many as 70 percent of the men students at a college. Many of their social activities and the values that they fostered were in conflict with the academic mission of colleges and universities. The connection of debating clubs to the curriculum and college life was only incidental. Intercollegiate debates began in the 1870s, and debates started to take on a new form. Departing from the florid rhetorical style of the literary societies, debaters sought to persuade by presenting facts and hard evidence.

These developments corresponded with a new attitude reflected in comments in college newspapers, that students of the 1870s lacked confidence in their ability to influence public life. At the University of Virginia a student suggested that "a great seat of learning" should become "aloof from the turbulences that environ us" and create "an atmosphere of scholastic and literary quietness." According to a New York University student, "Civilization derives its name from the life of cities; but it is not in the noise and glitter of their public life, but in the profound retirement of their private life, that we must look for the elixir of civilization, settled of its dregs."[24] These comments suggest that students had lost faith in their ability to rise and hold sway as leaders. But they lived in the period of transition and could not know that a new-style leadership was coming into being.

The reformed colleges and universities were clearly more secular than their unreformed counterparts, where Christian thought and belief continued to infuse the curriculum and college life. At the reformed institutions, religious ceremony existed at the edges of college life. Although some universities required students to attend Sunday service, most did not; in fact, most reformed colleges had no regular religious ceremony in which all their members participated. Hymns and prayers were a part of formal college convocations only. During the 1860s and 1870s however, many colleges retained or were established with a religious identity, especially in the Midwest and the South. In the mid-1870s a professor complained that Vanderbilt hired only Methodists, the University of Georgia wanted no Episcopalians, and Baptists controlled appointments at the University of Virginia.[25]

In the speeches of college presidents and students an entirely new theme—individualism—appeared in the 1860s and 1870s. Proclaiming in 1870 that practical education would show that "the richest learning will pay in a corn field or a carpenter's shop," John Gregory at Illinois Industrial saw a new monetary connection between higher education and individual success. Not merely to further self-development and to benefit the community, education was to benefit the individual for whom it was supposed to pay. Students shared the new thinking and hailed "the day when to all there shall be an equal chance; a fair field for the best men, let them start where they may, to get to the front."[26] The educational reforms of 1860–80 linked American higher education to American liberalism, which was rooted in eighteenth-century thought and supported the belief of the Revolutionary period that the artificial restrictions of mercantilism stifled colonial development. In the second half of the nineteenth century, Eliot, Gregory, and others, including students, applied the principles of liberal thought to individuals. They believed that educational restrictions such as those imposed by a required curriculum stifle self-development.

But republican thought was no longer disciplining individual efforts as it had in earlier decades. Excessive wealth was no longer feared as a corrupting influence on men and nations. Moreover, educational reformers set aside the academic goal of self-development and the metaphor of the whole man. In reformed colleges and universities, individualism and individuality prevailed. The practical college education supposedly enabled individuals to seek their destiny in American life—to make their education pay and to get ahead. It would be another ten years before educational leaders and politicians discovered how the self-assertion of the free individual could serve the public interest through institutions of higher education. Academic degrees, professional associations, civil service reform in 1883, and the establishment of government commissions of nonpartisan experts (the Interstate Commerce Commission was the first in 1887) would enable college students of the 1890s and beyond to gain public influence. In the 1870s only a few leaders, such as White of Cornell and Eliot of Harvard, proposed that colleges contain special schools to train leaders for public service.

In the 1860s and 1870s the older vision of self-development and community leadership attracted a tiny number of African-Americans to college. Most southern African-Americans had training in agricultural and artisan skills; the new African-American colleges and universities made it possible for them to develop a professional class of teachers, ministers, and doctors. Although African-American and white educators hoped that African-American communities would produce their own leaders, no educator was so optimistic as to predict an integrated society.

Many white educators supported African-American higher education also because they wanted to eliminate the influences of slavery and to offer a more complete education than freedmen's schools had provided. Freedmen's schools had not removed students from their homes, where they were surrounded, white educators assumed, by "injurious habits and influences," including role models who were impious, intemperate, and lazy. African-American universities offered white educators the opportunity to get students away from home and to make their education a total experience. At college, student behavior could be controlled both outside and inside the classroom.

White educators also wanted to create a corps of African-American teachers and professionals. Freed men and women preferred to be taught by members of their own race, and whites hoped that, as African-Americans became self-reliant, they would develop their own institutions to replace the freedmen's schools and their white faculties. Whites predicted that African-American teachers would have an impact both in and out of school. They would introduce "a pure morality into every circle [of their communities], thus perfecting a solid, permanent, and virtuous society." The influence of other professionals, although less potentially pervasive, was also vital to the development of African-American life along lines desired by Victorians. Medical and theology schools would supply trained men to replace folk healers and illiterate preachers, who ranted "heathenish vagaries" and tolerated "the grossest immoralities."[27]

Before 1860 only 28 African-Americans had earned B.A. degrees, and only one university, Lincoln in Pennsylvania, founded in 1854, existed for their education. During the postwar years the Freedmen's Bureau, northern missionary societies and philanthropists, and African-American churches helped to found many normal schools, industrial schools, and universities for the higher education of African-Americans. Among the first were Atlanta

University (1865), Fisk University (1867), and Howard University (1867). In Tennessee, the southern state where African-American institutions of higher education proliferated most rapidly, there were 11 colleges and 61 normal schools by 1870.

At first, the new African-American universities were universities merely in the sense that they contained several schools, frequently only a preparatory school and a normal school. Having opened a normal and a preparatory department in 1867, Fisk waited until the first four students had completed the preparatory course before opening its collegiate department in 1871. Throughout the nineteenth century most African-American colleges enrolled more preparatory and normal students than college students. In the late nineteenth century this was a common practice in many white institutions of higher education as well, especially in the South. For African-Americans, there were few college preparatory schools or academies outside of those provided by the universities. For whites, the Civil War had called southern youth into the army and forced many private academies to close.

Regulations at the new African-American universities showed that white educators tried to monitor every aspect of student life. Boarding students had rising bells and a scheduled time for lights out. Only during the four and a half hours of the day and evening set aside for eating and leisure could students visit one another in their rooms. Faculty supervised manners and decorum in the dining hall, and rooms were inspected for neatness. At coeducational institutions, a male student could be punished by formal reprimand in front of the student body for even touching the hand of a female student. Most colleges were affiliated with either a Christian missionary society or a white or African-American denomination. Students usually took mandatory Bible classes and attended required Sunday chapel and sometimes a weekday service. Students had to present a neat appearance and maintain a formal standard of dress. Many colleges told students to wear only somber colors. Students were to talk without slang or profanity and eschew tobacco, drink, gambling, and dancing.

These paternalistic regulations stemmed from northern white teachers' attitudes toward their students. Almost all the teachers thought the students displayed undesirable behavior and low intelligence. But the teachers did not believe that skin color made African-Americans permanently inferior to them. Years of slavery, they believed, had deprived freed men and women of the experience of Christianity, religious training, and living in a free society. The teachers hoped that the strictly regulated boarding schools would help freed men and women develop the habits of discipline necessary for life in a free society. Potentially, African-Americans could become Victorians and their equals.

The greatest problems facing African-American colleges were the attitudes of southern whites and the poverty of their students. African-Americans had to confront hostility and violence from white southerners every day. Public institutions were segregated, and in the postbellum years whites joined the Ku Klux Klan, which used violence to offset the impact of the Fifteenth Amendment. Besides terrorizing freedmen's school teachers, Klansmen also discouraged freed men and women from pursuing higher education. At Talladega College in Talladega, Alabama in 1870, the principal wrote a missionary society in New York requesting firearms to use in defending the college against threats of arson. Local African-American citizens turned back Klansmen marching toward the college by threatening that they would retaliate by burning down the town. Straight University in Louisiana, Hampton Normal and Agricultural Institute in Virginia, and Tougaloo College in Mississippi, however, were not so fortunate; each was damaged by arson attacks.

Poverty often prevented African-American students from completing more than a few years at the preparatory level in one of the new universities. Principals at many of the colleges appealed to benefactors for money for shoes because a cold winter could lower attendance drastically. Many students attended for a few months and then returned home to bring in their families' crops and to earn money. A Talladega student was able to attend college for three months out of three years, and a Fisk student attended school for only 26 months in 10 years of college enrollment. The biggest expense of schooling was not tuition but the wages lost to students' families.

Given the impoverishment of African-Americans in the South, it is not surprising that the .1 percent of their population graduating from college was far smaller than the almost 2 percent of whites who attended. One historian estimates that between 1876 and 1909 Tennesee's African-American colleges produced 525 graduates out of a population of over 470,000 African-Americans.[28] Colleges responded to their students' poverty by offering scholarships and keeping the cost of education low. Aid came from the North, occasionally from England, and even from sympathetic southern whites. For many southerners, support of African-American colleges and universities was a means of extending the segregation that they also maintained in elementary and secondary schools. Northern donors, who started giving large gifts to southern white and African-American colleges in 1867, often supported vocational rather than collegiate education for African-Americans.

Colleges kept costs low, mainly by requiring their students, and sometimes teachers, to do household chores and to work in workshops and fields. Until women were exempted in 1870, Fisk University required all professors and teachers to split wood and carry coal as part of their work duty. At most schools boarding students worked on a college farm that provided food for their table. At other colleges students had to work at manual chores, such as making brooms and caning chairs, for three to six hours per week.

No one expected students to become manual laborers. Economic need mandated, and educational theory justified, using the labor of students. Students at white colleges and universities, such as Cornell and Wellesley, were also required to perform manual labor. The theories of the Swiss educator J. H. Pestalozzi about learning by doing had influenced American educators since early in the century and were in force at several white institutions, including Oberlin College in Ohio and Oneida Institute in New York. It was hoped that manual work would help African-American college students overcome the heritage of slavery by increasing respect for manual work, encouraging industrious behavior, and building character.

In their collegiate departments, African-American universities offered a curriculum resembling that of old-time white liberal arts colleges. Elective courses were a rarity, and required courses usually included Latin, Greek, French, German, English, history, mathematics, natural science, and natural philosophy. Seniors continued these studies and also took on political science, mental science, and moral science, which were the standard courses that completed collegiate studies, being seen as a preparation for public life and leadership. As at white liberal arts colleges, extracurricular activities complemented formal studies. The faculty expected students to gain facility in public speaking and required them to present public addresses, orations, and declamations. Students also formed literary societies. Many followed the example of white societies and had names related to Greek and Roman ancient history; others chose names related to the Civil War or African-American history, for example, the Union Literary Society (Fisk) and the Phyllis Wheatley Literary Society (Atlanta University).

Normal departments in the new universities made one of the most important contributions to southern African-American life and to their students, of whom the vast majority were women. Much as in antebellum New England, a normal school education and a teaching certificate in the postwar South gave African-American farm women an independent life and livelihood. Those who married did so at a later age and chose husbands from a wider pool of available men. In the African-American community normal school graduates had a great impact. A principal estimated that 25 of her former pupils were teaching—and thereby changing the lives of—1,000 children. Without these teachers, African-Americans would have had to depend on northern or southern whites for their education. Normal schools not only provided vocational preparation for paying jobs but contributed to the building of a literate African-American population.

In the late 1860s a controversy arose over the course of study for male African-American students. Many teachers and students believed that the new colleges should offer the same prestigious and demanding curriculum then required of white collegiate students, including the Greek and Latin languages. Others, influenced by contemporary educational theories and their predictions about the roles African-Americans would play in southern society, thought a classical education would be of little value to southern

African-Americans. Gen. Samuel C. Armstrong, who developed the curriculum at the Hampton Institute in Hampton, Virginia, was a central figure in the controversy. His ideas made Hampton a model for industrial education, and its leading graduate, Booker T. Washington, became a spokesman for African-Americans in the 1880s. Many of Washington's ideas about the value of industrial education—which he instituted as first principal of the Tuskegee Normal and Industrial Institute, founded in 1881—stemmed from his studies at Hampton Institute and his friendship with Armstrong.

At Hampton Institute all students were required to work and the curriculum was supposed to make students identify with agricultural work, the livelihood of the majority of southern African-Americans. Armstrong wanted normal school graduates to labor among their people and to teach them the habits and work routines necessary for unskilled and semiskilled farm work. Armstrong seemed to prefer the less intellectually gifted of his students, whom he called "blockheads" or "plodders." He believed that they would do well teaching because they would have the most in common with their students, many of whom would lead a life of arduous farm labor. He feared that bright students with a liberal arts education would seek postgraduate training and would eventually have no interest working in the rural communities of their childhoods.

Hampton's curriculum offered neither Greek nor Latin, nor any modern foreign language. The study of English was divided into reading, spelling, composition, and grammar courses. Historical studies comprised English history, American history, and a short course in "universal history," the nineteenth-century version of world history. Science classes included geology, botany, physiology, and natural history, courses in the Bible, civil government, and moral science came under the "miscellaneous" category. Courses in history and civil government were occasions for teachers to present Armstrong's social philosophy. Students were taught that the history and evolution of the African-American race had given them their subordinate position, which was naturally 2,000 years behind that of the white race. These and other lessons taught Hampton graduates to prepare for life as it was and to accommodate themselves to conditions in the South. Change would come, but slowly—only as fast as the forces of history and evolution permitted.

Industrial education became a controversial issue between the African-American leaders Booker T. Washington and W. E. B. Du Bois, a Fisk graduate, late in the nineteenth century, and it is still a debated issue among contemporary historians. Advocates argue that classical education was impractical for a largely illiterate population and would have perpetuated the elitist attitudes associated with a classical liberal education. African-Americans had to have a practical education to serve their people. Opponents of industrial education point out the racist attitudes of some of its proponents and argue that industrial education was practical only where racial subordination and political exclusion were accepted. They believe that African-Americans needed a liberal arts education to develop leaders to protest oppression. Many postwar educators, however, took more flexible positions in this debate. For instance, the American Missionary Association (AMA) supported institutions whether they offered an industrial education or a classical education. The AMA's directors thought that exclusive support for either industrial education or classical education unnecessarily limited educational opportunities for the southern African-American community.

Many supporters of industrial education did not share Armstrong's racist views and conservative social philosophy. For example, Martha Schofield, founder of the Schofield Normal and Industrial School in 1868 in Aiken, South Carolina, opposed classical education for her African-American students, but she was no racist. In 1871 she led the fight for a municipal school tax, and she won a reputation as an advocate of woman's rights by objecting to being taxed when she could not vote. (The state government purportedly returned her taxes in response to her powerful letters of protest.) Aroused by an article that appeared days before the presidential election of 1876 in the *New York Daily Tribune*, "South Carolina at Peace . . . No Intimidation . . . Good Feeling between Whites and Blacks," Schofield responded with a letter to the editor detailing how whites were terrorizing African-American voters who intended to cast Republican ballots. Of the many recent murders of African-American men in Aiken, she estimated that as many as 70 had been politically motivated. To develop African-American leadership, Schofield tried to identify her more talented students and sometimes sent them to Hampton Institute.

She had concluded that many lessons at the new universities were "stuffing to a spiritless body" and was most troubled by a Latin class that she had observed. Of its two students, one seemed incapable of being raised "far above the plough handles," and the other looked as though he needed to be told about the evils that "tobacco, and whiskey and filth can do to the body." Schofield thought that white southerners had overemphasized the value of classical education. To an applicant for a teaching position at her school who had qualifications in "Hebrew, Saxon, Sanskrit, French, Anglo-Saxon, Early English Literature and History, Mineralogy, Botany and Geology," she wanted to say that "such stuff had kept the South a century behind the age."[29]

In the postwar United States, the calls for educational reform were everywhere—in the North, the South, and the West, in high schools and colleges, and in white and African-American education. When Schofield called for practical instead of a classical education for African-Americans, she was in the company of not merely Armstrong of Hampton Institute but also educational reformers from many prominent northern and southern universities and private colleges, such as North Carolina, Washington and Lee, and Cornell. All postwar educational reformers believed that a liberal arts education centered on the classics could not prepare students for life in their world. But practical education had different meanings for whites and African-Americans. In the postwar years many whites were trying to leave their rural communities and a college degree gave them a way out. For freed men and women, however, educators intended practical education to be preparation for work or teaching in an economically deprived, rural, agricultural world.

African-American students who enrolled in collegiate departments did so because they wanted to leave their childhood worlds and acquire a classical education. To the consternation of teachers like Schofield, these students saw the traditional classical curriculum as very desirable and did not want to be denied its lessons. Moreover, African-Americans frequently adapted classical studies to their own interests. Through the study of ancient history they discovered African-American history and a way to refute modern racist theories. For example, in the early 1880s a prominent African-American educator, Richard Wright, testified before the Senate Committee on Labor and Education about how the past had revealed to him the true history of his people. He had learned that the ancient Egyptians, who made so many scientific discoveries, were African-Americans. His studies had persuaded him that his people had high intellectual potential, for "differences of race, so called, are a mere matter of color and not of brain." The intellectual world opened up by college education could prevail over prejudice and folk superstition.[30]

For white women, the years between 1860 and 1880 were also a time of institution founding. Before 1860 there were few opportunities for women to pursue higher education. Since the antebellum years, a handful of private religious colleges, such as Oberlin in Ohio and Westminster in western Pennsylvania, had admitted women; they usually chose a literary course of study, which did not lead to a B.A. degree. At the several women's colleges founded before 1860, including Georgia Female College (1838) and Elmira Female College (1855), students as young as 12 were admitted to study a curriculum resembling that of an academy more than that of a liberal arts college with a classical curriculum.

After 1860 the opportunities for women to pursue higher education multiplied. The first of the great private women's colleges in the East were established—Vassar in Poughkeepsie, New York, in 1865 and Smith in Northampton, Massachusetts, and Wellesley in Wellesley, Massachusetts, in 1875. In the Midwest states receiving land-grant funds from the Morrill Act either began to admit women to their universities or founded state universities that admitted women from the start. Joining the University of Iowa, which had admitted women since its founding in 1855, were the universities of Wisconsin in 1867, Kansas, Indiana, and Minnesota in 1869, and Illinois, Missouri, Michigan, and California in 1870. By 1872, 97 colleges and universities admitted women, and by 1880 women represented one-third of all college and university students in the United States.

Educators adopted older ideas about women's destiny and their role in a republic to argue for women's higher education. A statement by Matthew Vassar was typical of Victorian educators: "The mothers of a country mould the character of its citizens, determine its institutions, and shape its destiny." But they also emphasized that a proper education promoted culture. Institutions of higher learning should help men and women grow into well-rounded individuals with their intellectual, moral, and aesthetic natures fully developed. Nevertheless, not all Victorians shared the belief that women could or should enjoy intellectual development. Maria Mitchell, a professor of astronomy at Vassar who was famous for her discovery in 1847 of a new comet (which was named after her), often reminded fellow women intellectuals that most "Americans don't believe in education for women." They wanted women, she said, to be useful in the kitchen and ornamental in the parlor and to know no more mathematics than they needed to be able to count. A male writer declared in an 1860 *Saturday Review* article that "equality of intellect in women . . . does not exist."[31]

The concept of self-development, or self-culture, opened up higher education opportunities for women even as it limited the content and methods of such education to means that were perceived as womanly. Among the institutions that imposed the mildest restrictions were the University of Michigan and Cornell University, which admitted its first women in 1875. At the 1873 cornerstone-laying of Sage Hall, the women's residence hall at Cornell, the remarks of Henry and Susan Sage were typical of the time. Mrs. Sage recited a four-line poem:

> I lay this cornerstone, in faith
> That a structure fair and good
> Shall from it rise, and thenceforth come
> True Christian womanhood.

Like most other Victorians, the Sages saw education as a Christian experience. Education led women students to realize their ultimate dependence on God and their consequent duties to home, family, and state. Supposedly, an all-knowing God had designed each sex to fulfill a specific, intended role. Men had greater rational ability, women a greater capacity for feeling and intuition. Men were destined for public life, women for home life. A sidestep into a temporary teaching career was acceptable for young women if they recognized that their eventual destiny was to marry and bear children. A college education did not fundamentally alter a woman's God-given role in life. As Henry Sage said, education did not change "the nature and functions of woman, or her most important sphere of duties in this life."[32]

In spite of their traditional views, the Sages also supported educational reform. Unfortunate circumstances had made Henry's mother and three sisters dependent on his support, so he was well aware of the practical reasons behind women's education. Through his membership in Henry Ward Beecher's Pilgrim Church in Brooklyn, New York, he had also become familiar with the reform thought of the era. He had met Beecher's women relatives, including Catharine Beecher and Isabella Beecher Hooker, and selectively borrowed many of their ideas about women's education. He shared Catharine Beecher's concern that an increasing number of single women needed an education to be able to support themselves, yet he rejected her call for women's higher education in domestic science. With Isabella Beecher Hooker and other woman suffragists, he hoped that increased rights and opportunities for women would lead to the general reform of American society. At the cornerstone-laying for Sage Hall, Sage observed that "man has used his power over [women], to say the least, unwisely and ungenerously." With coeducation he hoped that

the efficient force of the human race will be multiplied in proportion as woman, by culture and education, is fitted for new and broader spheres of action . . . when she is completely emancipated from unjust legal shackles, when she is as free as man is to seek her own path in life, wherever led by necessity or duty, hope or ambition, when opportunity and aid for culture in any direction are hers, then may we expect to see woman enlarged, ennobled in every attribute, and our whole race, through her, receive impulsion to a higher level in all things great and good![33]

To a great extent, women's education at Cornell in the 1870s and 1880s followed the Sages' vision. Modeled on the successful program of coeducation established at the University of Michigan in 1870, women at Cornell were free to pursue any academic interests. In the first coeducational class in 1875, women were admitted to the same studies as men, and they had access to all the university's resources, including its libraries and laboratories. Such was not the case at many coeducational universities. Admitted to the University of Missouri in 1870, women did not gain entrance to all university classes until the following year, and not until several years later did they enjoy complete use of the library and the right to attend the college chapel with their male classmates.

At Cornell extracurricular life was especially designed, however, to guide women students in womanly directions. Such pressure exceeded that at the University of Michigan, where women boarded off-campus, but was slight when compared to efforts at the recently established women's colleges. Both extracurricular courses and the design of Sage Hall attempted to promote the women students' physical and moral well-being. In addition to regular classes, students had to take courses in physiology and hygiene. For mandatory physical exercise periods, Sage Hall had a gymnasium and long corridors for rainy day walks. A brochure assured interested applicants that the residence hall had every up-to-date facility for healthy living, including gas lighting, steam heat, baths on every floor, and ventilation by windows and air shafts.

As at most colleges and universities in the 1870s and 1880s, more women applicants to Cornell were prepared for admission to the scientific course of study than to the classical course of study, which required Latin and Greek. In most states before 1890, public college preparatory education was scarce for both boys and girls, and private academies for men were more numerous than those for women. Lacking thorough preparation, women were ineligible for programs leading to the B.A. degree and had to matriculate in B.S. degree programs. At Winchester College from 1852 through 1885, 31 women (14.8 percent) and 515 men (93 percent) earned the B.A. degree, while 178 women (85 percent) and 39 men (7 percent) earned the B.S. degree.[34]

An exception was M. Carey Thomas. Admitted to the classical course at Cornell in 1875, she had been formally educated at a Quaker boarding school but studied Greek surreptitiously on her own. She received her B.A. degree in 1877, earned a Ph.D. degree in 1882 summa cum laude from the University of Zurich, and became dean of the faculty of Bryn Mawr College in 1884, and its president in 1894. Her performance on the Cornell entrance examinations earned Thomas a place in the junior class, and that first year she took courses in Greek, Latin, English literature, German, and analytical geometry. Statistics suggest just how atypical Thomas was. Between 1875 and 1895, 990 women attended Cornell, of which 270 received undergraduate degrees and 55 graduate degrees.[35] Most women did not complete the degree programs, probably because they were aspiring teachers who needed to take only particular courses. Future teachers saw college study as a means of enhancing their participation in this new and burgeoning field of women's employment. In 1870 women made up 61 percent of the teaching force, and 71 percent in 1900. Thus in the first decades of coeducation at Cornell, women students fulfilled the vision of the Sages. Although they could enter any course at Cornell, they actually prepared for careers that Victorians perceived as suited to woman's nature.

At colleges and universities like Cornell, sex-segregated study occurred on a de facto basis, but other institutions maintained sex-specific programs. Oberlin College in Ohio (1837) and Grinnell College in Iowa (1846) had a "ladies'" course, which awarded a diploma but not a degree. At state universities women sometimes could pursue degrees only in normal schools or departments, although they might be permitted to elect any course from the universities' various offerings.

The literary course was considered especially suited to women for both practical and intellectual reasons. It gave women more than adequate preparation for school teaching; in addition, women's supposedly more intuitive and less rational minds were considered less capable of the discipline required to study classical languages and more suited to the study of literature, art, and certain fields of natural science. For example, believing that he was flattering women, the head of the Richmond Female Institute wrote that women's minds leaped "from conclusion to conclusion with a delightful scorn of all reason." He called women's entry into men's occupations "unfortunate" for he believed that they should study arithmetic, literature, modern languages, music, and art, and leave higher mathematics, Latin, Greek, philosophy, and natural science to men.[36]

The ladies' course was only one way in which higher education was adapted to the special interests and needs of women. Another innovation of the postwar years was the establishment within colleges and universities of schools of domestic science. Domestic science was a result of education reform; it gave women specialized, practical education and credentials as experts. This reform paralleled the drive for more practical education that was leading to curriculum reform at men's colleges. To rural families, it seemed logical that while their sons were preparing for their future careers by studying agriculture at the state university, their daughters should prepare for paid employment as well as for home life in their college studies. In 1871 Iowa State College at Ames introduced domestic economy in the ladies' course, and in the midseventies the State Agriculture College of Kansas offered a program with courses such as "Household Management and Economy," "The Management of Children and Their Private Instruction," and "A Knowledge of the Laws of Health and Nourishing of the Sick." A complete domestic curriculum with courses surpassing those of the how-to variety would not be available until the founding in 1874 of the School of Domestic Science and Arts at the University of Illinois. Technical studies in the school followed the program for women's education that Catharine Beecher had described in *The American Woman's Home*. After two years of liberal arts study, students took courses in household economy, aesthetics, science, and architecture. Like Beecher, the director of the school believed that the improvement of American society started in the home. Wholesale reform of American society would occur when women learned "the strong moral influences exerted by good bread, wholesome food, and healthful, attractive homes."[37]

Whether free to attend classes of their choice at Michigan and Cornell or forced to march to class in a two-by-two line flanked by chaperones at Missouri, women at coeducational colleges faced considerable overt and covert hostility from male classmates, professors, and the general population. During the first years of coeducation at Michigan, women students could not easily find landladies willing to rent them rooms, and the congregations of churches that they attended shunned them. The formidable M. Carey

Thomas complained to her parents about her male classmates at Cornell, who sat "by fifty's on the steps of the different buildings and to pass between them into the lecture rooms is quite an ordeal."[38] Photographs of students in coeducational classrooms during the early years show men and women sitting in different sections or rows; the sexes never mingled. A professor at Michigan referred to all his students as gentlemen; when calling on a woman, he would address her as "Mr. so-and-so." Believing that the University of Michigan would founder after it admitted women, a writer for the student paper in 1870 derided both domestic education and liberal arts education. He predicted young ladies would want courses analyzing the chemistry of everyday substances like tea, coffee, and beef and would demand "a model kitchen" *and* "a nursery—not in [the] charge of Susan B. Anthony." He said in conclusion that he had forgotten that "the 'Coming Woman' is to give the home and home-life, the kitchen, dining room and nursery a wide berth, and deal with naught but the affairs of State."[39]

College life also reminded women that they were women. While men belonged to a class, women always were a group regardless of their class, as one woman's account makes evident "We were just coming out of Latin while the sophs were going up to trigonometry, and they met on the stairs and went at it. One sweet-faced boy said, 'For Heaven's sake Phelps, wait until the girls get out of the way!' But that worthy replied, 'Damn'em, they have no business here anyway, and let 'em take their chances!'"[40] The author of the quotation follows the usual college practice of referring to women as a group, but to men students as freshmen, juniors, and seniors. She initially refers to "we," the freshmen, but intends by the first "they" the freshmen and sophomore men.

Men students also excluded their women classmates from college rituals and organizations. Women did not wear class hats or beanies, participate in annual class-versus-class roughhouses, or attend annual class dinners. At the University of California men freshmen, sophomores, juniors, and seniors had certain benches and stairways on campus reserved for their use that members of other classes and all women students were prohibited from using. Having succeeded by 1879 in gaining admission to some of the less important campus clubs, some Cornell women tried to join the annual class dinner. After thwarting the attempt, a man asked in the university paper, "Are not the peculiar advantages of association of men with men weighty enough to cause a need here of some organizations not wholly coeducational in character?"[41] Cornell women proceeded to form their own student government, honor society, sororities, drama club, and orchestra.

Despite harassment most women found the coeducational experience worthwhile. Although probably sharing the prejudice of their time—that women's institutions and women professors were inferior—women students at coeducational institutions believed their education to be superior to that available at a women's college. One student questioned the ambition of Wellesley students, who seemed to want only "to get through college," and the attainments of their professors, who seemed "shallow." After graduating from Cornell, M. Carey Thomas weighed the disadvantages and advantages of coeducation.

There is much that is very hard for a *lady* in a mixed university and I should not subject any girl to it unless she were determined to have it. The educational problem is a terrible one—girls' colleges are inferior and it seems impossible to get the most illustrious men to fill their chairs, and on the other hand it is a fiery ordeal to educate a lady by coeducation—it is impossible to make one, who has not felt it, understand the living on a volcano or on a house top—Frank Heath's story and that horrible cartoon were samples—yet it is the only way and learning *is worth it*.[42]

Had Thomas attended a women's college 20 years later, she might have reached the opposite conclusion. But the late nineteenth century, fraternities, which had become the dominant force in campus social life, punished their members for speaking to women classmates on campus, inviting them to parties, and giving them fraternity pins. As female enrollments grew to 50 percent and more pressure also began to build at coeducational universities to limit women's admission and bar them from prestigious graduate programs, such as law and engineering.

At the new single-sex colleges, Vassar, Wellesley, and Smith, students entered oases removed from the general hostility to women's intellectual advance. In the early years, the New England women's colleges showed more dramatically than did coeducational institutions how Victorians could make education sex-specific. Also in the early years of higher education for women, the new women's colleges enrolled more women students than did coeducational colleges and universities. After 1880 the opportunities for coeducation expanded to such an extent that the enrollment of women in coeducational institutions began to exceed that in women's colleges by about 50 percent.[43]

The founders, presidents, professors, and administrators of the women's colleges wanted to prove that women students were capable of collegiate work comparable to that at men's colleges. As the initial announcement for Wellesley explained, its organizers wished "to offer young women opportunities for education equivalent to those usually provided in colleges for young men." These women's colleges did not attempt to offer women a distinctive women's curriculum of practical courses. Rejecting the idea of Vassar offering classes in cooking, nursing, and other vocational fields, a professor explained that "a complete womanhood is better than a trade."[44] To develop "complete women," the colleges established liberal arts curricula that resembled those of the leading private men's colleges. Although men's colleges were abandoning their Greek requirement and introducing elective courses into the junior and senior years, women's colleges did so cautiously. Their presidents believed that women first had to prove their ability in the traditional liberal arts curriculum before they could follow reformed curricula that required no classical languages. Only by taking this precaution could women prove their ability equal to that of men. Even so, women's college curricula allowed for some elective courses. After a mandatory freshman and sophomore year curriculum, juniors and seniors at Vassar could elect one-half their remaining courses.

Wishing to have their admissions standards approximate as closely as possible those of the leading New England men's colleges, women's colleges required classical study. Consequently, Vassar and Wellesley enrolled a considerable portion of their entering students in their preparatory departments. A Vassar professor reported that four-fifths of the entering students enrolled in this department in 1873. With a Greek and Latin requirement but no preparatory department, Smith had to settle for a first class of 14 students; the college lecture hall had been built to hold 300.

Nevertheless, the curricula at leading women's colleges were different from those of the leading New England men's colleges. Not surprisingly, women's colleges offered fewer Greek courses than men's colleges and more modern language courses. Women in the single-sex colleges preferred modern languages as did women in state universities. At the University of Illinois in the late 1870s, more than 40 percent of all students pursued nontechnical studies, and more than half of these were women studying English literature.[45] Literary study made good vocational sense for the large number of these women who were preparing for careers as school teachers, given the common school curriculum of the day. But literary study also prepared women for parlor life. Having widened and deepened their knowledge, college graduates could return to home life prepared to participate more richly in everyday intellectual pursuits.

The women's colleges also offered more natural science courses, especially biology courses, than did men's colleges. In fact, in the first four years after Vassar opened, a greater percentage of students chose science courses (39.3 percent of courses taken) than arts courses (11.6 percent) plus either classics courses (21.2 percent), modern language courses (20.6 percent), or social science courses (7.2 percent). By the first decade of the twentieth century, these preferences had changed. Science courses fell in popularity (to 25.4 percent of courses taken), as did classics courses (16.3 percent) and modern language courses (15.3 percent), while the popularity of arts courses (23.3 percent) and social science courses (19.7 percent) rose.[46] Science study seems to have been a distinguishing feature of midcentury women's intellectual life; it prepared young women for a vocation as well as an avocation. Their preference for science courses may have reflected their ambition to become high school

5.1 The Assembly-Room at Hampton Normal and Agricultural Institute. From *Hampton and Its Students by Two of Its Teachers* (Putnam, New York, 1874), p.50

5.2   College Row, Franklin and Marshall College, circa 1860. *Courtesy of Franklin and Marshall College Archives and Manuscripts*

5.3 In this 1865 lithograph of Vassar College the Calistheneum is to the Main Building's right and Maria Mitchell's observatory to the left. *Courtesy of the Vassar College Library, Poughkeepsie, New York*

5.4 This 1876 photograph shows the Senior parlor. The class of 1873 began the tradition of decorating their own parlor. *Courtesy of the Vassar College Library, Poughkeepsie, New York*

natural science teachers, a new field of employment opening to college graduates, as well as their desire to prepare intellectually for parlor life. Botany, entomology, and geology had already been accepted studies at the academy level for women, who, it was believed, could excel at certain types of scientific study. They presumably had the great patience and good eye for detail required for the tasks of the nineteenth-century biologist—observation, identification, collection, and classification. Maria Mitchell noted the attributes that would make women accomplished scientists: "her nice perceptions of minute details, all her delicate observations of color, of form, of shape, of change, and her capability of patient routine." She wondered why "the hammer of the geologist" and the "tin box of the botanist" were not found more often in women's hands.[47]

Victorian women's long-standing interest in preserving their own health and the health and growth of their children may also explain their choosing biology courses. Catharine Beecher devoted much attention to health matters in her *Treatise on Domestic Economy* (1841), and interest was growing in the 1860s and 1870s. Reflecting the general concern that women's health might deteriorate in college, the early women's colleges and coeducational universities provided for exercise and recreation. Like Cornell's Sage Hall, many residence and college halls had indoor corridors for walking. At Vassar one of the three buildings first erected was a "calisthenium," which contained space for calisthenics, a riding stable, and a bowling alley. At the University of Illinois women had to take a calisthenics class in which they performed exercises with wands and dumbbells. Their synchronized drill was reportedly a highlight of campus tours.

Even as religious observances were moving to the periphery of college life at men's colleges, the new women's colleges placed them at their center. The founders and benefactors of Wellesley College, Henry and Pauline Durant, were evangelical Protestants, and they wanted their college to be "Christian in its influence, discipline, and course of instruction."[48] Organized religion in men's colleges usually involved, at most, daily chapel and Sunday church services. Vassar and Wellesley offered a more thorough religious education. In 1870 a Vassar student complained, "How good they try to make us here— we actually are obliged to pray eleven times on Sunday and nine times every other day."[49] She might have exaggerated, but not by much. Required religious services included Sunday services, morning and evening chapel, and morning and evening periods for silent reflection or Bible reading. In addition, Wellesley students had to take a course in the Bible as part of their academic work, and Vassar students attended a mandatory Bible class on Sunday before church. Religious observances and celebration also permeated college life. Wellesley's professors, who were all women, had to belong to an evangelical church, and grace preceded each meal in the common dining room. Vassar's teachers began their faculty meeting with prayer. For its first

20 years, one day each winter at Vassar was set aside for the Day of Prayer for Colleges. After a day of devotional meetings filled with addresses and prayers by faculty members, students conducted an evening meeting in which any college member could offer a voluntary prayer.

Vassar required no religious test of its faculty, though its Baptist founder mandated that "the training of our students should never be intrusted to the skeptical, the irreligious or immoral." Nevertheless, the handful of faculty members with Unitarian sentiments often felt like an unwelcome minority— "black sheep among the orthodox," as Frances A. Wood put it. They found a leader in Maria Mitchell, who called the group "the Rads" (radicals). Dismayed on the one hand by doctrinal preaching that emphasized God's punishments and on the other hand by scientific speculation that a divine presence did not exist, Mitchell turned to preaching such as that by Unitarian O. B. Frothingham. He would call his congregation to "come into Thy presence this morning . . . and ascend with Thee into that higher realm where the sun is always shining, where the truth holds on forever, and where love—never wanes." At the Rads' Sunday evening meetings, Mitchell enjoyed discussing controversial subjects, for instance, the immortality of the soul. Written in 1868, this farewell poem to three of her students shows her rejection of contemporary skepticism.

> Sarah, Mary, Louise and I
> Have come to the cross roads to say good-bye;
> Bathed in tears and covered with dust,
> We say good-bye, because we must;
> A circle of lovers, a knot of peers,
> They in their youth and I in my years.
> Willing to bear the parting and pain,
> Believing we all shall meet again;
> That if God is God and truth is truth,
> We shall meet again and all in youth.[50]

Finding formal religious services insufficient, students founded organizations to satisfy their religious needs and curiosity. Vassar students held a 20-minute prayer meeting every day except Sunday and Thursday, the days when the college president held voluntary all-college prayer meetings. Attendance at the students' prayer meetings was so large in the first decade of Vassar history that the prayer group could not fit comfortably into an ordinary classroom, where they had to kneel amid fixed desks. Student religious clubs also proliferated. The first one, founded in 1867, was the Society for Religious Inquiry, where the college's evangelically minded students found a home and which more worldly students called the Society for Pious Conundrum.

To ensure that college studies would not lead women students in undesired directions, Vassar and Wellesley borrowed heavily from the antebellum academies—most notably, Mount Holyoke—in planning their physical plants and the rules governing students' lives. During their first decades, both colleges housed students in large college halls under the supervision of women teachers. Daily schedules left little free time after classes, study periods, morning and evening prayers, two required quiet times for silent prayer and reflection, and an exercise period. At most, students had five hours here and there during their waking hours each day to dress, bathe, eat, see friends, write letters, and pursue extracurricular activities. Wellesley students could receive visitors only on Monday, when there were no classes or meetings with faculty, and Vassar students could not go to town without permission and a chaperone. Discipline extended even to students' appearance and cleanliness. Teachers made sure that students bathed and checked the length of their dresses. For everyday wear, Wellesley rules in 1878–79 recommended dresses "short enough for easy walking and free from heavy trimming." When examining the length of evening dresses, the "lady principal" of Vassar criticized short hemlines with the observation that ladies were "not supposed to have feet."[51]

At Smith students were disciplined differently, largely because in the 10 years since the founding of Vassar opposition had developed to housing women in structures where they were completely isolated from contact with men and the everyday life of a community. When Smith opened in 1875, it had a large college hall housing classrooms and administrative offices, a nearby residence house for students, which had previously been a large private dwelling, and no chapel or library. Because students had to attend church and use the public library in Northampton, they were integrated into the life of the town. In the small residence hall, students lived under the supervision of a lady-in-residence and a woman professor. The daily schedule of required prayers with the college president, mealtimes, classes, and ten o'clock bedtime allowed time for students to go to town and receive visitors in their residence halls when they liked. Breaking with the organization of the antebellum women's academy, Smith College created a new model for women's colleges. They would cease to resemble nunneries and would be better connected to the world outside the campus. In the last years of the century, the architectural development of the Vassar and Wellesley campuses confirms that the Smith model for college organization was prevailing. College women no longer lived under the total sort of discipline that had prevailed during the antebellum years at both women's academies and men's colleges.

Student intellectual life at the women's colleges sometimes complemented the official curriculum and extracurricular activities and sometimes opposed them. The 1865 Vassar College prospectus predicted that students would start voluntary associations that would stay within the antebellum tradition of women's societies for charitable work and religious improvement—for example, sewing circles, or "Societies of Missionary Correspondence and Inquiry." The catalog stated that there would be no "oratory and debate" because these were not "feminine accomplishments."[52] Within the first years, however, students had founded a literary society named the Philalethean. Unlike the members of men's societies, Philalethean members merely prepared and read original compositions. By the 1870s, however, they were debating in private, and by the nineties there were interclass debates. In Wellesley's first years a group of students founded the O.P. Society for the purpose of writing poetry and studying the work of Other Poets. A lover of poetry himself, Henry Durant encouraged the club and introduced its members to the poets and publishers he invited to campus. Clubs multiplied at the women's colleges and showed the diversity of students' intellectual interests, which included chess, music, French conversation, natural history, gardening, Shakespeare, reading, and writing for college newspapers and literary magazines.

The student newspapers in particular show that women students were active critics of the organized intellectual life at their colleges. At Wellesley students objected not only to the many rules imposed by Durant but also to the curriculum. They thought they had come to a college, but they discovered that Durant had organized a women's seminary that was a college in name only. Like women college students elsewhere, Wellesley College students wanted a real college curriculum. By the late 1870s they understood that such a curriculum included elective studies, which would permit them to pursue some studies in depth. Voicing the general discontent over Wellesley's weak curriculum, a student in the class of 1879 complained:

Wellesley is not a college. The buildings are beautiful, perfect almost; the rooms and their appointments are delightful, most of the professors are all that could be desired . . . but all these things are not the things that make a college. . . . I am here to take a college course and not to dabble in a little of every insignificant thing that comes up. I am not the only one that feels it but every member of the freshman class has the same feeling and not only the students but even the professors.[53]

Visiting ministers at Vassar's Sunday church service talked about woman's sphere and duties so often that students dubbed these "Martha and Mary" sermons and smiled knowingly when unwary ministers mentioned the names of these exemplary women. An editor of the *Vassar Miscellany News* objected strenuously to one minister's comparison of the students to lilies, who were to "minister to the aesthetic nature of the manly oak." Other editorials objected to sermons that attacked the study of natural science because it led inevitably to infidelity. Visiting speakers were urged to assume that the students were "intelligent and human beings." One speaker who did was Phillips Brooks, who earned student praise for discussing the "personality of the times" and not "what women should do, for this, you must know, is drilled into us by every stick of a man who comes."[54]

Outside the New England women's colleges, most educators of the postwar years wanted to "let boys learn what they will practice as men and girls the things which they will practice when they grow up to womanhood."[55] Such rhetoric made women's pursuit of higher education sound less threatening and more natural. Indeed, most college graduates applied their education primarily to enhancing their own and their families' intellectual lives. Yet higher education prepared many women for untraditional lives. Although rates of marriage for college graduates and nongraduates began to converge in the early twentieth century, in the late century 35–50 percent of graduates remained single when less than 10 percent of all women did so. And when less than 19 percent of American women were in the labor force, as many as 70 percent of women college graduates worked at some time in their lives, usually for a few years before marriage. Most held positions as professionals, almost always as teachers and college educators.

As college education did for men, it opened to women opportunities for new-style intellectual leadership. Because of the sex-stratified nature of Victorian society, however, women new-style leaders entered positions with lower prestige and lower pay than did men. Women's colleges helped graduates extend their activities beyond the parlor, but not beyond the confines of their society and culture. Most educated Americans in 1880 understood that each sex had its own attributes, role, and destiny.

six

In Pursuit of Truth

In this and the next chapter our story turns to intellectuals. By intellectuals I mean the articulate few who devote themselves to shaping ideas and thought in the public world. Use of the word *intellectual* in speaking of these few in the midcentury years entails some risk. First, there is the issue of presentism. Until the first years of the twentieth century, Americans did not use *intellectual* as a noun to refer to a member of a certain class of people. Rather, they used the word as an adjective to refer to a quality of mind or the thinking capacity of the mind. Yet *intellectual* denotes more effectively than any other word the class of people that this chapter will discuss. Second, to readers of today, *intellectual* suggests mental activity conducted apart from everyday life. Most of us think that intellectuals affect our lives only indirectly. Such was not the case in the 1860s and 1870s.

To dispel contemporary prejudices and show that intellectuals held a central place in Victorian public life, this chapter discusses the issues that occupied the public mind as revealed in popular songs and poetry, best-selling novels, and periodicals with wide circulations and compares these sources with the writings of ordinary middle-class people. Literary works that did not reach a wide audience despite their timely subjects and high artistic merit—for instance, J. W. DeForest's *Miss Ravenel's Conversion from Secession to Loyalty* (1867) and Emily Dickinson's poems—have been bypassed.

In the mid-nineteenth century intellectuals and their public had a chicken-or-the-egg relationship. Although an elite by dint of their literary skills, education, and access to podium and printed page, intellectuals were inextricably linked to and dependent on their public. Rather than inventing the terms of public discourse, mid-Victorian intellectuals participated in it by confirming its basic beliefs and by developing the implications of those beliefs.

While Chapter 7 discusses the various approaches that different groups of intellectuals took toward their publics, this chapter dwells on the identity of intellectuals. Who were they, what issues did they discuss, and how did they discuss them? To answer these questions, we will examine several key words in public discourse, namely, *truth, death, and love.* We will also look at two central and controversial issues of the 1860s and 1870s—modern science and woman's rights.

For Victorians, the terms "men of letters," and "public men," and "scholars" reflected the expectation that intellectuals would be men. They might follow a variety of professions—author, editor, poet, journalist, minister, college president, and professor. To be an intellectual required no special training or degree. Still, Victorians assumed that their intellectuals had qualified themselves as public spokesmen by acquiring thorough knowledge of at least one subject. Knowledge could come from deep study as well as from other activities. For instance, Ralph Waldo Emerson's lectures displayed his wide reading and commitment to showing the realities beneath appearances. But practical experience also qualified men to speak before the public. Bayard Taylor drew material for his lectures and books from his extensive travels. Knowledge was also expected to have broad application to topics of public interest, such as proper civic conduct for educated men, temperance, or domestic life. In other words, intellectuals were public philosophers who although they might talk about practical matters, encouraged and pointed the way to moral and mental improvement. Intellectual endeavor was neither self-centered nor pursued for its own sake. Committed to the proposition that a moral citizenry would make a moral republic, intellectuals embraced their role as teachers of self-development.

In the 1860s and 1870s there were no words with positive connotations, and few with neutral connotations to describe women intellectuals. Women with opinions on public issues were frequently referred to negatively as "strong-minded" women, or they were called bluestockings, a term that associated them with the sexual libertinism, demagoguery, and radicalism of the French Revolution. In "A Chapter on Literary Women" by Sara Parton, who wrote under the pseudonym Fanny Fern, a man says that he wants a wife and not "a literary woman." Literary women were devilishly ambitious, he said, and "nondescript monsters; nothing feminine about them."[1]

By the 1860s women intellectuals were expanding their ability to reach the public beyond the printed media and were finding acceptance on the lecture platform. Still, the novelty of a woman lecturer often provoked comment and disapproval. Martha Schofield, who bravely ventured to the Confederate-captured territory of the Georgia Sea Islands during the Civil War, wrote a friend about public lecturing, "I would not want *my* sister or a dear friend of mine to appear in public like Anna Dickinson," the lyceum lecturer and abolitionist.[2] In *The Gilded Age*, Mark Twain and Charles Dudley Warner conveniently killed off their heroine before she could exploit on the lecture circuit the notoriety she had gained during her murder trial.

Both men and women intellectuals reinforced the meaning of the key words in Victorian public discourse. For example, popular poet Alice Cary wrote:

> But Truth is sure, and can afford to wait
> Our slow perception, (error ebbs and flows;)
> *Her* essence is eternal, and she knows
> The world must swing round to her, soon or late.[3]

Understanding this verse depends on the reader's knowledge of the meaning of the word *truth*. Cary could use the word without defining it because her readers already had in mind a definition that had been shaped by the prose, sermons, poetry, and hymnody of the day. Thus, an understanding of *truth* and other key words resulted from extensive exposure to them and the accumulation of meaning through their repetition. Besides frequently mentioning the key words, intellectuals also defined them intensively in their speeches and writings in their particular areas of inquiry.

In general, "truth" referred to a divine and timeless world of meaning that transcends human differences—in other words, God's truth. In the 1860s and 1870s many intellectuals used this idea of truth as a standard for criticizing their world. If people would stop their quibbling over theological doctrines, political parties, sectional differences, and scientific theory, they would find unity in pursuing devotion to truth. Though truth implied unity, that unity always implied the sacrifice of someone's interest. In "The Battle Hymn of the Republic" (1862), Julia Ward Howe used truth to link the northern cause with Union war aims and God's purpose. As northern soldiers were fighting and vanquishing the Confederacy, "His truth is marching on."

When intellectuals intensively discussed truth or any other key idea or concept, they gave focus to the welter of ideas found in general public discourse and embodied in its material life. For example, Victorian parlors were concrete testimony to the seeming muddle of their residents' intellectual lives. But this muddle is apparent only to uninformed observers. The occupants of Victorian parlors could perceive an underlying logic because intellectuals developed the implicit meaning of the objects displayed in the parlor and clarified the relationships among them all. For example, a scientist could explain in a lyceum lecture the divine message of a mineral displayed on a whatnot stand, and a missionary lecturer could give meaning to the stereograph image of an archaeological excavation in the Holy Land. Because both the mineral specimen and the stereograph spoke silently to truth. Victorians perceived their parlor decor not as a muddle but as a unified whole. And by extension, their concept of truth made the Victorian intellectual world orderly.

Although Victorians agreed generally on the definition of their key words, they could have slightly different meanings for different publics. The definitions of the key word *love* illustrate how intellectuals addressed these discrete—though overlapping—publics. Love, specifically the redeeming power of Jesus' love, appeared frequently in popular songs and hymns played on parlor organs and pianos. More specific meanings of love appear in the writings of Henry Ward Beecher, Phillips Brooks, and Dwight Moody. These three popular preachers spoke to different segments of the Victorian public. By family ties and religious heritage, Beecher was an evangelical Congregationalist. He became interested in antebellum reforms such as the temperance and antislavery causes, and he maintained these interests through the war and into the postwar years. Brooks, an Episcopalian, first acquired national attention through the sermon he preached over the casket of Abraham Lincoln during its stay in Philadelphia in April 1865. He became pastor of Trinity Church in Boston in 1869. Although he shared Beecher's antislavery and temperance positions, Brooks is better known for his ecumenism. He wanted to unite Christians in the love of Christ, and he asked parishioners to devote themselves to improving the lives of the poor. Both Beecher and Brooks were college-educated and well read; Moody's power as a revival preacher depended instead on his oratorical ability to communicate the power and joy to be found in Christian faith.

As celebrity preachers of the 1860s and 1870s, Brooks and Beecher reached audiences beyond the congregations of their churches. Beecher lectured on the lyceum circuit, and his sermons and editorials on a variety of topics, including slavery, northern war aims, woman's rights, art and museums, and modern science, appeared in the *Independent* and *Christian Union*. His novel *Norwood, or, Village Life in New England* was serialized in 1867 in the *New York Ledger*, a story paper with a circulation of 300,000. Brooks reached a wide audience by appearing before multidenominational audiences at the Chautauqua Institute and by exchanging pulpits with Boston ministers of various denominations, including Methodists, Baptists, and Congregationalists. In addition, he collected and published his sermons, which enjoyed a modest popularity. Diaries of New England schoolgirls reveal that they spent some of their leisure hours reading his sermons to one another. His Christmas carol "O Little Town of Bethlehem" immediately became a favorite. Of the three, Moody, as a revival preacher, reached the largest live audience by far. Those who were not among the thousands who attended a service during his two- or three-week long campaigns in major northern, southern, and midwestern cities could still participate in the Moody phenomenon. Newspapers gave extensive coverage to his revivals, and Moody or his supporters published collections of his works—including inexpensive hardback editions and even less expensive pamphlets. including sermons, favorite anecdotes excerpted from his sermons, and accounts of his revivals in specific cities—in inexpensive hardback editions and even less expensive pamphlets.

By the 1880s and 1890s, Moody's belief that the 1,000 years preceding the reign of Christ had not yet begun had given his preaching a more pessimistic quality than that of Brooks and Beecher, who both believed that the present day belonged to the 1,000 years of preparation for Christ's advent on earth. Nevertheless, in the 1860s and 1870s these three preachers had addressed common themes while reaching audiences that included Victorians of all professions and levels of wealth. For example, followers of Moody and Brooks occupied quite separate social worlds. In Moody's audience there might be a young migrant to Boston from rural New England. As a clerk working a 60-hour week and living in a boardinghouse, he lived at a geographic and social distance from his employer, who perhaps had just built a townhouse on elegant Beacon Street. Brooks's congregants attended the newly constructed Trinity Church (1877) in Copley Square. Planned as an urban cathedral, Trinity attracted Episcopalian worshipers from all sections of the city. Light flowed into the church through elegant stained-glass windows created by John LaFarge, and no pillars obstructed the congregation's view of their preacher, who addressed them from a raised pulpit decorated with scenes from the life of Christ sculpted in relief.

Moody's followers always engaged the largest possible lecture hall for his revivals. In Boston the Tremont Temple was built for him. An urban clerk would have been drawn to Moody's lecture by the advance publicity of a period of prayer in local churches and by the fliers and newspaper articles announcing the approaching revival meeting. If the clerk could not attend an evening or afternoon meeting, he could make it to one of Moody's lunchtime services. In the revival hall, Moody spoke from a raised stage that he occupied with Ira Sankey, the music director and soloist for gospel hymns, and many local notables, including prominent ministers, businessmen, professionals, and college presidents. Sankey's huge choirs—in Boston he organized 2,500 singers into five different choirs—gave audible force to the words of the gospel hymns that were selected to reinforce the message of Moody's sermons. After revival services, people who wanted to allay their own doubts about their fitness to accept Jesus' love could seek out specially trained ushers who conducted them into small rooms to speak with a revival worker, missionary, or minister. As Brooks explained, Moody sowed the seed of religious commitment that other ministers could cultivate. In Trinity Church and in Moody's revival meetings, worshipers heard religious messages that were similar in content but different in rhetorical strategy and appeal.[4]

Whether attending a church service or reading a sermon by Beecher,

Brooks, or Moody, people heard about love. This simple word evoked the theologically complex issues of atonement and salvation in Christianity. The three preachers were all turning away from the Anselmic theory of the atonement—which had prevailed among seventeenth- and eighteenth-century Protestant ministers—according to which God is wrathful and righteous and people have no ability to affect their divine destinies. The gentler God of mid-nineteenth-century Protestantism—developed from a view known as Abelardian—emphasized a loving God and his Son's relationship to those people who have the ability to attain salvation. Unlike earlier clergymen, all three preachers allowed more scope to the ability of humans to influence their own salvation and emphasized God's love—in other words, His promise of salvation to his people.

In their preaching, Brooks, Beecher, and Moody moved beyond doctrinal and theological exposition. Instead, they encouraged appreciation of and even identification with Jesus. Beecher advised ministerial students to write sermons that brought forth the image of Christ as a painting did. Love was the essence of preaching, for ministers were in love with Christ and told their congregations about Christ's love for them. Brooks wove his sermons around descriptions of events in Jesus' life that illustrated different aspects of His love. But Brooks did not go as far as Beecher, who insisted that God's central truth was love. Brooks warned prospective preachers that if they taught that there was "no truth but love," they would be guilty of sensationalism.[5]

In theological terms, the word *love* referred to the divine atonement promised when Jesus died to save the world. Moody often graphically illustrated the concept. In sermons he referred to an image from Calvary, when a Roman soldier's spear pierced Jesus' side and He bled. Moody explained that Jesus' blood symbolically cleansed all sin from the people whom he loved so well. After Jesus' sacrifice, it became Christians' duty to accept unhesitatingly the gift of salvation that Christ offers.

In a typical sermon, Moody explained the unconditional, all-embracing quality of Jesus' love by telling an anecdote about the reunion of an armless Civil War veteran and his sweetheart. Disturbed when she does not hear from her soldier, the sweetheart sets out to find him and dispel her doubts. Convalescing in a hospital, the soldier has not had a nurse write his sweetheart for fear that her love will wither when she learns of his amputations. Upon finding her soldier in the hospital, she is blind to his wounds. She immediately embraces him and reaffirms her love. As Moody interpreted the story, the sweetheart's love resembles Jesus' unconditional love. Repentent sinners should not hesitate in offering themselves to Jesus, because He will instantly accept all who come. As Moody did, Beecher and Brooks also asked their auditors to seek forgiveness and to realize their salvation in God. But the three preachers appealed to different emotions and levels of intellect.

Death was another popular subject in nineteenth-century thought, and analysis of the ways in which Victorian intellectuals used the word reveals how they offered intensive definitions of key words and expanded their meanings. In religious doctrine, love and death were linked. Death was the moment of departure when God's love and His promise of salvation could be made real. Extended deathbed scenes were the primary incidents in an enormous consolation literature that included poems and obituary memoirs, mourners' manuals, prayer guidebooks, and hymns about heaven. Midcentury Christians believed that the moments before death were the most exquisite moments of life. As friends and family watched during these last minutes, they could surmise from the words, behavior, and expression of their loved one whether or not he or she had repented, yielded to divine love, and embraced the promise of salvation. Many popular fictional works appealed to readers because they contained long, highly dramatized deathbed scenes in which the dying character resists accepting his or her fate. Finally, some insight into the love that Christ offers smooths the way toward acceptance of death and a peaceful end.

For Victorian Americans, the Civil War gave special meaning to their preoccupation with death. About 3 million men between the ages of 13 and 43 fought in the war—40 percent of northern white men and 61 percent of southern white men. In the bloodiest of all American wars, one in six northern soldiers and one in four southern soldiers died. There were 1.82 deaths per 100 of the total population of the North and the South, compared with 1.18 deaths per 100 in the American Revolution, the second bloodiest war, and .03 deaths per 100 in the Vietnam War.[6] In the 1860s and 1870s it was likely that every family had at least one relative participating in the war and facing the probability of death. No wonder that the popular songs of the period dealt with the contingency of death and the disruption of affection that occurred as fathers, husbands, sons, and sweethearts went to the war front and died.

During the midcentury years, Christians who emphasized the redeeming power of God's love believed that death did not cause permanent separation. A collection of hymns for home use, first published in 1871, started with the line, "My heavenly home is bright and fair," to which the chorus answers, "We'll be gathered home." The dying drummer boy in "The Drummer Boy of Shiloh" (1863) prays to his mother to receive him "to thy fond embrace— Oh, take me home to thee."[7] Popular novelists elaborated on the idea that heaven would reunite loved ones and contain all the joys and comforts of home. In *The Gates Ajar* Elizabeth Stuart Phelps showed how she reconciled herself to the loss of a young man whom she had loved. She created two central women characters: one shows Phelps's own initial emotional reaction to her loved one's death, while the other shows her final rational understanding of it.

In Phelps's story, a young New England woman, Mary, finds no consolation after learning of her brother's death. Her minister offers no words to reassure her about his destiny. Believing in an awesome God and the inability of humans to affect their divine destiny, the minister merely recounts the promise of heaven. The mourning rituals of the times—wearing black clothes, laying out the dead in the parlor, and receiving callers who urge the mourners to get on with their lives—have no meaning for Mary. Distressed and distraught, she refuses to participate in the communion ritual of her church and even doubts her God.

Fortunately, a visit from her pious young aunt, Winifred, and Winifred's daughter Faith saves Mary from unredeemable despair. Aunt Winifred, who knows her Bible thoroughly and has read deeply in theology, understands that the dead have not gone. They are near and with us, hearing what we say and watching what we do. We can feel and see the presence of the dead through signs of God's love on earth, such as flowers, birds, and trees. The aunt restores Mary's faith and contentment and agrees when Mary says "Roy remembers and loves and takes care of me; . . . he has been listening." When Mary asks, "Why, you don't think he may be *here*?" Winifred answers yes.[8]

To create an earthlike heaven, Phelps and other midcentury Christians drew on *love* as the operative word. Much as Beecher, Brooks, and Moody did, Aunt Winifred explains that God "loves me, and He loves mine. As long as we love Him, He will never separate Himself from us, or us from each other. That, at least, is *sure*."[9] God's love guaranteed that He had provided for the reunification of loved ones in Heaven. But Phelps went beyond the three preachers by having Aunt Winifred predict that people will find their loved ones greeting them at the door of heaven, their "other home," ready to lead them inside to "the light and the warmth." In heaven all the best parts of human nature will reign and "the self-centered and dreamy" parts will recede. The dead do not gossip; they converse and enjoy poetry, pictures, statues, music, and reading "—being influenced to be better and nobler by good and noble teachers of the pen."[10]

Besides raising theological issues of personal import, death could also raise issues of national significance. For example, when Lincoln was assassinated on 14 April 1865, five days after the surrender at Appomattox Court House, many intellectuals tried to find meaning in his death. They began to portray him as a sort of savior who loved his country and its principles so much that he died for its sins. Preaching over Lincoln's casket, Phillips Brooks described the President as a leader who embodied the better qualities of the northern people: he was unselfish and generous, a man of the people who loved his fellow men. In the war, he had acted as "the servant of God in striking down slavery." In Brooks's view, the promise of salvation lay in the reunification of a nation of free men, and Lincoln had died that truth might come.[11]

To understand why the Union and the Confederacy had to fight and cause the death of so many soldiers, northerners and southerners often consulted both Biblical history and republican political theory. Eighteen months before John Wilkes Booth fired his deadly shot, Lincoln said at the commemoration of the battlefield cemetery for the Union dead at Gettysburg that the soldiers had died so "that this nation, under God shall have a new birth of freedom— and that government of the people, by the people, for the people, shall not perish from the earth." Although Lincoln's avowal that republican government should not die became famous because of his position and fame and the concision and power of his words, his belief that the war involved large historical questions was common among the American people. In his novel *Norwood* (1867), Henry Ward Beecher explained why so many had died at Gettysburg: "War ploughed the fields of Gettysburg, and planted its furrows with men. But, though the seed was blood, the harvest shall be peace, concord, liberty, and universal intelligence. For every groan here, a hundred elsewhere ceased. For every death now, a thousand lives shall be happier. Individuals suffered; the nation revived!"[12]

Diaries of northern and southern soldiers and civilians also reveal the view that the Civil War was an episode in the historical republican struggle and that individuals had the duty of subordinating their personal concerns to the cause of securing the republic. A private in a Maine regiment wrote his wife in 1861 that he knew "how American Civilization now leans upon the triumph of the Government and how great a debt we owe to those who went before us through the blood and suffering of the Revolution; and I am willing perfectly willing to lay down all my joys in this life to help maintain this Government."[13]

Recuperating for over a year in a hospital from an almost fatal neck wound, an Ohio soldier said that he forgot his own troubles and recalled the larger meaning of the war when other patients sang "The Battle Cry of Freedom" (1862). The song describes soldiers rallying around the flag, shouting the battle cry of freedom, and becoming unified as they welcome thousands from east and west to the Union cause. In the words of the song, that cause is to "never be a slave" and, with fellow soldiers, to "hurl the rebel crew from the land we love the best, / Shouting the battle cry of Freedom. / (*Fortissimo*) The Union Forever, Hurrah boys, hurrah!"[14]

As casualties mounted and the horrors of warfare became evident, many people tempered their enthusiasm for war. The immediacy of privation and death began to outweigh the abstract goal of freedom. An Owego, New York, woman had said in an 1861 letter to her brother that the war opposed the "despotism of traitors" and involved issues of "right over wrong, of Justice over Injustice and Rebellion." After the terrible battles of 1862, she saw that "it is an awful thing for so many men to go there to be mowed down like the grass and their precious lives and blood poured out like water on the burning soil of those inhuman bloodhounds."[15]

Many people, in both the North and the South also held the idea that war, and this war in particular, represented a moment of historical choice. For northerners, the conflict posed the question, would there be union or disunion, freedom or no freedom, and for white southerners liberty or not? Northerners assumed that freedom was possible only if the Union was preserved; southerners assumed that their liberty depended on secession. For northerners, the federal government was a means to an end; for southerners, it was an insurmountable barrier to their end. In the words of a favorite Confederate song, "The Bonnie Blue Flag" (1861), southerners were brothers "fighting for our liberty! . . . Hurrah! for Southern Rights, Hurrah!"[16] Gail Hamilton (the pseudonym of Mary Abigail Dodge) told readers of the *Atlantic Monthly* in 1863 that this generation had to answer "the question of the world" in the conflict between "right and wrong, between progress and sluggardy." Death in this cause was noble, she counseled. "Ever since the world swung free from God's hand, men have died,—obeying the blind fiat of Nature; but only once in a generation comes the sacrificial year, the year of jubilee, when men march lovingly to meet their fate and die for a nation's life."[17]

Dodge's Biblical allusion reflects the common view of the war as an incident in divine history. For southerners, too, the war was a time of divinely inspired national retribution. Since David's battle with the giant Goliath, the just had been fighting for the right and triumphing with the help of God. A Louisiana woman wrote in 1861 that the Confederate cause was "right and God will give us the victory." After many Confederate defeats in late 1863 and 1864, a Virginia lieutenant said that southerners' arrogance had offended God. When people become humble, "I believe our cause will brighten and the sunny bright days of peace will return."[18] By 1865 Lincoln also saw the war as a divine judgment on the nation. If God condemned slavery, Lincoln asked in the Second Inaugural Address, had He given

to both North and South, this terrible war, as the woe due to those by whom the offense came, shall we discern therein any departure from those divine attributes which the believers in a Living God always ascribe to Him? Fondly do we hope— fervently do we pray—that this mighty scourge of war may speedily pass away. Yet, if God wills that it continue, until all the wealth piled by the bond-man's two hundred and fifty years of unrequited toil shall be sunk, and until every drop of blood drawn with the lash, shall be paid with another drawn with the sword, as was said three thousand years ago, so still it must be said "the judgments of the Lord, are true and righteous altogether."

Lincoln hoped that peace would bring reconciliation, that it would be a time "to bind up the nation's wounds; to care for him who shall have borne the battle, and for his widow, and his orphan—to do all which may achieve and cherish a just, and a lasting peace, among ourselves, and with all nations."[19]

146

Many northern intellectuals shared his hopes. Drawing upon her experience as a nurse in a wartime Washington hospital, Louisa May Alcott wrote stories that depict war as the prelude to reconciliation. Using a strategy typical of women intellectuals, Alcott communicated her hope for the nation by writing about individuals and their personal reconciliations. In her stories, when mothers and sweethearts find their sons and lovers, they reestablish their relations on a firmer and purer basis than had existed before their separation. In other tales about human relationships, Alcott showed that she thought and hoped for national reconciliation based on forgiveness between the North and the South. In "The Blue and the Gray," (1872) a wounded northern soldier destined to die holds out a hand of mercy to a vengeful Confederate. Initially, the Confederate has no forgiveness in him and blames the northerner for his amputated leg. But as death approaches, the Confederate realizes that wars cause good men to act savagely. It was not the northern soldier's fault that he was shot; it was the fault of the war, which "is nothing but wholesale murder." Contritely, the Confederate prays for forgiveness for shooting the northern soldier as he lay in the hospital ambulance and for trying to poison him in the hospital. To show that the contrition is real, Alcott has the Confederate leave his money to the dead northerner's "little Mary." In the last scene of the story, Alcott depicted her hopes for the nation by having a lamp shine "full on the blue and the gray coats hanging side by side."[20]

After the surrender of Robert E. Lee at Appomattox Court House, Virginia, on 9 April 1865, southerners had to come to terms with the death of their nation. Two months after Appomattox, Edmund Ruffin, an influential Virginia man of letters, shot himself, having refused to give up his "unmitigated hatred to Yankee rule."[21] Although Ruffin's solution was extreme, the defeat did prompt many southerners to ruminate about death and the meaning of the cause for which they had suffered and their men had died. "The Conquered Banner" (1865), a poem by Father Abram J. Ryan that became popular in the South immediately after its surrender, suggested that the defeat was an ending, and that the Confederate flag should be put away: "Touch it not—unfold it never, / Let it droop furled forever, / For it droops above the dead."[22]

After the war, southerners established their own days of fasting and thanksgiving and built cemeteries and monuments for their war dead. Starting in 1866, southern communities began to celebrate a Confederate Memorial Day in the spring. The day varied from community to community, depending on the dates of local anniversaries. Some communities in the Deep South chose 26 April, when Gen. Joseph E. Johnston surrendered to Gen. William T. Sherman. South and North Carolina observed Confederate Memorial Day on the anniversary of Stonewall Jackson's death, 10 May.

For a decade after 1865, white southerners formed ladies memorial associations (LMAs). Although men often prompted the formation of the LMAs, served on their advisory committees, and provided them with substantial financial support, women organized their activities and solicited funds. A few LMAs established battlefield cemeteries for Confederate dead, but most sponsored memorial monuments in local cemeteries where the war dead were buried in a separate area. In choosing designs for these monuments, the LMAs passed over contemporary designs—such as an angel with a finger pressed against her lips to suggest respectful silence—in favor of more timeless designs. Most chose Egyptian-inspired forms such as obelisks and pyramids, which evoked the Egyptians' strong belief in the afterlife. By selecting these designs, the LMAs expressed their hopes not only for the dead but also for their cause. The Confederacy was not to be in this world, but its truths could exist in the next. The LMA monuments derived their meaning from Victorian definitions of truth and death.

Our discussion now turns to the two most prominent disagreements of the 1860s and 1870s: the "problem of modern science" and "the woman question," as Victorians called them. These two issues threatened to destroy the Victorian intellectual consensus upholding divine truth, for they concerned crucial premises of that intellectual world.

The term "modern science" had several possible interpretations. First, it could refer to positivism. As Americans understood the theories of the French positivist philosopher Auguste Comte, human society could be known only by its facts. God had neither created nor ordained the institutions of this world; they were human creations. Second, modern science could be based on the social philosophy of the English philosopher Herbert Spencer, who argued that society was developing according to its own laws. Social predestination ruled as organizations evolved from simple to complex forms. Third, modern science could imply natural science and the Darwinian theory of random natural selection. Finally, modern science also referred to historical and archaeological research to reconstruct a record of Biblical times. Sometimes this research confirmed, and sometimes it undermined, the veracity of Biblical history.

Victorians referred to those who agreed with Comte, Spencer, and Darwin about how to interpret society as materialists, because they denied divine guidance and its role in the development of the universe and human life. Explaining the perspective of modern science, a New England schoolteacher said in 1874 that modern scientists did not see nature as a "revelation of God" and "a means of communing with Him."[23] Modern scientists contended that truth has no divine dimension.

The most extreme advocates of modern science proposed that the claims of science refuted those of religion. They called religious ways of knowing the universe superstitions that trammeled the advance of knowledge. In 1874

John W. Draper produced *History of the Conflict between Religion and Science*, which surveyed the state of science from the fourth century before Christ in Greece through the Reformation in Europe. In the final chapter he proclaimed that there must be freedom of thought. Religion had to yield its dominion to science. Quoting an ancient philosopher, Draper concluded, "As for Truth, it endureth and is always strong; it liveth and conquereth for evermore."[24] Draper did not invoke divine truth; he expected to find his truth in the natural facts of this world.

Whereas Draper suggested merely that religion should yield, a few modern science advocates went further. Among the extremists was the philosopher Charles Sanders Peirce, who argued that logic showed that nature was too vast to have a character as a human being did. Therefore, nature could not possibly be benevolent, just, or orderly, that is, it could not have any of the characteristics that people ascribed to it. Thomas Huxley, a British popularizer of Darwinian theory, invented in 1869 the term "agnostic" to describe his ignorance of anything beyond or behind the here and now. The American lawyer and orator Robert Ingersoll pushed the meaning of the term even further. He explained that the agnostic expressed more than his own unbelief. He goes another step, and he says, with great emphasis, that you do not know. . . . He is not satisfied with saying that you do not know—he demonstrates that you do not know . . . and compels you to say, at last, that your faith has no foundation in fact."[25]

Americans learned about modern science from a variety of sources. Journals and weeklies like the *North American Review* and the *Independent* published reviews, some appreciative, of books about modern science because their editors believed readers should keep informed about contemporary thought. Advocates of Comte and Spencer also found their views welcomed by newspapers that supported the Democratic party and opposed Republican party policies on business regulation, tariff protection for American industry, and reconstruction of the South. The managing editor of the *New York World*, for example, was David Croly, who also edited the positivist journal *Modern Thinker*. In the late 1860s the *Modern Thinker* published articles and reviews by John Fiske, one of the leading popularizers of Spencer's theory of social evolution. In addition, journals devoted to radical isms, such as *Modern Thinker, Woodhull and Claflin's Weekly*, and *The Revolution*, a woman's rights journal, published articles expounding the theories of modern science and attacking the foundations of Victorian belief.

Perhaps the most important outlet for the new thought was *Popular Science Monthly*, edited by Edward L. Youmans. It contained articles by leading British and American devotees of modern science; its first volume in 1872, for instance, serialized Spencer's *Study of Sociology*. As its prospectus explained, *Popular Science Monthly* was more than a journal containing articles about natural science; it was an active advocate of the scientific method. By this, its editor meant the study of facts. Scientists wanted "the most accurate knowledge that can be obtained of the order of the universe by which man is surrounded, and of which he is a part." Besides science, they could also study history, the social order, and all human productions—in other words, "the whole of Nature," including "all accessible and observable phenomena."

In the 1860s and 1870s, advocates of the scientific method often criticized other scholarly methods and theories. Materialists confronted religious idealists, who believed that natural phenomena testified to divine truth. Proponents of modern science and its methods launched salvos at what they called the literary method of study. It supposedly had done little to dispel "the illusions and obscurities which have shrouded the nature of man and human society." The science advocates also disagreed with the claims of religious idealists that truth has a divine dimension and can be perceived by the trained eye in all things.[26]

These arguments and others like them gave people good reason to associate science with skepticism and hostility to religion. The title of Draper's book postulated a necessary conflict between religion and science. And Youmans always denigrated manifestations of popular religious belief, no matter how sincerely expressed. Anyone who attended a camp meeting he called an "ignorant blockhead," and he predicted that the claims of religious idealists would have to yield as science drove "on with its researches, regardless of any thing but the new truth it aims to reach."[27]

The dogmatism and belligerence of many in the modern science camp made science a hot topic in the postwar years. Articles and lectures on modern science and its supposed conflict with religion filled the media, and periodicals introduced science columns and departments. Even so, skeptical or agnostic modern science advocates were never more than a minority among intellectuals. In *We are Our Neighbors* (1875) Harriet Beecher Stowe trivialized the intellectual challenges posed by modern science advocates, the "Darwinians and scientific men" who "have an easy sort of matter-of-course way of announcing that the Bible is nothing but an old curiosity-shop of by-gone literature."[28]

Throughout the 1870s most intellectuals held to their vision of divine truth. They concluded that modern science, far from posing a threat to their religious beliefs, simply demonstrated the promise of better things to come. Leading natural scientists, social scientists, and ministers, including Beecher and Brooks, maintained that evolution showed the beneficence of divine purpose, and Christ remained as the eternal measure of truth. Most Protestants still believed that the world was getting better and better. The social scientist and modern science advocate J. Stanley Jevons argued that social evolution showed a "deep-built scheme working toward goodness and happiness." The more he studied evolution, the more he became persuaded that a human was "no automaton, no mere lump of protoplasm, but the creature of a Creator."

Having their cake and eating it too, intellectuals adopted the lessons of modern science without perceiving how they could overturn divine truth. As the Congregationalist journal *Advance* argued in 1877, "The Bible and science are but the extreme right and left wing of that movement which embraces the truest thought, the noblest sentiment and the best works of these progressive times."[29]

Despite the confidence expressed in modern science, there was a problem—and a big one. When scrutiny of biblical texts and archaeological digs in the Holy Land revealed that the Bible was not literally true, believers had to find another foundation for their faith. At the same time, the Darwinian theory of evolution and positivistic social science theory were intellectually credible ways of understanding the world and its development. Intellectuals had to choose whether they would see God at work in evolution or not, and whether they would see divine truth in mundane phenomena or not. These theories robbed religious faith of its taken-for-grantedness. By creating a choice between theistic and agnostic theories of human and social development, they made holding religious conviction in the 1860s and 1870s quite a different experience than it had been in the 1840s and 1850s.

Most people continued to believe, but they were troubled. Even those who rejected Darwin's theory that humans had descended from lower beings did so nervously. Marietta Holley, whose popular subscription novels sold door to door to rural and lower middle–class readers, had a laugh in her *My Opinions and Betsey Bobbet's* (1872) at New York City intellectual circles where knowledge of Darwin was assumed. Even as she joked about the pretensions of big-city intellectuals, Holley showed that she expected her readers also to have some knowledge of Darwin and his theories. Popular jokes made fun of the supposed relationship between human beings and apes. A southern monthly asked, "Why is Abe Lincoln, among his children, like a certain river in Virginia." The answer: "Because considered with reference to his children, he is the Pamonkey (Pamunky)"[30] Even Mary Chesnut humorously contrasted the Prince of Wales with a gorilla.

From the pulpit, Brooks, Moody, and Beecher confronted the challenge of modern science with a strategy based on their placement of love at the center of their preaching. At times Moody played up the antitheistic claims of modern science; the more potent they seemed, the more urgent became his call to Jesus. Thus, he saw the 1870s as "one of the darkest ages of unbelief." He also took the most anti-intellectual stance of the three preachers. Commenting on historical and archaeological research into Biblical history, he stated that "we haven't any authority to take out just what we like, what we think appropriate, and let dark reason be our guide."[31] Brooks and Beecher advised future ministers to involve themselves in the intellectual controversies of the day. Beecher forthrightly announced that he had become a convert to Herbert Spencer's version of social evolution. Brooks acted more cautiously and counseled ministers neither to embrace nor to deny modern science and its claims in their sermons. Responding with greater sophistication than Moody, Brooks suggested that ministers don the armor of professional competence to protect religion from the bombardment of science. He wanted religion to avoid confronting scientific claims. If it did not, it could only "pronounce upon the results of scientific inquiry in a summary way which it would never tolerate with reference to its own peculiar subjects of study." For all three ministers, preaching about love won souls to Christ without confusing minds. Christ was a refuge, Brooks argued, from the competing claims of science and religion. And Christ empowered ministers to see the "disputed truth of the moment in His light and as an utterance of Him."[32]

Not all intellectuals viewed modern science with as much optimism as did Beecher and Brooks; some perceptive critics and advocates perceived its revolutionary potential. Charles Hodge of Princeton Theological Seminary rejected Darwinian evolution entirely in his *What Is Darwinism?* (1874). He asked, "Is development an intellectual process guided by god, or is it a blind process of unintelligible, unconscious force, which knows no end and adopts no means?"[33] Yale's Noah Porter, who accepted a theory of natural evolution, agreed with Spencer, John Fiske, and other materialists that their theories severed the divine from truth. But unlike these intellectuals, who were glad to throw off religious absolutes, Porter predicted that doing so would result in intellectual confusion and chaos. If the theories of modern science were true, if humans were not divine in their nature but merely masses of molecules, then their intelligence had merely a material existence. Law, the state, and the family could no longer be seen as divinely rooted institutions; as human inventions only, they could perish at the whim of the moment. The result would be "caprice in morality, tyranny in government, uncertainty in science."[34]

Porter and many others believed that the issue of woman's rights portended just such caprice in morality. In the 1860s and 1870s the "woman question" was one of what rights or privileges women were entitled to. Did women have a right to the wages they earned and the property they inherited? Should they receive higher education, and if so, what kind? Should they have the right to vote? Although most supporters of woman's rights answered these questions affirmatively, they did not expect—or want—to overturn the fundamental institutions and beliefs of society. They believed that each sex had its own special nature and distinct attributes, that the family had a divinely inspired origin, and that divine truth reigned. What supporters of woman's rights did expect was that granting rights to women would lead to social reform. Homes would be more secure places, better-educated mothers would produce better-educated children, and women voters would introduce the perspective of their sex into political debate.

In the last years of the Civil War the woman question became one of the most controversial, publicly contested issues. As the war ended, woman's rights advocates revived their campaign, which they had subordinated for the war's duration to the cause of emancipation for slaves and the success of the North. Heated debate arose as Elizabeth Cady Stanton and Susan B. Anthony campaigned to have the word *men* deleted from the Fourteenth Amendment, to secure passage of a Kansas state referendum in favor of woman suffrage, and to have sex removed as a barrier to voting by the Fifteenth Amendment. A profusion of books, pamphlets, journal articles, and lyceum lecturers appeared in support and opposition.[35] Opponents of woman's rights, and of woman suffrage especially, argued that these reforms would fundamentally alter social arrangements. To prove their arguments, antireformers had merely to point to the life and ideas of Victoria Woodhull.

Woodhull and her sister Tennessee Claflin were notorious in the 1870s. Through Claflin's talent for running séances for spiritualists, the sisters won the admiration of railroad tycoon Cornelius Vanderbilt, who helped them establish in January 1870 their own brokerage house, which made them wealthy within six months. Confident of her own abilities, Woodhull found no project too large. In the spring of 1870 she announced that she would run for the presidency of the United States as a candidate of the Cosmo-Political party, and she founded *Woodhull and Claflin's Weekly* (1870) to help inform the public of her views. Until the weekly printed Woodhull's accusation that Henry Ward Beecher had committed adultery with Elizabeth Tilton—which prompted Anthony Comstock, at the time a special agent for the U.S. Post Office, to close down Woodhull's paper for violating the Comstock Act, which banned obscene materials from the mails—the weekly printed articles on a wide range of issues, from reform of world government to reform of women's clothing styles. The issue for 22 April 1871, for instance, contained articles on the Fourteenth Amendment, the technology used in the Franco-Prussian War, and the wedding presents received by an English princess. Many of the causes advocated by the weekly outraged Victorians' religious, economic, and sexual beliefs. The paper had a columnist who was the leading American advocate of Auguste Comte's positivism; it advocated legalized prostitution; and after the sisters assumed leadership of the American branch of Marx's International Workingmen's Association in 1871, the paper printed Marx and Engels's *The Communist Manifesto* (1848) for the first time in the United States.

That same year, before Victoria Woodhull crossed the line between fame and notoriety, the wing of the woman suffrage movement that advocated amending the Constitution to include the right of women to vote welcomed Woodhull into its fold. She had impressed Anthony with a speech before the House Judiciary Committee arguing that women had the right to vote as citizens under the Fourteenth and Fifteenth amendments. She wanted to hold a convention of woman suffragists to plot revolution. "We will over-slough this bogus republic and plant a government of righteousness in its stead, which shall not only profess to derive its power from the consent of the governed, but shall do so in reality."[36]

Woodhull earned most of her notoriety for her advocacy of free love and the household that she kept in New York City, where she purportedly lived with two husbands. During 1871 and 1872, in New York, Boston, and other American cities, her lecture "Principles of Social Relations" employed the rhetoric of republicanism to criticize existing laws of marriage. If a law does not protect people in their right to love but interferes, she proclaimed, "it is *infamous* law and worthy only of the *old-time* despotism: since individual tyranny forms *no* part of the guarantee of, or the right to, individual freedom." These statements were more than enough to violate contemporary understandings of truth, but then she announced herself a free lover. "I have an *inalienable, constitutional* and *natural* right to love whom I may, to love as *long* or as *short* a period as I can; to *change* that love *every day* if I please, and with that right neither *you* nor any *law* you can frame have *any* right to interfere."[37]

Woodhull's public statements on marriage illuminate why most people opposed woman's rights in the 1870s. Her opponents saw her proposals not as reforms but as stepping-stones to a world of free love. Her ideas put supporters of woman suffrage and higher education for women in the position of always having to answer the charge that such reforms would overturn the fundamental order of things. Opponents of woman's rights thought that Woodhull's arguments proved that social revolution lay just beyond these reforms. She overturned truth by denying that human institutions were divinely sanctioned. To her, state, family, church, and school were not institutions mandated by God to promote moral growth. Woodhull took to an extreme the liberal idea that self-development was possible only when the state imposed no artificial restraints on the individual. To her mind, the government of the 1870s barred self-development by limiting an individual's freedom to form conjugal alliances.

Woodhull not only offended sexual propriety; she also shook Victorian ideas to their roots. If marriage was impermanent, could there be a home? If there was no earthly home, could there be a heavenly one? Further, if men and women had the right to start and end marriages at will, would sexual and social anarchy ensue? And most frightening to Victorians, if women could leave their husbands to pursue other men, did that not mean that they were sexually alive and forceful? What would the world be without their passive contribution of purity? Woodhull was proposing that men and women had similar sexual natures and that people should be free to seek their own happiness. If she was correct, there was no divine truth to proclaim what men and women should do and to ensure an orderly world.

In spite of her impact and notoriety, by the late 1870s Victoria Woodhull had retreated from American public life. She recanted some of her former beliefs and even declared marriage a divine institution. After emigrating to England in 1877, she married an heir to a banking fortune and lived the last half of her life in comfort and respectability as a supporter of uncontroversial reform causes. Conventional morality would not be rocked again by intellectuals espousing free love until the years before World War I.

Unlike the issue of free love, the debate about the conflict between religion and science did not slip into abeyance. After 1880 science remained at the center of the intellectual stage. And the scientific approach to investigation that Youmans had outlined in 1872 came to dominate natural science as well as the social sciences in the last decades of the century. After 1885, at the latest, no respected scholar in America would say that his or her research proved or disproved divine truth. Both theists and agnostics embraced theories of evolution, and most optimistically continued to think that social and natural development was a process of improvement rather than one of random change or degeneration. Thus, with one difference, Alice Cary's words still held as true in 1876 as they had in 1860:

> From transient evil I do trust
> That we a final good shall draw;
> That in confusion, death, and dust,
> Are light and law.[38]

After the rise of modern science, however, many people read Cary's verse differently; not everyone was certain that the "light" of her last line shone from a divine source. Without heavenly light, truth slowly dimmed and the Victorian intellectual consensus started to crumble as the new century began.

seven

Intellectuals and the Public

Most Victorian intellectuals agreed in theory that they should undertake the twofold task that one of the characters in Harriet Beecher Stowe's *My Wife and I* (1871) proposes: they should arouse and strengthen "the public mind . . . to resist" and teach people to discriminate by establishing "a just standard of moral criticism no less than of intellectual."[1] In practice, different groups of intellectuals adopted different strategies for undertaking this task. Women could not use the same strategies as men, and after 1865 southerners had to avoid offending northerners when exercising their public conscience. Moreover, a minority of northern intellectuals, who called themselves liberals, set their critical standards very high in the hope of reforming education, literature, art, architecture, and thought. In this chapter, we will examine how these four main groups of intellectuals—women, southerners, liberals, and mainstream male thinkers—sought to arouse the minds of their publics, and we will look at the standards of criticism they established.

The vast majority of midcentury intellectuals reached their public through lecturing on the lyceum circuit and publishing in general-interest, family-oriented periodicals, of which *Harper's Weekly* and *Scribner's Monthly* were the leading representatives. With circulations of 200,000 at their height, these periodicals reflected the educational endeavor in which most intellectuals of the day participated. As family magazines, they always upheld a moral viewpoint rooted in Protestant Christianity. The editors of *Scribner's Monthly* explained that they wanted "to make a magazine that is intelligent on all living questions of morals and society, and to present something in every number that will interest and instruct every member of every family into which it shall have the good fortune to find its way."[2]

Family magazines serialized novels and books and contained articles or columns on politics, science, geography, current events, religion, and humor. Some family magazines and weeklies were intended for a specific religious audience. The *Independent* and *Christian Union*, for instance, appealed largely to religious liberals, mainly Congregationalists and Presbyterians who supported reform causes such as the antislavery and temperance movements. Other periodicals targeted certain family members, for instance, *Godey's Lady's Book* was for women, and *Our Young Folks* for children.

A common school education was all that was required to read and understand the content of these periodicals, which sought to inform rather than improve analytical abilities or challenge widely held assumptions. Judging these periodicals by Stowe's criteria, they successfully made the public aware of current events, but their critical standards tended to value moral probity over intellectual quality and acuity. The periodicals did not stimulate profound political thought or encourage artistic creativity or literary genius. Rather, they embraced the products of Victorian culture, including its revival preachers, story papers, sculpture by John Rogers, and poetry by Alice Cary, and relayed them, with no very trenchant comment, to their readers. On cultural matters, the periodicals were relatively democratic. The principle of *vox populi, vox dei* reigned, with two exceptions: the periodicals defined "the people" as the Victorian public, and they insisted that what this public wanted should be moral.

The family magazines had an institutional look-alike in the Chautauqua Assembly in Chautauqua Lake, New York, founded in 1874. The assembly illustrated a particular strength of mid-Victorian intellectual life: its outreach to the middle class. Intellectuals who supported Chautauqua took as their task the education of the public mind. Prominent ministers, such as Phillips Brooks, addressed the assembly, and professors from Harvard, Johns Hopkins University, and Boston University lectured in its institutes. Every summer intellectuals joined their public at the assembly and helped attendees satisfy their desire for self-culture and education. On a Chautauqua vacation, pious Protestant Americans enjoyed both the seriousness of pleasure and the pleasure of seriousness. The assembly's newspaper, the *Chautauqua Assembly Herald*, promised that a vacation in the community "combines pleasure with profit" and could "preserve the mind from weariness, dissipation, and ennui."[3]

The Chautauqua Assembly began as a two-week summer institute for Sunday school teachers. In the first years its Methodist founders had to warn away those prospective vacationers who expected to find a camp meeting at which they could express intense religious feeling. Within six years the program had expanded to six weeks and established itself as a general education program.

The founding of Chautauqua was an indication that Methodists and Baptists—who from the late eighteenth century through the antebellum years had scorned education and denied that it could further piety—were changing their opinions. These denominations were developing liberal wings that looked favorably on cultural participation; in the years between the Civil War and 1900, they also began to support institutions of higher education. Methodists organized Vanderbilt University (1872) in Nashville, Tennessee, and John D. Rockefeller, a Baptist, endowed the University of Chicago (1891). Its first president, William Torrey Harris, had founded in 1879 the Chautauqua School of Languages, where students could learn Latin, German, French, Hebrew, and Greek. At Chicago, Harris established the university as a research institution while also starting the first university extension school in the country.

The faithful at Chautauqua often needed reassurance that cultural participation would not tempt them from the path to salvation. No summer was complete without a lecture entitled "Is Culture a Substitute for Religion?" The lecturer would answer no, of course. He would tell the audience that the ideal Christian followed the faith and practices of religion while pursuing self-culture through the study of history, art, literature, and natural science. Culture was no substitute for, but a complement to, religion.

After 1880 the Chautauqua Assembly inspired imitations in many northern, midwestern, and southern communities. The term "chautauqua" also came to mean a traveling road entertainment featuring musical and vocal performances, lectures, and sensational scientific demonstrations. Although the original Chautauqua and some of its clones—the Monteagle assembly in Tennessee and the Mount Gretna assembly in Pennsylvania, for instance—still draw summer vacationers who attend lectures and musical entertainments, the popularity of the assemblies declined after the 1930s.

Visitors to Chautauqua in the 1870s usually arrived by a lake steamer, which followed a Sabbatarian schedule. At the assembly they found a community of boardinghouses, private cottages, hotels, dining halls, public buildings, and pavilions. Tents and canopies attached to buildings extended their public spaces into the open air. The decoration of open-air pavilions—classical columns, capitals, and pediments—and their august names, such as the Hall of Philosophy, announced that serious learning was pursued inside. Public recreation areas also reflected the serious, religious nature of the place. Along the lake was a complete reconstruction of Palestine, including all of its Biblically important natural features. There was also a tent museum of Biblical and Oriental geography, which showed the dress and customs of the Assyrians, the Egyptians, and others. But some amusements had no serious dimension. Chautauquans picnicked, played baseball and tennis, and enjoyed the lake and forests. A first-time visitor to Chautauqua in 1880, Unitarian Edward Everett Hale, exclaimed, "This place is simply marvellous. It is a great college for the middle classes."[4]

7.1 A montage of scenes of Chautauqua Lake, New York, *Harper's Weekly*, 21 August 1880. *Courtesy of the Winterthur Library: Printed Book and Periodical Collection, Henry Francis du Pont Winterthur Museum, Winterthur, Delaware*

Given the Chautauqua founders' religiously liberal belief that divine meaning was to be found in all things, the assembly's program was as comprehensive as possible. Visitors usually came for one of the several institutes or conventions held each summer. There was the original institute for Sunday school teachers, as well as conventions that dealt with modern literature, science, and philosophy. National organizations, including the Civil War–era Christian Commission, the Woman's Christian Temperance Union (1874), the Young Men's Christian Association, and the National Education Association (1859), also found the assembly a convenient location for their annual meetings or reunions.

Many Chautauqua lectures were dedicated to solving some of the problems that modern thought posed for Christian believers. In lectures like "The Place of Science in Symmetrical Culture" and "The Importance of Science to the Religious Thinker," Chautauquans learned that they should pursue scientific study. Lecturers also encouraged appreciation of new scientific discoveries by explaining their potential to illuminate the relationship of the natural world to divine truth. A lecture like "The Earth as an Astronomical Body" conveyed up-to-date scientific knowledge, while others made science interesting and less threatening to theistic laypeople by including demonstrations of apparatus such as microscopes, telephones, and phonographs.

Other lecturers confronted the atheistic claims of positivists and other contemporary thinkers. Borden P. Bowne, a professor of philosophy at Boston University, gave a series of lectures in 1880 on German philosophy. He refuted the prevalent view that German philosophers had atheistic tendencies and explained that their theories shed new light on the phenomenon of faith. Ministers and professors also tackled the problem of Darwin and explained how a knowledgeable person could believe in both God and evolution. One minister assured Chautauquans in 1877 that evolution assumed the existence of a creation, and creation the existence of a Creator. Another speaker, William N. Rice, a professor of natural science from Wesleyan University who in 1867 had earned the first Ph.D. degree awarded in the United States, explained that evolution "dethrones not God. It does not show us that the universe goes on without a Divine plan. It only show us that God's plan is vaster and more comprehensive than our poor thoughts had before been able to recognize."[5]

The Chautauqua lecture platform and newspapers were closed only to those who denied divine truth. For example, Chautauquans never heard from any follower of Victoria Woodhull, although they debated the woman question. The June 1880 *Chautauqua Assembly Herald* published letters to the editor suggesting that arguments in favor of woman suffrage should be aired. Responding to an article that had opposed woman suffrage, readers wanted to know why women should not have the vote and be ordained as ministers. During the summer of 1881 a debate on the issue was included in the program.

The assembly also reached out to a national public. Through printed materials, anyone could take Chautauqua lessons year-round. The assembly founded a publishing house, which made works of religious interest available at a low cost. One of the most successful Chautauqua programs was the Chautauqua Literary and Scientific Circle (CLSC), the first successful correspondence course in U.S. history. Advertised in the *Sunday School Journal*, the program attracted 8,400 subscribers in 1878 alone. Members undertook a four-year guided reading program that surveyed English history, Greek civilization, English literature, Biblical history and scholarship, astronomy, and physiology. CLSC members formed themselves into local reading groups, discussed the assignments that appeared in *The Chautauquan*, and mailed in tests and written assignments. Within a few years after its founding, the CLSC had developed an organizational structure and rewards that resembled those of colleges. Reading groups became classes in which members started as freshmen and progressed to the senior level, and each class adopted its own flower and slogan. Upon completion of the program, seniors received diplomas at a graduation ceremony held at Chautauqua Lake.

The assemblies and the CLSC program probably appealed to Protestants who were excluded, by either age or income, from the organized higher education movement of the day. CLSC members could follow the Victorian self-improvement imperative through education, confident that what they were doing was right. The professors who selected the CLSC reading program and the Chautauqua name guaranteed that learning was valuable and that it would sustain piety.

In the midcentury years, most people assumed that the term "woman intellectual" was an oxymoron. Women intellectuals had to overcome the disabilities that their womanhood and domestic life supposedly had imposed on them before they could command a respectful public audience. Julia Ward Howe, author of "The Battle Hymn of the Republic," an organizer of women's clubs, and an officer of the American Woman Suffrage Association, told women how they could best run their association at the first meeting in 1873 of the national Association for the Advancement of Women (AAW). She advised them to forgo the petulant and domineering ways that they had acquired as mistresses of their homes and to become docile and cooperative so that their association would prosper. A positive local newspaper report of the AAW's fifth meeting in Cleveland, Ohio, praised the "moderation and judgment" displayed in the discussions, which had promoted ideas "well worth the attention of male scientists and philosophers." Altogether, the meeting proved to the reporter "that sensible women can come together in the interests of their sex without incurring the censure and ridicule of those who listen to their deliberations."[6]

The prospect of public scrutiny heightened women intellectuals' fear of presenting their ideas in public. Women often published anonymously or under pseudonyms. Sara Parton, a novelist and columnist for the *New York Ledger*, published under the name Fanny Fern, Mary Abigail Dodge under the name Gail Hamilton, Harriet Beecher Stowe occasionally under the name Christopher Crowfield, and Marietta Holley as "Josiah Allen's Wife."

Pseudonyms also allowed women to publish their ideas on issues that convention decreed was beyond their ken. Mary Abigail Dodge used the name Cunctare for her reports to the *Congregationalist* on the proceedings of the House of Representatives and the Senate. And like men, women used anonymity and pseudonyms when they published stories that violated standards of propriety. Louisa May Alcott wrote *Little Women* in her own name and thrillers for story papers under her pseudonym, A. M. Barnard. Using a similar strategy, women lecturers camouflaged controversial subjects with benign-sounding titles. Elizabeth Cady Stanton's lecture "Home Life" presented arguments for liberalized divorce laws, equality between men and women, coeducation, and self-control in sexual relations. At Vassar College in 1872, Sara Jane Lippincott, who wrote as Grace Greenwood, gave her blandly titled lecture "Indoors," which advocated woman's rights. Feeling deceived, the Vassar president wrote his wife that Lippincott had presented "a coarse worldly view, altogether below the Vassar standard of delicacy & seriousness."[7]

The concepts of woman's sphere and woman's special nature determined to a great extent the issues that women intellectuals addressed. With the exception of the women's newspapers that supported woman's rights, no women's periodical, and few women intellectuals, discussed electoral politics. Most women intellectuals respected the distinction between home and public life, and their choice of subjects reflected their legal exclusion from national political life. Still, women intellectuals were public intellectuals and philosophers. For example, Harriet Beecher Stowe's *Uncle Tom's Cabin* and Augusta Jane Evans Wilson's *St. Elmo*—the first and third best-sellers of the century, respectively—turned conventional womanly concern for home and family into social and political criticism. The northerner Stowe argued against slavery, while the southerner Wilson posited a foundation for postwar national unity. Gail Hamilton, Fanny Fern, and Jennie June (Jane Cunningham Croly) supplied story papers and respected monthlies with articles about the lives of working men and women, as well as about typical middle-class domestic concerns such as cooking, gardening, and marriage. Their readers learned about the problems of a six-day work week for clerks, women in prison, domestic violence, and the urban poor. The strategy developed by these women intellectuals during the 1860s and 1870s served for a century as a springboard for women to propel themselves into public life.

In the South, the war gave some white women an exemption from the decree that women should be concerned with domestic matters only. More conventional southern women, like Constance Cary, a columnist for the

Southern Illustrated News in Richmond, wrote on women's homefront activities and helped develop a wartime ethic and appropriate standards of behavior. These writers debated whether women should enjoy the company of men who were avoiding military service and whether dances were appropriate entertainment when soldiers were dying on the battlefield. Addressing economic issues, these writers offered recipes and tips for coping with the scarcity of food and household goods and criticized merchants who took advantage of shortages to raise prices. During the war southern women took the lead in advocating that the common good should prevail over private gain in setting prices. Less conventional women wrote about the warfront and described both the bravery of Confederate soldiers and the horrors of battle. Attempting to rally morale, Sally Rochester Ford wrote *The Raids and Romance of Morgan and His Men* (1864), and Augusta Jane Evans Wilson included eyewitness accounts of the Battle of Manassas in her novel *Macaria* (1864). Poets who published in local newspapers composed venomous verse about the Yankee enemy and did not avoid mentioning battlefield gore. Through their poetry women transported themselves to the battlefront and joined the fight. A southern woman, a Mrs. Clark, wrote in "The Battle of Manassas" that soldiers had pledged their lives to the Confederate cause at Manassas, "But the wine in which we pledged them, was all of ruby red!"[8]

Although northern women did not write about the battlefield or excoriate the Confederates to a similar extent, they did write so prolifically during the war years that a journalist for *Frank Leslie's Illustrated Weekly* commented in 1863 that "woman has now taken to her pen."[9] Women filled newspapers and magazines with poems and articles telling women readers that their prayers could help the Union cause and advising them about practical opportunities to help the war effort. In the *Atlantic Monthly* for 1863, Mary Abigail Dodge, under her pseudonym Gail Hamilton, criticized northern women for not rising to the heights of understanding and effort that the times demanded. Women were merely rolling bandages instead of rallying their men to military service and steeling themselves to make the ultimate sacrifice.

Women intellectuals' wartime activism built on the achievements in the 1850s of women novelists such as Maria Cummins, Sara Parton, Harriet Beecher Stowe, Mary Virginia Terhune, and Susan Warner. These writers had begun to dominate American novel writing and fiction sales; in 1858 they wrote half of the nonfiction books that the *American Publisher's Circular* named as "among the greatest successes." After these women novelists gained a degree of acceptance for women's public presence as intellectuals, increasing numbers of women published. By 1871 women were writing almost three-fourths of all novels published.

The Civil War provided women with an additional impetus and rationale for their participation in public life. The heroine of Alcott's *Hospital Sketches* (1863) announces in the first sentence of the book, "I want something to do."

Helpful relatives suggest, some humorously, that she write a book, teach, take a husband, become an actress, or "go nurse the soldiers." Just as Alcott did, the heroine takes the wartime assignment and serves in a Washington hospital. In real life, Alcott caught a serious case of typhoid fever after six weeks. Drawing on her experiences, she then wrote *Hospital Sketches*.

Although the war eased women intellectuals' entry into public discourse, strictures about the subjects that they could address remained. Alabamian Augusta Jane Evans Wilson wanted to write a history and justification of the Confederacy but deferred to ex–Vice President Alexander Stephens upon learning that he had undertaken a similar project. When her novel *St. Elmo* became a best-seller, she had her sweet consolation.

Women lecturers found acceptance more slowly than did women writers. A supporter of emancipation, freedmen's causes, and woman's rights, Anna Dickinson was the most popular woman lecturer during the war and immediately afterward, and she commanded the highest fees. She spoke on timely subjects that appealed to the public. She herself aroused interest because many still thought of a woman lecturing to mixed assemblies as a promiscuous act. A young admirer of Dickinson believed she had been

called to do this great work. . . . Only once in a century or more is woman called to so great a work, and never in the history of our nation has a young woman had such a mission. No, my dear Sadie, she could not do as much good at her own fireside— We must remember that times like these demand of each one of us every effort in the great cause—and because her powers and responsibilities lead her out of the common path, we have no right to condemn so long as they only produce good. . . . There is something sublime and heroic in a young woman thus stepping out of her supposed sphere and bearing the criticism of the nation for the good of her country.[10]

Despite Dickinson's success, the Chautauqua Assembly did not invite a woman to speak on a topic other than one related to Sunday School education until its third summer. Then Frances Willard, a representative of the Woman's Christian Temperance Union, was invited to speak, but she was cautioned to keep her support for woman suffrage private if she wanted a cordial reception.

In 1873 women intellectuals founded the Association for the Advancement of Women. Its organizers, who were active in a New York City women's study club, felt that the time had come for "the earnest few" to gather for a deliberative assembly and to learn about "practical methods for securing to Women higher intellectual, moral, and physical conditions, with a view to the improvement of all domestic and social relations."[11] Four hundred women came to the first meeting in New York City, and subsequent annual conventions drew even more; over 1,000 women attended the 1877 meeting in Cleveland. Although the association never focused on any subjects offensive to southerners—freedmen's education, for example—no southern state sup-ported an AAW chapter until 1879.

Speakers at the annual AAW conventions presented papers on women's domestic lives, education, and social problems. Many papers called for an end to dress styles that were harmful to women's physical development, for increased opportunities for higher education, and for reform of penal legis-lation. The most advanced women intellectuals advocated equality in mar-riage and an expanded role for women in public life, but not a similar identity for men and women. AAW members envisioned an elite spearheading Amer-ican progress and argued that it should include women as doctors, lawyers, teachers, college professors, scientists, and government officials on the boards of schools, prisons, and reformatories. Women's special qualities com-plemented men's and guaranteed that solutions to social problems would draw on and reflect the unique qualities of each sex. AAW members agreed with Antoinette Brown Blackwell, the first ordained woman minister in the United States, that "men and women are equals, but not identicals, associates but not rivals."[12]

The most thoroughly debated issue at AAW meetings was higher educa-tion. All AAW members wanted increased educational opportunities for women so that they could have a greater impact on American life, but they disagreed about whether higher education should be sex-defined. Elizabeth Cady Stanton took a minority position and argued that colleges should edu-cate "what man and woman have in common and leave the rest to nature . . . to preserve and educate that subtle difference called sex." The majority of members supported sex-specific education.[13] They wanted women to learn domestic economy, or at least to take classes in subjects such as physiology, chemistry, and natural philosophy that had been adapted to women.

AAW members also lent their support to reforms that would reduce the participation of the supposedly unthinking many in American politics. They backed civil service reform and educational qualifications for suffrage, mea-sures that would limit the power of urban political leaders, who drew their support from patronage and the votes of recently enfranchised immigrants. Although woman suffragists argued for that reform on the basis of woman's right to vote, they also thought that woman suffrage promised to balance the votes of uneducated immigrants with those of educated women. Yet merely a few AAW members supported woman suffrage. The topic was not often discussed at meetings, perhaps because in the 1870s, it was too controversial an issue. Women intellectuals shared the prejudices of the day and shaped their theories of democracy accordingly.

When the southern states seceded and formed the Confederate States of America, they revolutionized the intellectual life of the United States. After they formed the Confederacy, southerners slowly realized that they needed more than a constitution to make a nation. Recognizing the need for a Confederate national culture, *The Countryman* contended in 1862 that "it is idle to talk of a great nation without a national literature."[14] The formation of a national identity for the Confederacy involved, first, rejection of dependence on the North and, second, the creation of Confederate ideas.

In forming its intellectual life, the Confederacy faced problems that stemmed both from wartime exigencies and from the historical development of the region. Southerners lived rural lives, and their intellectual life had developed through oral, face-to-face communication. As the editor of the *Southern Literary Messenger* pointed out, southerners took their ideas mostly from discussion. "A planter of Virginia or South Carolina" was more disinclined "to reading than a shoemaker of Massachusetts or a coal digger of Pennsylvania."[15] Rural life did not support the growth of formal institutions; 93.1 percent of southerners lived in rural areas in 1860, and 90 percent in 1880. Consequently, illiteracy was higher in the South than in the North, and few communities supported lyceums and lectures. Men and women carried on their intellectual life in parlor and porch discussions, and men on occasions of community ceremony and conviviality, such as election-day debates and circuit court sessions. Nevertheless, big cities like Charleston and Richmond had their gentlemen's libraries and literary societies, and southern literature and rhetoric of the time show the deep knowledge of ancient history and political theory that a literate few commanded. At the dedication of a memorial for the Confederate dead in Richmond, LMA members and supporters heard a poem that referred to Sophocles' tomb and even more arcane, the Greek poet Simonides.[16]

Although southern newspapers and journals had complained before the war about their region's intellectual dependence on the North, no one had remedied the deficiency. Northern publishers produced most southern books and journals, and northern teachers staffed southern schools. In retrospect, we know that southern intellectuals had only slightly more than four years to fill the void that secession had produced—to create a Confederate literature and forge a national identity. Having to do so in wartime made the task even more difficult; the blockade, disruption of southern transportation, and war-induced shortages hindered and then prevented the dissemination of the printed word. Magazines, newspapers, and books reached few readers. Popular songs like "The Virginia Marseillaise" and "The Bonnie Blue Flag," sung by civilians and soldiers alike, taught southerners more about the rightness of their cause than did novels and magazines.

Despite the difficulty, Confederates tried to take control of their own intellectual life. They staffed their schools with southern teachers, published Confederate textbooks, and tried to stop reading northern novels and journals. Established as well as newly founded southern journals served the interests of their new country by praising things southern and denigrating things northern. The editor of the *Magnolia Weekly*, a Richmond publication, was sure that an outburst of literary creativity was due to "the exertion of the giant intellect of the South after being freed from her Northern bonds." He criticized a play as sensational and thus more suitable for the theaters of northern cities, where pandering to the "tastes of the wicked and depraved is made a special feature."[17] *The Countryman* served the war cause by printing news of Copperhead activity and riots in the North, refuting criticism of southern generals, humorously criticizing socializing officers and draft dodgers, and giving advice on how to substitute plentiful goods for those in short supply, for instance, okra seeds for coffee beans.

Postbellum southern literature shows that Appomattox had ended the fighting only on the battlefield; southerners continued to fight the North with words until 1880. Resuming publication after its wartime hiatus, *De-Bow's Review* assumed the subtitle, "Devoted to the Restoration of the Southern States and Development of the Wealth and Resources of the Country." Albert Taylor Bledsoe dedicated the *Southern Review* to "the despised, disenfranchised, and downtrodden people of the South." Newspaper editors continued to uphold the accepted position that slavery had permitted the achievement of southern civilization and insisted that slaves had supported the war effort by working loyally on the homefront. Throughout the 1870s most intellectuals believed the South should not follow the example of northern economic development. They believed that the prewar growth of manufacturing and trade had caused northern politicians to disregard liberty. Answering the demands of economic development, they had permitted the federal government to compromise liberty by levying protective tariffs and granting subsidies for transportation projects. The southern people did not want to become, an editor hoped, like northerners—bowing "the knee to" Baal, the god of materialism.[18]

By 1880 most of the strident pro-Confederate journals had ceased publication or changed their tune, and southerners no longer had a journal in which to express Confederate political ideas if they had wanted to. But new views were appearing. Breaking with traditional southern support for a planter elite, newspaper editors Henry Grady of the *Atlanta Constitution* and Henry Watterson of the *Louisville Courier-Journal* began to call for a new generation of leaders who could promote "material greatness."[19] Southerners began to remember the Confederate cause by celebrating the war itself and the distinctive geography and history of their region, not the distinctive political ideas the South had held. *Sunny South* and the *Louisville Home and Farm Weekly*, which reached large, almost exclusively white southern readerships, regularly featured stories of battles and their heroes. Aside from their focus on the South and its history, these publications resembled northern family periodicals.

Until the mid-1870s southern writers had difficulty addressing a national audience. The fault lay with both southerners, who insisted on their distinctive ideas, and northerners, who found in southern literature nothing more than evidence for why the war was fought. For example, although a reviewer in the *North American Review* found *My Cave Life in Vicksburg* (1864) interesting, he commented that the book contained "striking glimpses of the semi-barbarism and the dulness of human feeling produced by slavery."[20]

A comparison of two novels by one southern author who successfully reached a national audience in the postwar years reveals a strategy that was open to southern intellectuals. Augusta Jane Evans Wilson's novels *Macaria* and *St. Elmo* have many similarities of style and convention, and both carry a political message. Publishing under her maiden name, Wilson wrote the first novel to inspire support for the Confederate cause, and the second to show how the nation could be reconstructed in the postwar period.

Wilson's heroines resemble the heroines in other midcentury novels written by women. They are conventional, strong-minded, adventurous, generous, hard-working, thoroughly Christian, and hopelessly in love with heroes seemingly beyond reach. In *Macaria*, because of a blighted relationship between the heroine's father and the hero's mother, the hero and the heroine are star-crossed lovers, destined to love but never to marry. Just before the hero dies from a fatal battle wound, they embrace and console themselves by remembering that they will be together in the afterlife.

The hero of *St. Elmo*, after suffering the rejection of a beautiful, but mercenary young woman, turns on the world, flees from his family, debauches himself in the Near East and Paris, and breaks the heart of every young woman he meets. After returning to his home in the South, he falls in love with a young orphan, the heroine, whom his mother has befriended. After the heroine realizes her love for the hero, she avoids his polluted embrace and follows her literary ambition to New York City. There she becomes a best-selling author who turns down proposals from eligible men, including an editor of a respected literary journal and an English nobleman. Finally, she learns that the hero has reformed. After his hard, dark, and brooding evil shell cracks and falls away, his true self shines forth. He reveals that he could not resist the power of the heroine's goodness, and he proves himself to be an exemplary Christian man by joining the ministry and pledging his life and love to the heroine. On the last page, he "put his hand under her chin, drew the lips to his, and kissed them repeatedly."[21]

Although Wilson gives her novels a conventional plot, the relationship between a man and a marriageable young woman, she wrote in a self-conscious style that showed her own great erudition and thereby established her credibility on subjects other than love and marriage. Her central female characters spout quotations from ancient history and philosophy, Biblical history, classical and even Scandinavian mythology, and political theory from the Enlightenment forward. Wilson wrote as if she wanted to prove wrong the influential editor she created in *St. Elmo*. He advises that a novelist who attempts to educate readers will "either declaim to empty benches or be hissed down." Readers "expect you to help them kill time, not improve it."[22]

Wilson helped readers improve themselves by inserting in her romantic narratives political speeches by the heroines and their like-minded friends. In *Macaria* characters declaim the nobility of the southern cause and the ignominy of the North. They see the South as "the guardian of liberty," which the Union government has destroyed by suspending habeas corpus, abrogating freedom of speech and the press, and drafting soldiers into its army against their will. In the novel, the word *union* becomes a synonym for "political duplicity, despotism, and the utter abnegation of all that had been once called American freedom."[23]

Real liberty, Wilson insisted, depends on the federal government respecting the sovereignty of the states and the limitations imposed on its powers by the Constitution and the Bill of Rights. To Wilson and other southerners who believed that the republic and its heritage belonged to the white population, denying liberty to slaves and equal civil rights to free African-Americans seemed to be no contradiction. To them, slavery had created social cohesion and the fullest liberty (for whites) because it obviated the need for an "antagonistic system of labor" such as that found in the North.[24]

St. Elmo contains no diatribes against northern political theory or justifications of the Confederate cause. Only in a mild way does the novel criticize northern society. In an almost forgettable passage, New York City newsboys taunt a young boy of the upper classes as he lies pathetically on the ground with a broken ankle. Here Wilson hinted that all was not well in northern society, and that she continued to see potential antagonism between capital and free labor.

Far more important is the novel's celebration of ideal womanhood. Unlike southern white men, white women had not surrendered on the battlefield. Dazed by their defeat, southerners embraced their ideal of womanhood as a kind of talisman. It had the power to lead white southerners back to their idealized past and to protect them from the radical changes that the war had brought. By lauding southern women, Wilson and other southern writers also implicitly criticized the North, and specifically criticized the woman's rights theory that southerners associated with the North. From the antebellum period through the postwar years and beyond, southerners saw the North as the source of faulty woman's rights doctrine, which threatened to overturn their patriarchally based society.

During the war Wilson had argued that "the women of the South must exercise an important influence in determining our national destiny." But in her postwar novel *St. Elmo*, she set aside her explicitly regional emphasis and said that "intelligent, modest, Christian women [are] the real custodians of national purity, and the sole agents who could arrest the tide of demoralization breaking over the land." Through her heroine, Wilson defined "every woman's right which God and nature had decreed the sex." She argued that women had

the right to be learned, wise, noble, useful, in woman's divinely limited sphere; the right to influence and exalt the circle in which she moved; the right to mount the sanctified bema [altar] of her own quiet hearthstone; the right to modify and direct her husband's opinions, if he considered her worthy and competent to guide him; the right to make her children ornaments to their nation, and a crown of glory to their race; the right to advise, to plead, to pray; the right to make her desk a Delphi, if God so permitted; the right to be all that the phrase "noble, Christian woman" means. But not the right to vote; to harangue from the hustings; to trail her heaven-born purity through the dust and mire of political strife; to ascend the rosta of statesmen, whither she may send a worthy husband, son, or brother, but whither she can never go, without disgracing all womanhood.[25]

Compared to the demands of woman suffragists, Wilson's position on woman's rights appears tame. But it was not. Her belief that women have the same intellectual abilities as men and that they should receive an equally rigorous education placed her in the vanguard of supporters of southern women's education and in the company of northerners, including AAW members, who argued for expanded opportunities for women in higher education. But in believing that a wife's counsel to her husband depends on his judgment of her worth, Wilson, like other southern women, even strong-minded ones, was accepting the patriarchal basis of southern society. They expected wives to subordinate themselves to their husbands' authority to a degree that no northern woman intellectual supported. Even northerners who opposed woman suffrage thought that in ideal families husbands consulted their wives before they cast their ballots.[26]

Wilson argued in *St. Elmo* that social cohesion depends on the activities of women of the upper classes. Her heroines are models of social responsibility who realize their obligations and initiate good works, such as supporting free public schools, founding orphanages, and caring for the sick. By alleviating the problems of the lower classes, upper-class women were eliminating potential sources of social unrest. Wilson strengthened her argument by creating servants and working people who show no desire to rise above their dependent status; they appreciate the philanthropy of their betters and accept a benevolent, but rigidly structured social hierarchy. In her ideal patriarchal society, social harmony prevails. No street urchin would be so ungrateful as to taunt a member of the upper class.

St. Elmo became a runaway best-seller; readers named country homes after the hero's estate and gave the name of the novel to cigars, a punch, and hotels. To reach a national audience, Wilson did what other southern writers had to do in the postwar years: she did not defend the part of the South that northerners had vanquished in the war, namely, Confederate constitutional theory and slavery. Yet her novels are thoroughly southern. She carefully described southern geography, architecture, and regional types and focused on characters' personal lives and relationships. Although some southern writers, such as Albion Tourgee, gained a northern audience by denouncing white southerners' response to Reconstruction, most southern writers who gained national attention in the 1870s followed a strategy similar to Wilson's.

St. Elmo stands at the very beginning of a new literary movement, the local color movement, that became increasingly important in the 1880s and 1890s. Its major representatives from the South were Joel Chandler Harris, who published his first Uncle Remus tale in the *Atlanta Constitution* in 1879, George Washington Cable, and Mary Murfree, all of whom described a new South untainted by slavery and appealing for its quaint folkways and scenic beauty.

Editors of periodicals also recognized their readers' interest in the South. In 1873–74 *Scribner's Monthly* published a lavishly illustrated series called "The Great South," which revealed the postwar economic development of the region as well as its curiosities, such as the alligators of the Florida Everglades. By the mid-1870s other major periodicals including *Harper's Monthly* and *Atlantic Monthly* were sending writers south and publishing southern writers. By the 1880s a national literary reconciliation was well under way.

Although writers from other regions did not face the political problems that southerners did in reaching a national audience, they too found audiences interested in regional peculiarities. Among the popular local colorists of the 1860s and 1870s were Mark Twain, who first won recognition with "The Celebrated Jumping Frog of Calaveras County" (1865), and Bret Harte, who described western life in mining camps. In his most popular poem, "The Heathen Chinee" (1870), he created the figure of a crafty Chinese gambler who would become the subject of articles in weeklies and of cartoons and stereographs.

A number of midcentury Victorian intellectuals had something more in mind than merely keeping cultural development on a moral track. They believed that their fellow intellectuals had set too low a standard of intellectual criticism. Rather than embrace the dominant culture of the day, these dissident intellectuals, who called themselves liberals, criticized it for intellectual shallowness, mediocrity, and excessive piety. Symptomatic of the cultural disorder were American reading tastes and social analysis. Devoted to reading "tales, sketches, and anecdotes," most people thought they could solve the problems of "the universe by turning a crank."[27]

The major group of disaffected intellectuals included E. L. Godkin, Charles Eliot Norton, and Frederick Law Olmsted. They made their institutional headquarters in New York and Boston, where they and other key members were associated with the *Nation*, the *Atlantic Monthly*, and the *North American Review*. Their movement was broad-based. Its academic members had positions in new private universities such as Cornell and Johns Hopkins, state institutions, including the universities of Wisconsin and Michigan, and older colleges such as Harvard and Yale. From public cultural life the movement included the founders and supporters of art museums, libraries, and civic parks. In political and social life, liberal intellectuals supported the American Social Science Association and its causes, including a reformed civil service and more efficient charitable efforts.

The leaders of the liberal movement saw themselves as standing apart from the mainstream of American life. They distinguished themselves from those they called capitalists, who let money determine their loyalties, from the middle class, which was content with mediocrity, and from the lower class, which did not understand the true principles of American democracy. Liberals called those for whom they spoke "the educated few" or "the best men," and cared little that their number was small. Despite their great disaffection from the American public, liberals committed themselves to what they thought were the truest democratic ideals.

Godkin, Norton, and their supporters found a major source of their liberalism and democratic ideals in the political philosophy of the Englishman John Stuart Mill. They argued that nations should properly be areas of political and economic freedom within which citizens are guaranteed equal participation and equality before the law. Governments should limit their authority to protecting political freedom and should not interfere with citizens' enjoyment of economic freedom. States should not pass legislation that benefits one group at the expense of another, such as protective tariffs. In other words, states should follow a policy of laissez-faire, in the spirit of Adam Smith. He and the moral philosophers whom he influenced argued that self-interest understood correctly promotes recognition of one's obligations to others. In the antebellum period Smith's liberalism as modified by Whig thinkers and reformers had led to the establishment of government-sponsored institutions—such as the common school, which prepared children for the freedom that they would enjoy as adult citizens.

Acting on these views, American liberals supported government power when they perceived the actions of one group compromising the national area of freedom, but opposed government force when they perceived it compromising liberty within that area of freedom. In practice, they supported the northern cause in the Civil War, advocated an end to slavery, and opposed the South and its commitment to principles that they considered undemocratic. After the northern victory, they supported reconstruction of the South, including its occupation by Union forces, and passage of the Fourteenth and Fifteenth amendments. But predicting that continued application of federal power in the South would jeopardize freedom, they acquiesced in the end of Reconstruction in 1877. Liberals assumed that African-Americans had all the political rights they needed to function as free men, and so they did not endorse further federal oversight of southern elections. They considered the freedmen to be another immigrant group like the Irish or Chinese and concluded that their future would be "bound up undoubtedly with that of the white man, and does not now require separate consideration."[28]

Liberals used the same rationale when analyzing the relationship of the government to labor violence and strikes. Seeing labor actions and violence as interference in the free play of the marketplace, they recommended strong government action to quell the labor actions that brought railroad traffic to a halt in 1877. But liberals proposed that government restrict its sphere of action when they perceived that sphere expanding to compromise economic freedom. Liberals thought government should not recognize the demands of American workers for a 10-hour day and the right to strike.

Although philosophically defensible, these views seem quite narrow and waspish in the context of the economic woes of the 1870s. The economic downturn after the panic of 1873 affected unskilled workers and urban workers most severely. Employers tried to cut costs by shrinking their work forces, cutting wages, and lengthening hours. Despite widespread unemployment and a rise in the number of street beggars, the *Nation* argued against aid for even the truly needy. The principle of the matter loomed large: "Free soup must be prohibited, and all classes must learn that soup of any kind, beef or turtle, can be had only by being paid for." Responding to the railway strikes of 1877, the *Nation* cautioned that the government had to maintain its military force and teach immigrants "that society as here organized, on individual freedom of thought and action, is impregnable, and can be no more shaken than the order of nature." The best that can be said for these liberals is that their criticism cut against capitalists as well as workers. The reference to turtle soup—expensive fare—implied that capitalists also should not ask government for special privileges.[29]

Although they were committed to freedom of action and freedom of thought, liberals understood that educated people would support certain limitations on their freedoms. As Lincoln had done when he compromised the unqualified enjoyment of First Amendment rights during the war years, and as legislators did when they supported the Comstock Act, liberals gave priority to the preservation of a community of freedom. The *Nation* advised restricting individual expression when it threatened the community. Addressing the violence of 1877, the journal cautioned philanthropists and social reformers to remember that some questions were closed to discussion and had but one side. The debate over the rights of labor threatened civilization and its tenets, "which raise man above the beasts."[30]

Further, when liberals discussed freedom, they thought exclusively of public life, not private life and personal relations. Although Victoria Wood-hull may have drawn on liberalism to propose radical alterations in the nature of the Victorian family and sexual relations, these liberals did not apply their political thought to areas that they deemed personal. Liberals wanted to improve their world; they did not want to overturn its social foundation in marriage and the family. As the *New York Times*, which often took the liberal viewpoint, said of itself, it proposed "no themes subversive of the principles on which the sacredness of family ties and the existence of society alike repose," although it was "fearless and independent in championship of the right."[31]

Godkin, Norton, and other liberals took issue with the prevailing intellectual standards. As liberals, they opposed any force that they perceived as a threat to reason. Although not all liberals were agnostics, most disputed religion's exclusive claim to truth. These were secular intellectuals who held their own religious beliefs privately and decried the invasion of unthinking theism or denominational loyalty into public affairs. They believed that American public discourse of the day obscured real truth, and they located the cause in the public institutions of midcentury America that embraced the many—lyceums, common schools, and periodicals. Expressing typical liberal opinions, a *North American Review* writer said: "Our national evil genius is mediocrity. And the form it takes with us is the undue respect that we have for commonplace work. . . . The whole spirit of ordinary journalism, ordinary schooling, ordinary preaching, ordinary writing on science, philology, metaphysics, is simple mediocrity."[32]

Liberals called American culture second-rate, secondhand, crude, cheap, and shallow and thought it was filled with little patient thought but much self-proclaimed profundity. But these deficiencies stemmed from the very nature of the United States and its intellectuals. Echoing Alexis de Tocqueville's criticism in *Democracy in America* (1835, 1840), liberals attributed the country's shortcomings to its lack of a hereditary class. Without patrons to support them in their efforts to establish standards of taste, intellectuals were tempted to play to popular taste and follow the dictates of the marketplace. They offered—as was said of Henry Ward Beecher—merely "vague aspirations" and a "lachrymose sensibility."[33] Periodicals led readers to believe that self-culture could be realized through mere acquaintance with many interesting facts and and never taught them how to think. As the liberal editor of *Popular Science Monthly* said: "Excess of reading without regard to its quality is a pernicious dissipation, and, besides wasting precious time, it disqualifies those who indulge in it from that serious effort of thought which is the first condition of mental improvement."[34]

Intellectuals had to realize that their task was hard thought at the risk of being unpopular. They could not mingle in the lives of the common people

by adopting their sympathies, writing for them, and enjoying their pleasures. Instead, intellectuals had to gain strength by associating with their
own—socially, in clubs for like-minded men, and professionally, in journals
and universities. Through these institutions, serious men could consolidate,
feel themselves a power, and influence public opinion.

It was quite consistent with liberals' self-image as true democrats that they
should be self-appointed. Intellectuals could participate in democracy merely
by stepping beyond partisan politics and the prejudices of religious sectarianism and offering the reading public clear, accurate and thorough analysis
of all aspects of public life. Their formative influence on public opinion
could lead Americans to realize that religious sentiment often clouded truth
and that haphazard reading did not lead to self-culture. True self-culture
required a program of discipline, self-sacrifice, and hard work. Cultured
Americans of good character would know how to deal with the problems of
modern life.

In a republic, liberals thought, intellectuals are the class meant to take the
place of a hereditary aristocracy, and they often described themselves as the
aristocrats of the American democracy. Not seeking to copy the English gentry, this aristocracy supported "Liberty and Union" and held true to the
founding ideals of the nation. Although liberals in Boston and New York
formed their own clubs, they sought to influence other communities through
their journals. These reached a readership of like-minded men who were
often among the better-educated members of a community and were apt to
be initiators of local reform activity.

The liberals' expectation that their followers outside of Boston and New
York would share their concerns and follow their national leadership reflected the centralizing force of the Civil War years. Even so, their social
understanding of influence and power remained consistent with an older
view of American life. They held to the republican view that a group of men
distinguished by wealth or standing led the intellectual life of a community,
and they called these men, as they did themselves, true democrats.

In 1865 liberal intellectuals helped to found the American Social Science
Association, an organization that embodied the changes in the definition of
intellectual leadership that were occurring in the postwar years. Through the
association, intellectuals applied the new thought of their day to the reform
of American life. The ASSA was the first national association for general
reform, and it built on reformers' hopes that the Civil War had begun a national social reformation.

When the AAW was founded eight years later, it joined the ASSA as a
sister organization; many of the women members belonged to both groups.
The associations' members shared the same attitudes toward reform and electoral politics, and they drew on similar intellectual imperatives. The AAW's
first purpose, however, was the advancement of women and their inclusion

in the organized intelligence of the community. Its members assumed that women's advance would lead to general reform of American society.

Both AAW and ASSA members believed that society resembled an organism. Its growth, when not impeded, would develop all its parts into a harmoniously functioning whole. The analogy of society to a growing thing suggested that social change ideally occurred without abrupt breaks or departures; revolution was not implied. Although social development was a natural process, people could facilitate its progress when they understood the determining social laws and ensured that institutions conformed to them. The AAW and the ASSA therefore sponsored the collection of facts that would reveal the laws governing social development. Members of these associations wanted to make the public aware of these laws and to reform or establish institutions to be in conformity with them.

All AAW and ASSA members deemed undesirable the individualism that stemmed from the strain of American romanticism espoused by Henry David Thoreau. They believed that human accomplishment, growth, and freedom depended instead on association and cooperation. Some social science reformers found their inspiration in the theories of those who expounded the conservative or institutional side of romanticism. These spokesmen included minister Horace Bushnell and political scientists Francis Lieber and Theodore Dwight Woolsey, who argued that people could develop their capacity for freedom within society because its institutions—including family, schools, and government—restrained the bad aspects of human nature while allowing the good to develop.

Other intellectuals came to a new appreciation of society during the war years through reading August Comte and the works of his American disciples, such as John W. Draper, who explained that "civilization does not proceed in an arbitrary manner or by chance, but . . . passes through a determinate succession of stages, and is a development according to law." Rejecting the assumption that facts signify divine truth, Comtians argued that social scientists could not know the origin of things or their final destination beyond this earth. The laws of development had meaning only for the here and now. Mary Putnam Jacobi, a doctor of medicine and member of the New York City Positivist Society, explained in 1878 the research methods of positivists. She said that they substituted "the study of the invariable *laws* of phenomena for that of their *causes*, immediate or final."[35] Rejecting an idealistic philosophy, Comtians like Draper and Jacobi embraced realism.

Within the ASSA both positivists and romantic idealists found an organization that supported their reform goals. Many of its members had belonged to antislavery, temperance, and woman's rights organizations before the war, and during the war they had supported the U.S. Sanitary Commission, which cared for the wounded and operated soldiers' hospitals. Many intellectuals claimed that their war experience was behind their new acceptance of the national government as a proper vehicle for accomplishing collective ends. Caught up in the enthusiasm of victory, however, they were forgetting that even before the war many reformers had called upon the powers of the national government. In the 1850s most antislavery advocates supported free-soil initiatives and the Republican party, which proposed to use federal power to ban the extension of slavery to new territories. The defeat of the South, however, reaffirmed the federal government's legitimacy and, especially after ratification of the Fourteenth Amendment, confirmed its role as the protector of liberty. Writing in the *North American Review* in October 1865, Samuel Fowler observed that the war had defeated not only the South but the Jeffersonian philosophy of government, which was based on the theory that states protected local and individual liberties.

Anticipating a more active federal government after the war, intellectuals concluded that they had to influence it through means other than politics, which they perceived as hopelessly corrupt. Comtian social analysis seemed to promise them a place at the head of postwar reform. Looking forward, and applying the lessons of Comte, Draper observed in living organisms "a continual tendency to a concentration of power and a development of intellect." Like a living organism, society had many lower parts devoted to duties "of a wholly material nature" and a higher part devoted to "the operations of intellect. Of these it is the especial, the unavoidable duty to exert a direct influence over all." Jacobi agreed and said that progress can only occur when "the elite of humanity" commit themselves to "the discovery of new laws."[36]

The reform commitment of college professors, philanthropists, newspaper editors, journalists, scientists, ministers, educators, and reformers—both positivists and romantic idealists—drew them into the ASSA. Members wanted their organization to be the organized intellect of society and felt that its task was to discover the laws governing society's functioning. They believed that social harmony, a state in which all individuals' interests blended without friction, could exist. That it did not exist yet was only because people did not know the facts necessary for the correct functioning of government, the economy, and society. After the ASSA brought the facts to public attention, members assumed that society would start developing on its course toward natural harmony. The ASSA proposed to address the "Sanitary Condition of the People, the Relief, Employment, and Education of the Poor, the Prevention of Crime, the Amelioration of the Criminal Law, the Discipline of Prisons, the Remedial Treatment of the Insane, and those numerous matters of statistical and philanthropic interest which are included under the general head of 'Social Science.'" The various departments of the association investigated topics in law and jurisprudence; education, including public schools and civic monuments; public health, including parks and ventilation in buildings; social economy, including labor, trade, and the "causes of Human Failure and the Duties devolving upon Human Success."[37]

During the early and most productive years of the ASSA, its chief goal was reform of the civil service, which seemed to be the political precondition for achieving the larger reform agenda. As political liberals, ASSA members believed in a democratic society but did not believe it was well served by majority rule. They did not hold to *vox populi, vox dei*, not even when it was supported by the commonly held assumption that "the people" were all Victorians. ASSA members wanted an American social and cultural life for the people, but they did not want social and cultural life to be of and by the people. Conceding, many times grudgingly, that the majority ruled in electoral politics, they looked for solutions to the social problems they thought were important outside of the political process and in the control of the committed, educated few.

In a way, civil service reformers revised republican political theory. Like republican theorists of the early nineteenth century, they believed that each community naturally produced an educated class. But in their analysis, patronage-filled civil service positions had deprived this class of a leadership role. Seeing national political life as debased, midcentury reformers proposed that nonelective government officials be chosen on the basis of merit through an examination system controlled by an appointed commission. With a nonpartisan civil service, at least part of the executive branch of government—city, state, and federal—would be removed from the control of politicians and handed over to appropriately educated officials.

The rhetoric of civil service reform contains strong language drawn from republican sources that ASSA members used to express their disaffection from American political life. George William Curtis, a leading supporter, associated civil service reform with the Civil War and the American Revolution. He described the spoils system of appointing government officials as "a monster only less threatening than slavery." Americans neglected their heritage of freedom if they did not hold themselves "as much the enemies of the despotism of a party as our fathers were enemies of the tyranny of a king." Politicians were no democrats, but "vampires who suck the moral lifeblood of the nation."[38] Although reformers like Curtis gave civil service reform passionate support, it did not have widespread appeal until a disappointed office-seeker assassinated recently elected President James Garfield in 1881. Then public outrage led to the passage of the Pendleton Act (1883), also known as the Civil Service Act, which made performance on examinations the criterion for appointment to lower-level positions in the federal civil service.

The debate over the criteria for selection of government officials marks a turning point in nineteenth-century political and intellectual history. Only a few intellectuals opposed the reform. Mary Abigail Dodge, writing under her pseudonym Gail Hamilton, thought that participation in political parties and government service was a vital part of civic education. The reforms proposed by liberal intellectuals would end this benefit to the American people and change the nature of American democracy by trammeling "the feet of an intelligent people."[39] Reformers believed that government practice no longer supported the view that President Andrew Jackson had articulated in the 1830s; they did not see government officials primarily as representatives of the people and considered the functions of government so complex that common men could not direct them. Civil service reformers found evidence in the scandals of the postwar years that office holders followed partisan and personal dictates. Reformers believed that education would give government officials the special knowledge necessary for their positions and that examinations administered by a nonpartisan commission would insulate office-seekers from the corruption of party politics.

The allies of civil service reformers, the leading educational reformers of the day, proposed that colleges and universities train prospective government officials. At his inauguration in 1876 as the first president of Johns Hopkins University, Daniel Coit Gilman suggested that universities contain schools to give future politicians and civil servants the "intellectual and moral discipline to advance the public interest irrespective of party, indifferent to the attainment of official stations."[40]

Although the ASSA remained in existence until 1909, its vitality was drained in the early 1870s by the debate between positivists and romantic idealists. But the association did spawn many new organizations, including the National Prison Association, the National Conference of Boards of Health, the National Conference of Charities and Correction, and the American Public Health Association. Not expecting moral regeneration to lead to social reform, members of these organizations replaced the sentimental inspiration behind antebellum reform efforts with a scientific rationale. Scientifically inspired assistance was efficient, argued the postbellum reformers, because it accepted the limits of charity and was based on a correct understanding of reform. Postbellum reformers believed that individual benevolence led to temporary and incomplete results, and they complemented their donations to the needy with a long-term plan for the alleviation of poverty. True benevolence developed the "education and knowledge of better principles to remove permanently the causes of existing evils."[41]

Although this commitment to eradicate poverty seems positive, the new charitable efforts often did not serve the poor and needy any better than had the old. Awful events shocked well-meaning people. When a little boy froze to death on the streets of New York City, the editor of *Harper's Weekly* questioned whether the emphasis on efficient charity had not eliminated human caring and resulted in "machine charity." Although he agreed with scientifically minded reformers that indiscriminate giving encouraged indigence, he decried the boy's needless death. Forgetting that many indigent people were non-English-speaking immigrants, he suggested that responsible citizens distribute to the poor whom they encountered on the streets cards bearing the names and addresses of relief agencies.[42]

After the early 1870s, the influence of Comte faded and Herbert Spencer's increased, though not yet to the high levels it would reach in the 1880s. Leading the Spencerians, Edward Youmans attacked the idealist sentiments of many ASSA members and charged that they misunderstood the nature of social science. He contended that the ASSA, while claiming to follow the imperatives of social science, was actually collecting facts to justify the activities of philanthropists and reformers who wanted to interfere with the functioning of social laws. In violation of the principles of true social science, reformers were forcing the government to assume parental functions and to encroach on the province of parents and the home. Youmans decried the "universal passion for experimenting with society under a superstitious delusion in regard to the omnipotence of legislation."[43] Although the debate between Spencerians and idealists weakened the ASSA and gained a great deal of attention, the controversy created more smoke than fire. Its heat was insufficient to destroy any of the charitable agencies that helped to alleviate the problems of the poor in many American cities. And when the smoke began to clear in the 1890s, it became clear that intellectuals had begun to espouse a new social science philosophy that reconciled the environmental determinism of positivism with the individual autonomy posited by idealism.

Although all intellectuals spoke as Victorians and generally agreed with the task that Harriet Beecher Stowe had proposed for them—to educate the public morally and intellectually—some interpreted this task in a democratic sense and others in a republican sense. Some accepted *vox populi, vox dei* albeit with modifications; others rejected it altogether. This division among intellectuals roughly parallels other developments in midcentury culture and corresponds roughly to the division between middle-class and upper-middle–class culture. Intellectuals who saw themselves as removed from the many of the middle classes had an upper middle–class audience. Its members learned how to express their success and how to separate themselves from the stasis of the many. For example, readers who chose serious literature over sentimental best-sellers and preferred reproductions of classic masterpieces over original works depicting hens and chicks were expressing their elevated taste. And they knew that they were doing so because of the cultural criticism that filled liberal journals, which recommended the choice of these books and artworks. But not all intellectuals looked favorably on the efforts of liberals and their followers and affirmed the aspirations of the upwardly mobile. Humorists like Marietta Holley, who identified with the rural and small-town Victorian public, had great fun exposing the pretensions of social circles that adopted European culture. She caricatured young ladies trying to be impressive in parlor entertainments and disdaining popular ballads like "Somebody's Darling" in favor of Italian arias that they muttered "in a unknown tongue."[44]

Finally, liberal intellectuals spoke for those Victorians who were beginning to redefine their religious faith. Except for positivists, few liberal intellectuals were avowedly agnostic, but many privately drifted into mild unbelief. All liberals distrusted emotional professions of religion, and none testified to having had a personal religious experience. As natural science theory and Biblical criticism stripped truth of its divine aspect, liberals' definitive pronouncements about the laws of society and nature gave their public a secular and seemingly secure basis for moral thought and action.

Whether northerners or southerners, positivists or idealists, men or women, liberals or Chautauquans, all Victorian intellectuals judged the world in absolute terms and understood that fixed laws determined social development. These two postulates brought together our four major groups of intellectuals, whose activities and thought made the mental world that we know as Victorian.

eight

Centennial Milestones: 1876 and Beyond

In 1876 Americans commemorated the one-hundredth anniversary of the signing of the Declaration of Independence. Civic-minded gentlemen and ladies organized the six-month-long International Centennial Exhibition in Philadelphia, and communities across the nation held Fourth of July celebrations. Most American cities turned the Fourth of July into a two- or three-day holiday. Municipal newspapers described the torchlight parades that took place on the Fourth and the night before. Military units joined city officials, trade and voluntary associations, and fire companies in forming huge parades all of which reflected the diversity of American cities: their trades, neighborhoods, and nationalities. In Pittsburgh ice wagons, florists' wagons, coal wagons, butchers' wagons, and many other tradesmen's wagons joined the march. In Jersey City the line of Irish societies alone extended for two miles. In New York City on the night of 3 July, the voluntary associations marching to Union Square included German and Scandinavian societies, the German Centennial Union, the Order of American Mechanics, the Sons of Washington, St. Patrick's Mutual Alliance, St. Augustine's Temperance Society, the Centennial Club, the Society of Bakers, the Arcadian Literary Society, the Alpha Lodge of Odd Fellows, the Catholic Temperance Society, and St. Anthony's Benevolent Society. Houses, shops, and businesses lighted by Japanese lanterns and festooned with bunting lined the parade route. Upon reaching their destinations, the marchers waited until midnight. When bells pealed the beginning of the second century of independence, the crowds erupted into cheering, whistles sounded, factories blew their whistles, and ships sounded their horns. Spectators set off fireworks, and formal displays of fireworks lit up the skies.

On the Fourth of July itself, businesses and shops in most northern and western cities were closed. People enjoyed more parades and congregated in public buildings, city squares, and parks to sing national hymns and airs and hear recitations of patriotic poems and orations by their public men and intellectuals—ministers, politicians, men of letters, professors, and college presidents. Most of these men were locally prominent, but some had national reputations. Sen. William M. Evarts spoke in Philadelphia, George William Curtis on Staten Island, and Henry Ward Beecher in Peekskill, New York. After these intellectuals had reflected on the meaning of the Declaration of Independence, U.S. history, and contemporary events, the crowds celebrated yet again at parties, picnics, and regattas organized by political clubs, ethnic societies, and workingmen's associations.

Analysis of the festivities of the Fourth and the six-month-long Centennial Exhibition reveals how Americans, especially Victorian Americans, applied their serious thought to national issues and what the particular meaning of republicanism and liberalism were for Victorians, workingmen, women, and African-Americans. Some of these meanings emerge from what people said and did during the Centennial year, and others from what they did not say and do. The Centennial celebrations reveal American national ideals and to what extent they were realized in American life of 1876. What intellectual resources did people draw on to celebrate the first 100 years of American independence?

Orations delivered at Centennial celebrations are a useful starting point, for they reflect the mood of the day, the way Victorians thought about their world, and the fundamental Victorian concepts of national political life. The titles of Fourth of July orations tell that optimism reigned: "The Genius of America," "The Magnificent Present," "The Matchless Story," "The Progress of Liberty," "The Free Institutions of Our Republic," "What the Age Owes to America," "The Advance of the Century," and "The Iliad of Patriotism" were typical. A handful of speakers rejected the prevailing rosy view. Titles such as "Warnings for the Future" and "The Cost of Popular Liberty" betray their authors' fear that the republican form of government might soon perish.[1]

Most speakers followed a historical method of analysis as they reviewed the past to face the issues of the present and chart the path to the future. They found in the past a basis for national unity. Southerners and northerners alike affirmed the achievements of the Revolutionary generation which supplied all the states with a common heritage. An audience in Memphis, Tennessee, heard that the Fourth belonged "to no North, no South, no East, no West. . . . The South gave to the country him who wrote the charter of our liberties. The South gave to the world a Washington. Let the name of

Washington be indissolubly and forever linked with those of Hancock, Adams, Franklin."[2]

From this past flowed republican ideals, especially the ideal of self-sacrificing civic virtue. Both optimistic and pessimistic speakers frequently referred, as one did, to the "thoughtful, patriotic, self-sacrificing-men who built this great temple of civil and religious liberty."[3] Speakers worried that contemporary politicians no longer adhered to the demands of civic virtue. Instead of serving the national interest by setting private interest and gain aside, politicans sought private profit at national expense. For example, in 1876 the House of Representatives impeached President Grant's secretary of war, William Belknap, after collecting evidence that he had received bribes for selling the right to do business at trading posts in Indian territory.

All orators agreed that public officials and private citizens were putting the United States in peril by violating republican principles for the sake of personal gain. To restore civic virtue, a few speakers recommended that educated and prominent men end their retreat from democratic politics and reenter political life. A New Orleans minister thought that "if the men of culture and refinement, who wear kid gloves and fine clothes, are going to live in a Republic, they must be content to crowd the polls, side by side with the men from the factory and the engine, in their coarse blouses."[4] Most orators, however, proposed simply reform of the civil service. They wanted to establish a nonpartisan bureaucracy that elected officials would not be able to staff from motives of patronage and graft. No advocate of civil service reform recognized that it would make government officials independent of the American people and their elected officials—that is, that they were proposing to purify the republic by making it, in a sense, less democratic.

Speakers attributed the decline of civic virtue to the success of the American economy, which permitted the accumulation of excessive wealth. According to an orator in St. Louis, "the pursuit of wealth" had become "a mania."

It is as if money had been showering from the sky, and men had postponed all other thought than to pick up a fortune before the miracle was over. Thus, the very ease with which the republic prospered has been an injury to its permanent welfare; since that ease gave quiet to patriotism and excited avarice. As a result avarice is to-day the ruling passion of Americans. More with us than with any other nation does money regulate the scale of society. Money is our rank, our morality.[5]

Although they condemned wealth, orators lauded American prosperity, and most effusively praised the material comforts that average citizens enjoyed in the United States. One speaker explained that the work of building the nation, clearing its land, building cities, and connecting them with railroads had fallen to average citizens. Common people had reaped the harvest of their labors and now lived comfortably. "There is more material for thought, for comfort and for home loving to-day, in the ordinary workman's house, than there was a hundred years ago in one of a hundred rich men's mansions," Henry Ward Beecher declaimed.[6]

But the strands of republican thought drawn forth on 4 July 1876 were intertwined with liberalism. Speakers used republican ideas to analyze the past and criticize the present, but they used liberal ideas to analyze the present and predict a rosy national future. When drawing on those ideas, they set aside one implication—freedom from restraint, which had dominated public discourse since the 1780s. Instead, they emphasized the promise that liberalism held for the future and drew on their liberalism to laud the sort of freedom that permitted individual prosperity. They praised the country for being one in which "the way to ascend is so easy." With so many opportunities to improve their lot, men had no good reason to be discontented. If a man did not rise, Henry Ward Beecher explained, he had only himself to blame; he was probably intemperate or had some "radical defect" of birth, schooling or home education. Yet the economic advancement that speakers predicted and wanted was not from the rags of the Five Points district to the riches of Fifth Avenue. A workingman who was temperate and followed the example of virtuous parents assuredly would own a house with carpets, chromos on the walls, and books "nestling on the shelf." In short, he would have a home—"the sweetest place on earth."[7]

In Centennial addresses men invoked the ideas associated with republicanism and liberalism for one purpose—to laud prosperous workingmen and the middle class. Liberalism denied that poverty was a permanent condition for all but the few, and republicanism located virtue, the security of the republic, in the great middle of the American polity. No speaker, whether Republican or Democrat, Protestant or Catholic, western, easterner, or southerner, mentioned either the impoverished sections of great American cities or the mansions rising in urban upper-class neighborhoods and seaside resorts. This significant omission suggests that they thought extremes of wealth and poverty were no blight on American life. There would be a peaceful future if rich and poor learned the true nature of the American republic.

Many speakers reiterated that education was crucial to the survival of the republic. Pulpit, press, and common school had to teach the beliefs on which American prosperity depended—the most important of which was equality before the law for rich men, poor men, and all immigrants who came to the United States in search of its freedoms. A Tammany Hall Democrat said that "all men, poor and rich, artisan and millionaire, shall be equal in the eye of the law, so that the Declaration of Independence shall not be a mere sounding phrase, but a wholesome fact."[8]

The economic and social unrest that had troubled America for three years gave rise to the concern with workingmen in Centennial addresses. In 1873 a depression had hit; 3–4 million Americans were still unemployed, two times the percentage of unemployed citizens during the Great Depression of the 1930s. Dissatisfied workingmen, to whom Beecher alluded, had rioted in New York City in 1874 and in western Pennsylvania in 1873 and 1874. Moreover, educated Americans feared replication of recent European episodes of social revolution, most notably the Paris Commune of 1871. They hoped that U.S. workingmen would not follow these revolutionary paths.

Nine months after the Centennial Exhibition closed, the greatest strike that had ever occurred in the United States erupted in West Virginia and spread across the nation. The great railroad strike of 1877 was only the first of a series of strikes and riots that afflicted the country throughout the 1880s and 1890s; working people were expressing their anger and distress over the periodic economic downturns that resulted in wage cuts, unemployment, and impoverishment. In the last decades of the century economically distressed farmers and laborers turned away from the promises of republicanism and liberalism propounded on the Centennial and toward the alternatives proposed by the Knights of Labor and the Populist party.

For the rest of the century, debate over labor, capital, and the structure of business occupied Americans. While the public men of 1876 were still explaining current social problems in terms of republicanism and liberalism, other little-known intellectuals who would gain prominence in the 1880s were beginning to imagine a country where capital and labor existed in harmony and there were no extremes of poverty or wealth. The 1870s ended with the publication of Henry George's *Progress and Poverty* (1879). Unlike the Centennial speakers, George did not think that individuals were poor because they were intemperate, lazy, or immoral. He traced the cause of poverty to incorrect understanding of economic laws. If people rightly understood these laws and taxed the excessive wealth that had accumulated in land, there would be a golden age of material prosperity and an explosion of intellectual energy and unimaginable feats of invention. "With want destroyed; with greed changed to noble passions; with the fraternity that is born of equality taking the place of the place of the jealousy and fear that now array men against each other; with mental power loosed by conditions that give to the humblest comfort and leisure; and who shall measure the heights to which our civilization may soar?"[9] Until the economic and labor troubles of the 1870s, almost all Victorians would have thought that George's words accurately described the potential of their society.

To focus too tightly on the social and labor unrest of the 1870s is to overlook the tremendous moment of national unity that occurred on the Centennial Fourth. Its festivities brought a diverse American people together in celebration of independence. Most recognized independence as an ideal that individuals could realize through temperance, industry, and thrift. Parade and picnic organizers prohibited participants from imbibing alcohol because such celebrations were occasions for the display of respectability. In any event, many Americans wanted parades to be orderly. Following routes and rules specified by civic authorities, the participants were not to march at will through the city, damage stores and businesses along the route, provoke riots, or tease or taunt bystanders. Those who wanted parades to be orderly, temperate affairs were offended by certain celebrations on the Fourth and other holidays by immigrant groups and less prosperous workingmen. They disapproved of animal baiting and bare-knuckle boxing because such amusements displayed cruelty and physical violence; respectable and orderly celebrations and festivities did not. Thus, Fourth of July parades actually reflected a consensus on how individuals and groups should act in public.

This consensus, however, was shallow; two major groups of Americans had fundamental disagreements about celebrations of independence. Workingmen viewed holiday processions as occasions for the display of their independence and respectability and believed that their many parade groups showed their crucial role in the American republic. They believed that their contributions to its political life and economic productivity secured its survival, prosperity, and virtue. In contrast, Victorians wanted the Fourth of July celebrations to reflect their serious ideals, and they saw themselves as the most important members of the American republic. When they celebrated independence, they celebrated their own central role in guaranteeing the survival, prosperity, and virtue of the nation.

In addition to the local Fourth of July celebrations, Americans celebrated the one-hundredth anniversary of the signing of the Declaration of Independence at a tremendous international exhibition. The International Centennial Exhibition ran from 10 May to 19 October 1876 and was held on a 450-acre fairground in Philadelphia's Fairmount Park, adjacent to the Schuykill River. Although the exhibition was closed on weekends, and most factory workers and shop clerks worked a 6-day week, over 9 million people, or 1 in every 19 Americans, attended. In the fairgrounds there were 5 main buildings, a women's pavilion, 24 state buildings, 15 buildings erected by foreign nations, and 228 other buildings for privately sponsored exhibits, concessions, restaurants, and toilets. The exhibits included products of factory and field, artistic and mechanical creations, and displays of U.S. history and the natural history of North America.

The Victorian ladies and gentlemen who planned the Centennial Exhibition intended it to be both a celebration of the diversity of the American people and a manifestation of their ideal of serious entertainment. As guidebooks and official brochures explained, the exhibits illustrated the material and moral development of the United States. Even the design of the exhibition's drinking fountains was taken seriously. A main cross-thoroughfare of the fairgrounds was Fountain Avenue. On it were located three major drinking fountains sponsored by temperance associations. A grand one was the 100-foot-high Memorial Fountain of the Catholic Total Abstinence (CTA) Union. At its center stood a rock mound topped by a 16-foot-high statue of Moses. Water cascaded over the rock into a pool. On the pool's circular wall were sculpted portrait heads in relief of Catholic foreigners who had participated in the American Revolution, including the Marquis de Lafayette, Tadeusz Kościuszko, and Stephen Moylan. The pool rested on a granite platform in the shape of a Maltese cross. Each of the four arms ended in a marble pedestal upon which stood a statue of a prominent American Catholic of the nineteenth century. People slaked their thirst at the drinking fountain located in a sculptural niche in the base of each pedestal.

While recognizing ethnic diversity, the CTA fountain also suggested that the values and beliefs of the Victorian world overlapped with those of the working class. At midcentury, workingmen's newspapers, the Knights of Labor, and Catholic temperance advocates all denounced drink as a threat to individual independence and family stability. They advised members and readers to put shebeens—drinking places in Irish neighborhoods—and saloons behind them. But the fountain spoke only to some Catholics: those who, whether Victorians or working people, had accepted temperance as a desirable behavior. Once again, Victorians welcomed diversity on their terms when it did not threaten their core beliefs.

Also giving visible testimony to the diverse origins of Americans were the exhibition's statues representing other ethnic, religious, and racial groups. Presbyterians sponsored a statue of Scottish immigrant John Witherspoon, president of the College of New Jersey (Princeton) during the Revolution. On the Fourth, German-Americans dedicated a statue of the naturalist and statesman Baron Alexander von Humboldt, and on Columbus Day, Italian-Americans dedicated a statue of Christopher Columbus. African-Americans commissioned a statue of Richard Allen, who had purchased his freedom from his owners in Delaware, fought in the Revolutionary War, and founded the African Methodist Episcopal Church. B'nai B'rith sponsored a sculpture called *Religious Liberty*; on its pedestal were inscribed the opening phrases of the First Amendment to the Constitution.

Outside the gates of the exhibition grounds, entertainment was designed to amuse. Whereas the buildings of the exhibition were substantial edifices inspired by the forms and motifs of Greek, Roman, and Gothic architecture, the buildings of "Centennialville," as one wag called it, were of wood construction. One commentator on the Centennial Exhibition contrasted the "splendid and imposing structures" of the fairgrounds with "the cheap and tawdry" buildings of this mushroom town. Every evening Centennialville and its saloons filled with tourists. Strolling musicians serenaded people enjoying sideshow attractions and watching men test their strength in contests like weightlifting. Winning such a contest brought a prize: perhaps a photograph of Rutherford B. Hayes, the Republican candidate for president, Samuel Tilden, the Democratic candidate for president, or George Armstrong Custer, the famous Civil War cavalry commander and Indian fighter on the Great Plains. That year he became even more famous: on 25 June Crazy Horse led the Sioux into the Battle of Little Bighorn, where they outmaneuvered and killed Custer and his troops.[10]

Organizers of the Centennial Exhibition and Fourth of July festivities hoped that the 1876 anniversary of independence would promote national unity by burying the differences that had led to the Civil War. To read the Declaration of Independence on the Fourth of July in Philadelphia organizers picked Virginian Richard Henry Lee, namesake of the member of the Continental Congress who had proposed independence in 1776. Despite this gesture, the Centennial was celebrated largely on northern terms. At the exhibition a huge historical canvas, *The Battle of Gettysburg* by the artist Rothermel, hung in the U.S. section of Memorial Hall. Old Abe, the war eagle mascot of the 8th Wisconsin Infantry, attracted crowds around his perch in Agricultural Hall. Northern men of letters, including William Cullen Bryant, John Greenleaf Whittier, and Oliver Wendell Holmes, contributed odes and hymns to the celebration. Whittier's hymn rejoiced in the "rended bolt and falling chain" of slavery, and Bryant's hymn thanked "the Guardian Power, who kept / Our sacred league of states entire."[11]

Many white southerners continued to feel that the Fourth of July was not their holiday; Confederate Memorial Day had more meaning for them. Although southern African-Americans had celebrated the Fourth since the Civil War, in most southern cities whites had not had Fourth of July parades since 1861, and in 1876 businesses remained open. Georgia, Virginia, the Carolinas, and Louisiana did not send exhibits to Philadelphia or sponsor state buildings. Yet on the Centennial Fourth, small signs suggested that southern animosity toward the North was abating. In important southern cities such as Savannah, Selma, Nashville, and Memphis businesses did close on 4 July and white citizens paraded. In Richmond the state flag and the national flag flew together on the state capitol for the first time in 16 years.

Throughout the nineteenth century, public readings of the Declaration of Independence were a standard feature of Fourth of July celebrations, but the one-hundredth reading was special. At the ceremony near Independence Hall in Philadelphia, Richard Henry Lee read from a tattered, framed copy of the original document. Because of the poor acoustics in the square, few in the audience of 5,000 could hear his words. Even so, cheers broke out at its conclusion, and men in the audience threw their hats into the air. The master of ceremonies then proposed nine cheers for the Declaration, and the crowd responded enthusiastically. Eventually, it quieted down to listen to Bayard Taylor's recital of a lengthy ode composed for the occasion and Sen. William M. Evarts's oration, "What the Age Owes to America."

There are many phrases in the Declaration that orators could have celebrated on the Centennial. During the midcentury years northern college professors, who often opposed the Democratic party and supported the Whig party, argued against the Enlightenment theories of natural rights expressed in the Declaration's first two paragraphs. They believed that the civil state was part of God's plan for the universe and the moral development of humankind. Another focus of attention during the nineteenth century and in the present century, mainly by radicals, has been the phrase about a people's right to rebel against an established government when it destroys the ends for which it was established. Bypassing these important passages, most Centennial orators chose to focus on the phrase "all men are created equal." They proposed that a great accomplishment of the nation's first 100 years had been the transformation of equality from an ideal into a fact of political life. George William Curtis told his audience: "For more than eighty years that Declaration remained only a Declaration of faith. But fellow citizens, fortunate beyond all men, our eyes behold its increasing fulfillment. The sublime faith of the fathers is more and more the familiar fact of the children. And the proud flag which floats over America to-day, as it is the bond of indissoluble union, so it is the seal of an ever enlarging equality, and ever surer justice."[12]

Curtis saw an "enlarging equality" in the ratification in 1865, 1868, and 1870 of the Thirteenth, Fourteenth, and Fifteenth amendments, which had made the promise "all men are created equal" more explicit. In the United States people would never again be enslaved. States had to extend to all people equal protection of the laws and could not take away "life, liberty, or property, without due process of law." Finally, neither the states nor the federal government could deny citizens the right to vote because of their "race, color, or previous condition of servitude."

Most Americans thought that the Thirteenth and Fourteenth amendments extended the guarantee of equal rights to all. By equal rights, most people meant the right to buy and sell one's own labor, the right to own and to dispose of property, and the right to claim the protection of the government to enforce the first two rights. Almost all Americans agreed that equal rights had nothing to do with making sure that all people began their lifelong acquisition of property from the same starting line or with equality of condition. The phrase "all men are created equal" did not and should not preclude some individuals from rising in wealth and others from sinking into poverty.

The Fifteenth Amendment also extended the franchise by saying that the right to vote should not be "denied or abridged by the United States or by any State on account of race, color, or previous condition of servitude." But in 1874 the Supreme Court ruled in *Minor* vs. *Happerstett* that states need not grant all citizens the vote. In this particular case, the Court ruled that a state could grant the suffrage only to its male citizens. A vocal and influential minority of educated Americans held for the next fifty years that voting was no right but a privilege, even though the amendment itself referred to the *right* to vote. Adherents of this viewpoint usually opposed woman suffrage and/or supported an educational requirement to limit the immigrant vote.

For African-American men the Civil War amendments removed explicit racial barriers to their right to vote and granted them equal rights. Still, Fourth of July celebrations and the Philadelphia exhibition showed that equal rights under law existed in a segregated society. De facto segregation prevailed, in both the North and the South, and in the South de jure segregation was becoming more and more common. Restaurants and theaters patronized by whites usually denied admittance to African-Americans. The Centennial Exhibition seemed at first glance to be an exception. African-American Edmonia Lewis's sculptures of Richard Allen and Cleopatra were well received by white spectators and commentators, and no segregated area for African-American art existed. But Frederick Douglass, who had been invited to sit with President Grant and other dignitaries at the opening ceremonies, was barred from the platform by guards until a white senator recognized him and assured them that Douglass was meant to sit there. On the Fourth of July many orators referred to the abolition of slavery and to the Fourteenth and Fifteenth Amendments. But almost none mentioned the contribution of individual African-Americans to national history. One who did was George Washington Williams. He proposed to an Independence Day crowd that "to take the negro out of the history of the Revolution is to rob it of one of its most attractive and indispensable elements; it is to impoverish it by the withdrawal of some of its most wealthy and enduring facts."[13] In 1882 he would publish *A History of the Negro Race in America: From 1619 to 1880*, the first history of African-Americans.

Women organizers of the exhibition also discriminated against African-Americans. The all-white Women's Centennial Commission invited African-American Philadelphia women to form a separate subcommittee to solicit funds from "colored people." In protest, the African-American women denounced the commission for reviving "the bitterest colored prejudices."[14] Faced with adverse publicity in the press, the commission relented, and the African-American women's subcommittee was allowed to raise funds from whomever its members wanted to ask.

Parades also reflected the racial divisions of American society. In most southern cities African-Americans held their own parades and festivities on the Fourth. In the North newspapers did not report separate African-American parades. African-Americans who marched at all in northern civic parades probably did so as representatives of their own social and benevolent societies. White prejudice was not the only reason that African-Americans marched in segregated units. Although anti-African-American prejudice, as well as anti-immigrant and anti-Catholic prejudice, prevailed in the United States in 1876, African-Americans were behaving like other minority groups in forming their own parade units. In 1876 most Americans entered public life as members of associations and clubs organized on the basis of religious loyalty and/or national origin.

Nonetheless, African-Americans faced a future different from that of Irish-Americans and German-Americans, who were unaffected by white Americans' inability to imagine an integrated society. An illustration in *Frank Leslie's Historical Register of the Centennial Exhibition* (1877) showing a crowd of African-American men, women, and children surrounding Francesco Pezzicar's statue *The Abolition of Slavery in the United States* confirms this. The statue portrays chains dropping from a heroic and muscular figure of an African-American man as he extends his arms in jubilation at his emancipation. His loincloth contrasts with the finery of the middle-class African-American audience clustered around the statue. In the background are older African-Americans—a bearded man and his wife stand in their country clothes with their eyes lowered, as if in thanks for the passing of slavery days. The contrast in the clothes of the two groups of African-American viewers shows the progress from peonage to prosperity. But no whites join the African-American audience around the statue. The illustrator allows African-Americans upward mobility into middle-class Victorian life, but not into white Victorian life.

White Americans also excluded African-Americans from national political life. In the South the right of African-American men to vote was often denied. The Ku Klux Klan had been founded in 1865 as a fraternal organization, but by 1868 its members were using force and terror to reduce the size of the Republican vote. In the mid-1870s the federal government refused to prosecute southerners who violated the right of African-Americans men to cast their ballots. To discourage African-Americans from voting, white Democrats often incited riots. For example, before a county election in Vicksburg, Mississippi, in December 1874, whites started a riot in which at least 35 African-Americans and two whites died. Because the governor of Mississippi expected similar violence in 1876, he requested that President Grant send federal troops to protect voters. Afraid that the use of federal force would cost northern Republican candidates votes, Grant refused the governor's request, and violence surrounded the election.

In 1876 the Supreme Court overturned key provisions of the civil rights enforcement laws of 1870 and 1871. These laws had made it a federal offense to try to deprive a person of civil or political rights, and they had given the president the power to use the army to enforce this provision and to suspend the writ of habeas corpus in areas that he declared to be in a state of insur-

8.1 Statue of a freed slave, Memorial Hall, Centennial International Exhibition, Philadelphia, 1876, in *Frank Leslie's Illustrated Historical Register of the Centennial Exhibition* (New York, 1877). *Courtesy of the Winterthur Library: Printed Book and Periodical Collection, Henry Francis du Pont Winterthur Museum, Winterthur, Delaware*

rection. By invalidating the enforcement laws, the Court ruled that the Fourteenth and Fifteenth Amendments applied not to individuals but to states. These rulings reflected contemporary thinking about liberty. As widespread support for the Comstock Act had showed, most Americans believed the preservation of liberty in a community was more important than the right of an individual to freedom of speech. In the 1876 rulings the Supreme Court decided that the guarantee of liberty to a majority, through the maintenance of federalism, outweighed the guarantee of civil and political rights to a minority. In the Victorian era, subordination of the individual to the whole was a distinguishing condition of public life as well as of parlor life.

As southern states completed the process of Reconstruction and the federal government withdrew its forces, southern "redeemer" governments felt free to violate the spirit of the postwar amendments. They found constitutional means for depriving African-Americans of the right to vote. Poll taxes and grandfather laws, by denying the ballot to a cash-poor people whose enslaved grandfathers had not been citizens, made unnecessary the Klan's tactics of terror.

The inauguration of Republican Rutherford B. Hayes on 3 March 1877 completed the process of reconstructing the South. To settle the disputed presidential election of 1876 and avoid a constitutional impasse, a congressional committee awarded enough contested electoral votes to Hayes to make him the victor. Republicans and Democrats in Congress agreed that a Republican should be president and that southern states should regain control of their own internal political affairs. The federal government removed its remaining troops from the southern states and did not use military force again in the nineteenth century to guarantee to African-Americans equal rights and the right to vote. The Republican accommodation with southern Democrats was in accord with the opinion of the majority of white Americans and their elected representatives at Washington, D.C. All but a handful of northern whites accepted that African-Americans would have to take whatever place in southern political life the white-controlled political parties and state governments allowed them. On the issue of equality, Fourth of July speakers in 1876 were far too optimistic.

While the war brought African-Americans freedom, citizenship, and for men the right to vote, women made no similar gains in the postwar years, even though woman's rights and woman suffrage were two of the most passionately debated issues of the day. During the Centennial year advocates of woman suffrage found themselves excluded from official celebrations; so they organized protests and demonstrations to draw attention to the legal status of women. On the Fourth, Julia Ward Howe and other members of the American Woman Suffrage Association (AWSA) gave speeches arguing for a larger role for women in public life. At Independence Square in Philadelphia, Susan B. Anthony and four other members of the rival National

Woman Suffrage Association (NWSA) disrupted the official ceremony. As the crowd huzzahed the reading of the Declaration of Independence, Anthony audaciously led a delegation through the confusion of the cheering to the podium. There, she handed Vice President Thomas B. Ferry a "Declaration of Rights for Women." Then the protesters marched to a platform in front of Independence Hall and read their declaration.

The women's declaration repeated many of the claims that the Declaration of Principles of the Seneca Falls convention had made in 1848. It argued that "the history of our country over the last one hundred years has been a series of assumptions and usurpations of power over women, in direct opposition to the principles of just government." Of these principles, the leading ones were "the natural rights of each individual" and "the equality of these rights." While the Declaration of Independence had listed the specific offenses of George III against the colonists' natural rights, the women's declaration specified how the federal government and state governments were depriving women of their rights. Although state constitutions contained the word *male* and denied women the vote, federal and state governments compelled women to pay taxes. Convention and law also excluded women from juries and denied wives the right to testify against their husbands. Although by 1876 many states had passed laws giving married women the right to their wages and inherited property, some states, especially in the South, had not. In many states married women also could not sign legal contracts or deeds. For example, in Philadelphia in 1876 Susan B. Anthony, one of the few unmarried members of the NWSA, had to sign the lease agreement for the NWSA's offices. The declaration also protested the low wages paid for women's jobs and the municipal laws and police practices that attempted to control prostitution by punishing women for loitering in the streets after certain hours.

In its conclusion, the women's declaration drew on a tradition of republican thinking about independence and absolute power to denounce universal manhood suffrage—in its words, "a more absolute and cruel despotism than monarchy." The declaration ended with a statement with which few Victorians agreed—that woman was made not for man but "first for her own happiness, with the absolute right to herself." Still, the declaration often justified woman suffrage by invoking central Victorian beliefs, namely, the special natures of men and women, and the sanctity of motherhood. An aristocracy of sex, the declaration said, exalted "brute force above moral power, vice above virtue, ignorance above education, and the son above the mother who bore him."[15]

Although the NWSA's declaration did not attack the institution of marriage and was thus less radical than Victoria Woodhull's position, the NWSA still represented a minority view. In 1878 a NWSA-backed joint resolution was introduced in the Senate. The Susan B. Anthony amendment, as it came to be called, proposed that the Constitution be amended so that neither the state governments nor the federal government could deny a citizen the vote on account of sex. In 1920, 42 years later, this amendment finally became one of the supreme laws of the land.

At the Centennial Exhibition the Women's Pavilion embodied a more moderate, and more widely supported vision of woman's rights. The Women's Committee had come into being in 1875 when exhibition organizers realized that displays of foreign nations would take all the space in the main building originally allotted to women. After the Women's Committee was appointed, its members raised $30,000 for a pavilion and selected its exhibits. Organizers of the committee relegated the woman's rights display of the AWSA—a protest of "taxation without representation"—to an obscure exhibit space, and the NWSA decided not to locate its headquarters inside the Women's Pavilion, or even on the fairgrounds.

The Women's Committee thought that women deserved more recognition for their role as homemakers, and so it arranged for the display of many articles of women's home manufacture and handicraft. The most noted piece was an Arkansas woman's sculpture in relief in butter, *Dreaming Iolanthe*, the heroine of a contemporary short story. The exhibition included the handiwork of women of leisure as well as the domestic manufactures of peasant women from other countries. Queen Victoria sent a piece of her embroidery, and Japan displayed the lacquer and inlay work of its women.

Other exhibits suggested that women were capable of extending their domestic role by enlarging the area of responsibility and duty that they already assumed in their roles as mothers and wives. The committee wanted to refute the contemporary notion that women should be excluded from the public world of social responsibility and work. To show that women of leisure did not spend their lives in idle pleasures, the exhibition demonstrated that middle-class women had taken on public responsibilities. One display featured photographs of benevolent organizations throughout the United States and Europe that women had founded or managed, including homes and schools for orphans, hospitals, reformatories, and homes for indigent and elderly women.

Other displays promoted the view that women should not be excluded from the modern mechanical and technological world of work and that prevailing notions of women's frailty were false. On one side of the pavilion stood an engine house where a young woman operated a six-horsepower steam engine. It supplied power to other machines, including spinning frames and looms and a Hoe cylinder press on which AAW members printed a newspaper. The articles in the newspaper discussed the issues raised by women's operation of the machinery in the exhibit.

As the paper often pointed out, women in the work force usually held low-paying jobs, and those women who held the same jobs as men were paid as much as two-thirds less. By demonstrating women's competence, the exhibit

8.2 Women's Pavilion, Centennial International Exhibition, Philadelphia, 1876, in *Thompson Westcott's Centennial Portfolio: A Souvenir of the International Exhibition at Philadelphia* (Philadelphia, 1876)

was silently calling for increased opportunity and better-paid jobs for women. If women were better paid, AAW members proposed, they could afford to make wiser marriage choices. They would not be deserted so often and would not have to resort to prostitution to support their families. Able to earn a living wage, single mothers would be better mothers.

Speaking for the down-to-earth housewives of small-town and rural America, Marietta Holley confirmed that the message that the Women's Pavilion had meant to transmit had been received. Samantha, the philosopher-heroine of her novels, endorses the exhibition effort:

That buildin' stands there to-day as a solid and hefty proof that wimmen are sunthin' more than the delicate, and helpless zephyrs and seraphines, that they have been falsely pointed out to be. . . . It is a great scientific fact, that if men go canterin' blindly down that old pathway of wimmen's weakness and unfitness for labor and endurance and inability to meet financikal troubles and discouragements again, they must come bunt up ag'inst that buildin' and recognize it as a solid fact, and pause before it respectfully, ponderin' what it means, or else fall.[16]

Despite Samantha's enthusiasm for the Women's Pavilion and the Centennial Exhibition, they showed, along with the parades and speeches of the Fourth of July celebrations, that in the public life of 1876 women occupied a restricted place. When orators referred to upward mobility, they were talking about men; none mentioned women who worked outside the home. There is no newspaper report on the Centennial celebration that mentions any group of women parading or individual women joining other parade units. On the exhibition grounds, women's displays were confined to their own building, and no public sculpture commemorated an actual woman. The images of women that did appear in public sculpture were idealized figures symbolizing justice, freedom, or liberty. The restricted terms of women's participation in the Centennial festivities parallel those that governed their everyday public life. Middle-class women entered public life most frequently to perform benevolent work on behalf of others; most working women in the nonagricultural labor force had entered public life to work as domestics or in factories, especially those manufacturing textiles and clothes. Working for their charities and in their jobs, women were in a sense cloistered, confined to roles and responsibilities associated with domesticity.

When George William Curtis told his "fellow citizens, fortunate beyond all *men* (emphasis added)," of their "enlarging equality," in every likelihood he did not mean humankind when he used the word *men*; he was referring to a fact of life in the United States of 1876. Victorians found it debatable whether women were entitled to equal rights, and they assumed that men should preside over public life and secure the economic welfare of their families.

In 1876, the United States of America was once more one nation, truth still reigned, and most Americans were certain that adherence to republican principles could create a future in which independent men rose and prospered. Victorian Americans had drawn on their cultural storehouse to deal with momentous events such as the Civil War and emancipation. To perpetuate their world, they had created new institutions—freedmen's schools, public parks, women's colleges, to name a few—and reformed others. Yet, as we have seen, there were signs portending deep and radical changes in the Victorian intellectual world. Challenges to divine truth were revising and even refuting core Victorian beliefs. The invention of the telephone and electric lighting soon would transform the material and social dimensions of everyday intellectual life. Still, as the 1880s began, most Victorians insisted that there was a divine truth that should and ought to be that it was moral, and that all right-thinking people could appreciate it. They continued to think in absolutes; their world of thought and action remained a serious place. The Centennial year 1876 had been a time to celebrate the continuation of an era, not its end.

Chronology

1859 Charles Darwin's *On the Origin of Species* published.

1860 Population of the United States is 31,433,321; 153,604 immigrants arrive. South Carolina legislature votes to secede from the Union 20 December.

1861 In January–February six more southern states secede. Provisional government of Confederate States of America established 8 February. Jefferson Davis elected president of Confederacy 9 February. Abraham Lincoln inaugurated sixteenth president of United States 4 March. Confederate forces fire on Fort Sumter, South Carolina, 12 April.

1862 Land-Grant (Morrill) Act enacted 2 July. Following Union victory at Antietam Creek, Maryland, Lincoln issues preliminary Emancipation Proclamation 22 September. Julia Ward Howe's "The Battle Hymn of the Republic" published.

1863 Emancipation Proclamation goes into effect 1 January. At Gettysburg, Pennsylvania, Union army defeats Gen. Robert E. Lee and the Northern Army of Virginia 1–4 July. Siege of Vicksburg, Tennessee, ends with 9 July surrender of Confederate defenders to Gen. Ulysses Grant. Rioters in northern cities, 13–16 July, protest the draft; in New York City, Irish workingmen burn the draft office and Colored Orphan Asylum; the mob lynches at least 12 African-Americans. 18 July African-American soldiers enter battle for the first time in the Civil War; the 54th Massachusetts Infantry, a regiment composed of African-Americans, leads an unsuccessful attack on Fort Wagner, South Carolina. Lincoln delivers the Gettysburg Address 19 November at dedication of a battlefield cemetery for the Union dead.

1864   Atlanta, Georgia, falls to Union army 1 September. Gen. William T. Sherman marches across Georgia. Lincoln reelected president 8 November over George B. McClellan.

1865   Freedmen's Bureau established 3 March. Lincoln delivers Second Inaugural Address 4 March. Lee surrenders his army to Grant at Appomattox Courthouse, Virginia, 9 April. John Wilkes Booth assassinates Lincoln at Ford's Theater, Washington, D.C., 14 April. Vassar College, Cornell University, and Atlanta University founded. American Social Science Association founded. The *Nation* commences publication. Ku Klux Klan founded as a fraternal organization. Thirteenth Amendment, which declares slavery unconstitutional, ratified. First three *Freedman's Readers* published.

1866   Over President Andrew Johnson's veto, Congress passes Civil Rights Act 9 April; extending citizenship to African-Americans, it guarantees their rights to own and rent property, to make contracts, and to have access to the courts as parties and witnesses in legal suits.

1867   Howard University and Fisk University founded. University of Wisconsin admits women. (The University of Iowa was the first state university to do so, in 1855.) *Ragged Dick*, Horatio Alger's most successful book, published. Augusta Jane Evans Wilson's *St. Elmo* published; it would be the third-best-selling novel of the century after *Uncle Tom's Cabin* and *Ben Hur*.

1868   Fourteenth Amendment ratified. Grant elected eighteenth president of the United States 3 November. Elizabeth Stuart Phelps's *The Gates Ajar* published. Volume 1 of Louisa May Alcott's *Little Women* published.

1869   Charles William Eliot becomes president of Harvard University. Railroad tracks from east and west meet at Promontory Point, Utah, forming a transcontinental railroad. Volume 2 of Alcott's *Little Women* published. The universities of Indiana, Kansas, and Minnesota admit women.

1870   Golden Gate Park in San Francisco founded. Fifteenth Amendment ratified. Victoria Woodhull runs for president of the United States and founds *Woodhull and Claflin's Weekly*. Museum of Fine Arts in Boston and the Metropolitan Museum of Art in New York City are founded. The universities of California, Michigan, and Missouri admit women.

1871   Congress appoints Commission on Civil Service Reform 3 March; Congress later ignores its recommendations, and the commission is dissolved. William Marcy Tweed, grand sachem of Tammany Hall, is indicted 26 October for stealing from New York City treasury; conviction and imprisonment follow. Noah Porter becomes president of Yale College.

1872   Grant reelected 5 November. *Popular Science Monthly* commences publication, with Edward L. Youmans as editor. Congress establishes Yellowstone National Park.

1873   Financial failure of Jay Cooke and Co., a banking house, on 18 September precipitates depression that lasts until 1878; many employers respond to economic slowdown by cutting wages; strikes follow in New York City (1874) and western Pennsylvania (1873–74). The Act for the Suppression of Trade in, and Circulation of, Obscene Literature and Articles of Immoral Use, commonly known as the Comstock Act, enacted 3 March. Sage College for women at Cornell University founded. Association for the Advancement of Women founded. Mark Twain and Charles Dudley Warner's *The Gilded Age: A Tale of Today* published.

1874   Brooklyn, New York, park system founded. John W. Draper's *History of the Conflict between Religion and Science* and John Fiske's *The Outlines of Cosmic Philosophy* published. Women's Christian Temperance Union founded. First Chautauqua Institute held during August at Chautauqua Lake, New York. School of Domestic Science and Arts at the University of Illinois founded.

1875   Dwight L. Moody and Ira D. Sankey begin their revival tour of American cities, including Philadelphia and Brooklyn as well as Princeton, New Jersey, at invitation of Princeton students. Wellesley College, Smith College, and Vanderbilt University founded.

1876   International Centennial Exhibition opens 10 May in Philadelphia. Crazy Horse and Sitting Bull, leading 1,000 warriors, defeat Gen. George A. Custer and a cavalry regiment at Little Bighorn River on 25 June; no whites survive the battle. Alexander Graham Bell demonstrates the telephone. Mark Twain's *The Adventures of Tom Sawyer* published. House of Representatives impeaches Secretary of War William Belknap for receiving bribes for sale of trading posts in Indian territory. Johns Hopkins University founded, with Daniel Coit Gilman as president. American Library Association founded.

1877   Rutherford B. Hayes inaugurated nineteenth president of the United States 3 March; after dispute about the November election returns, southern Democrats in Congress accept his election in return for an end to Reconstruction. Workers on the Baltimore and Ohio Railroad go on strike 10 July; more railroad workers join the strike; governors mobilize state militias, and President Hayes sends federal troops when state forces are unable to quell the strikers. First intercity telephone communications systems established.

1879   Thomas Edison improves electric light bulb. Henry George's *Progress and Poverty* published.

1880   Population of the United States is 50,155,783, and 457,257 immigrants arrive.

Notes and References

Introduction

1. For trade catalogs, I consulted the extensive holdings in the library of the Winterthur Museum and Gardens, Winterthur, Delaware (hereafter cited as WM&G). Except for the correspondence between Turner MacFarland of Richmond, Virginia, and J. Willcox Brown of Fredericksburg, Virginia., 1866–73, which is privately owned, most of the manuscript collections I consulted are located in the Joseph S. Downs Collection, WM&G. They included the journal of Gotham Bradbury of Farmington, Maine, 1881–83; the diaries of T. Stewart Brown of Philadelphia, Pennsylvania, 1863–65; the letters of Elizabeth Brown to T. Stewart Brown, 1861–63; the diary of Francis Burgess of Harford, New York, 1864–65; the journal of Martha Fletcher of Delanco, New Jersey, 1864–67; the diary of Mrs. Capt. William Cowles of Petersburg, Virginia, 1866–68; and the diary of Maria M. Fifield of Salisbury, New Hampshire, 1857–59 and 1860–62.

2. See David A. Hollinger's discussion of discourse in *In the American Province: Studies in the History and Historiography of Ideas* (Bloomington, Ind., 1985), 130–51.

3. There are many other valuable histories of the Civil War and Reconstruction years, the middle class, and Victorian culture that I have drawn upon extensively. The suggested reading section lists the most helpful of these books and comments on the more significant debates that concern historians. Grier's book came into my hands just as I was finishing chapter 1 of this book in October 1988. Our studies are mostly complementary and mutually reinforcing. As an outsider to material culture studies, however, I question some of the generalizations that come naturally to those inside the field, and as an intellectual historian, I have been careful to derive my definition of key words—*culture*, for instance—from the discourse of the day.

4. This discussion builds on that of Daniel Walker Howe, "Victorian Culture in America," in Daniel Walker Howe, ed., *Victorian America* (Philadelphia, 1976), 3–29.

205

5. James C. Mohr, ed., *The Cormany Diaries: A Northern Family in the Civil War* (Pittsburgh, 1982), 130; C. Vann Woodward, ed., *Mary Chesnut's Civil War* (New Haven, Conn., 1981), 518.

6. Henry T. Williams and Mrs. C. S. Jones, *Beautiful Homes, or, Hints in House Furnishings* (New York, 1878), 3.

7. Although augmented by findings from my own research, the following discussion largely follows that of Stuart M. Blumin, "The Hypothesis of Middle-Class Formation in Nineteenth-Century America: A Critique and Some Proposals," *American Historical Review* 90 (1985): 299–338. Blumin's book, *The Emergence of the Middle Class: Social Experience in the American City, 1761–1800* (New York, 1989), came to hand as I was revising the final draft of this book.

8. Blumin, *Emergence of the Middle Class*, 117–19.

9. Catharine E. Beecher and Harriet Beecher Stowe, *The American Woman's Home, or Principles of Domestic Science* (1869; reprint, Hartford, Conn., 1975), 19.

10. Blumin, *Emergence of the Middle Class*, 190.

11. Mrs. Maria Oakley, *From Attic to Cellar: A Book for Young Housekeepers* (New York, 1879), 124.

12. *Papers and Letters Presented to the First Woman's Congress of the Association for the Advencement of Women* (New York, 1874), 16.

13. Mrs. Henry [Eunice White] Beecher, *All around the House* (New York, 1878), 5.

Chapter One

1. Williams and Jones, *Beautiful Homes*, 138.

2. Various sources underlie this analysis of the parlor as an institution of intellectual life. Manufacturer's trade catalogs are mines of information about the middle-class marketplace during the years 1860–80. For parlor decoration, catalogs offered furniture, lighting devices, toys, games, books, engravings, chromolithographs, stereographs, and sculpture, to name the most obvious articles. This bountiful catalog marketplace offered abundant variety and innumerable choices. For instance, a single furniture catalog of parlor suites describes 700–800 items, each available in a number of styles. Visual images, including paintings, their inexpensive reproductions, and photographs, are another type of sources used in this analysis. Contemporary published and unpublished writings, including diaries and letters (see Introduction, note 1) and advice books, also describe parlors and their activities.

But all these sources have limitations. Given Victorian artistic conventions, paintings and photographs usually depict an ideal, rather than an accurate image of daily life. Learning about the values and beliefs of Victorians by examining the objects displayed in trade catalogs may lead to overreading; it is all too easy to attribute meanings to objects that their owners perceived neither consciously nor unconsciously. Diaries and letters do reveal a writer's ideas and assumptions, but they are still incomplete. Writers usually do not mention daily activities they take for granted. Finally, the first task of advice book authors was to tell people how to behave, not to describe life as it was actually lived.

Even so, these sources do supply crucial information for a portrait of Victorians' intellectual life. Besides offering advice, advice books often warn against certain decorating practices. These admonitions can provide glimpses of actual behavior that the authors had observed. Offerings in trade catalogs also can reveal some information about daily activities that diaries and letters omit.

And since many pieces of Victorian furniture were heavy and difficult to move, it can be presumed that visual images of parlor decor accurately reflect furniture arrangement.

3. Julia McNair Wright, *The Complete Home: An Encyclopedia of Domestic Life and Affairs* (Philadelphia, 1879), 193.

4. Described in Robert Taft, *Photography and the American Scene, 1839–1889*, 2d ed. (New York, 1964), 138.

5. Williams and Jones, *Beautiful Homes*, 4.

6. *Cassell's Household Guide: Being a Complete Encyclopaedia of Domestic and Social Economy*, 4 vols. (London, 1870), 1:17.

7. Harriet Prescott Spufford, *Art Decoration Applied to Furniture* (New York, 1878), 214.

8. For example, see G. W. Tomlinson, *Catalogue of Card Photographs* (Boston, 1864).

9. Eucleian Society, *The University Glee Book* (New York, 1860), 7.

10. Lord Byron is another possible exception. He did not, however, have as large a hold on the Victorian imagination as Napoleon did, and his portrait appeared infrequently in trade catalogs.

11. Mohr, *Cormany Diaries*, 73.

12. Edward Everett Salisbury, "Principles of Domestic Taste," *New Englander* 36 (1879): 313.

13. Richard Crawford, ed., *The Civil War Songbook: Complete Original Sheet Music for 37 Songs* (New York, 1977), 120. For the top 20 list, see William Mahar, "March to the Music: Twenty Top Hits of the Sixties," *Civil War Times Illustrated* 22, no. 5 (1984): 12–17, 41–44.

14. Mahar, "March to the Music," 61.

15. Quoted from hymns published during the years 1860–80, reprinted in Albert Christ-Janer, et al., *American Hymns Old and New*, 2 vols. (New York, 1980).

16. Wright, *Complete Home*, 194.

17. Although social commentators since at least the time of John Adams have recognized this phenomenon, anthropologists have until recently let the theories of Thorstein Veblen dominate their analysis of consumption. Grant McCracken is among the first anthropologists to seek explanations of consumption beyond Veblen. See his *Culture and Consumption: New Approaches to the Symbolic Character of Consumer Goods and Activities* (Bloomington, Ind., 1988).

18. James Parton, "On Popularizing Art," *Atlantic Monthly* 23 (1869): 349–57.

19. Clarence Cook, *The House Beautiful* (New York, 1877), 271, 88.

20. Charles L. Eastlake, *Hints on Household Taste* (1872; 5th ed., Boston, 1877), 137.

21. Jenny Juneiana (Jane Cunningham Croly), *Talks on Women's Topics* (Boston, 1864), 86.

Chapter Two

1. Lee Soltow and Edward Stevens, *The Rise of Literacy and the Common School in the United States: A Socioeconomic Analysis to 1870* (Chicago, 1981), 155, 69, 70, 79.

2. See Noah Porter, *Books and Reading, or, What Books Shall I Read and How Shall I Read Them?* 2d. ed. (New York, 1882); Wright, *Complete Home*, 4.

3. Porter, *Books and Reading*, 33.

4. Mohr, *Cormany Diaries*, 161.

5. Hamlin Garland, *A Son of the Middle Border* (New York, 1914), 187; John Kent Folmar, ed., *"This State of Wonders": The Letters of an Iowa Frontier Family, 1858–1861* (Iowa City, 1986), 68; Daniel Woodall to his sister, 2 April 1862, Daniel Woodall Papers, Historical Society of Delaware (hereafter cited as HSD), Wilmington, Delaware.

6. Wright, *Complete Home*, 214.

7. Porter, *Books and Reading*, 340.

8. As quoted in Carl H. Moneyhon, ed., "Life in Confederate Arkansas: The Diary of Virginia Davis Gray, 1863–1866, Part 2," *Arkansas Historical Quarterly* 42 (1983): 148; Oakley, *From Attic to Cellar*, 151.

9. Gail Hamilton (Mary Abigail Dodge), *Skirmishes and Sketches*, 2d. ed. (Boston, 1866), 45; Amelie V. Petit, *How to Read: Hints in Choosing the Best Books* (New York, 1880), 194–97.

10. Porter, *Books and Reading*, 7–8.

11. Mark Twain and Charles Dudley Warner, *The Gilded Age: A Tale of Today* (1873; reprint, New York, 1969), 140–41, 147.

12. Petit, *How to Read*, 50.

13. Quoted in John Austin Edwards, "Social and Cultural Activities of Texans during the Civil War and Reconstruction, 1861–1873" (Ph.D. diss., Texas Technical University, 1985), 19–20.

14. C. H. Fowler and W. H. De Puy, *Home and Health and Home Economics* (New York, 1880), 61.

15. Wright, *Complete Home*, 198; Hamilton, *Skirmishes and Sketches*, 44. One reader said that she was not totally won over to the "sentimentality and morbid religiosity of Sunday school literature" because of the "good wholesome stories provided for me at home" (Elizabeth Moorhead, *Whirling Spindle: The Story of a Pittsburgh Family* [Pittsburgh, 1942], 233).

16. Edward L. Wheeler, "Deadwood Dick, The Prince of the Road, or, The Black Rider of the Black Hills" (1877), in E. F. Bleiler, ed., *Eight Dime Novels* (New York, 1974), 78.

17. Horatio Alger, *Ragged Dick and Mark the Match Boy* (1867; reprint, New York, 1962), 46; Mary Abigail Dodge to Sophia Hawthorne, 29 November 1865, New York Public Library; Porter, *Books and Reading*, 222.

18. See "Books for Boys and Girls," *St. Nicholas* 2 (January 1875): 190, "The Last of the Children's Books," *The Nation*, 30 December 1869, 587, and William Graham Sumner, *Earth-Hunger and Other Essays*, ed. Albert Galloway Keller (New Haven, Conn., 1914), 368, 377–78, all discussed and quoted in Gary F. Scharnhorst, "Good Fortune in America: The Life and Works of Horatio Alger, Jr. and the Fate of the Alger Hero" (Ph.D. diss., Purdue University, 1978), 219–22.

19. Garland, *Son of the Middle Border*, 186; Herbert Quick, *One Man's Life* (Indianapolis, 1925), 174, 175.

20. The contemporary women's movement and scholars interested in broadening the canon of American literature have revived interest in these and other women authors. Frank Luther Mott, *A History of American Magazines, 1865–1885*, 5 vols. (Cambridge, Mass., 1938), 3:105; Moneyhon, "Life in Confederate Arkansas," passim; list of books in the Delanco library, in the journal of Martha Fletcher 1863–65, of Delanco, New Jersey, WM&G.

21. Porter, *Books and Reading*, 222. For complaints about novel reading, sample annual reports of the Boston Public Library.

22. Quoted in Frederick F. Schauer, *The Law of Obscenity* (Washington, D.C., 1976), 10–11.

23. Edward Dicey, *Spectator of America* (1863; reprint, Chicago, 1971), 19–33, and passim.

24. *Harper's Weekly*, 25 December 1869.

25. Woodward, *Mary Chesnut's Civil War*, passim; Folmar, "*This State of Wonders*," passim; the diary of Francis Burgess of Harford, New York, 1864–65, WM&G.

26. See Folmar, "*This State of Wonders*," entry for 3 May 1864, diary of Francis Burgess of Harford, New York, WM&G.

27. Quoted in Edwards, "Social and Cultural Activities of Texans," 22.

28. Mohr, *Cormany Diaries*, 399; statistics from Soltow and Stevens, *Rise of Literacy*, 52–53.

29. Edmund Townsend to his brother Samuel Townsend, 3 September 1863, Townsend Folder, HSD; *Regimental Enquirer*, 8 April 1864, in Daniel Woodall Papers, HSD; quoted in Fletcher Melvin Green, "Johnny Reb Could Read," in Fletcher Melvin Green, *Democracy in the Old South and Other Essays*, ed. J. Isaac Copeland (Nashville, 1969), 179.

30. *Regimental Enquirer*, 8 April 1864, in Daniel Woodall Papers, in HSD.

Chapter Three

1. As quoted in Jane C. Croly, *The History of the Woman's Club Movement in America* (New York, 1898), 456–57.

2. Folmar, "*This State of Wonders*," 40, 67.

3. A. H. Saxon is responsible for these calculations. See his *P. T. Barnum: The Legend and the Man* (New York, 1989), 107, 108.

4. Quoted in Francis G. Couvares, *The Remaking of Pittsburgh: Class and Culture in an Industrializing City, 1877–1919* (Albany, N.Y., 1984), 38.

5. Carlton P. Brooks, "The *Magnolia*: A Literary Magazine for the Confederacy," *Virginia Calvacade* 32 (1983): 153.

6. Mary P. Ryan, *Women in Public: Between Banners and Ballots, 1825–1880* (Baltimore, 1990), 80.

7. *An Historical Sketch of the Origin and Progress of the Society of the Sons of St. George* (Philadelphia, 1872), in T. Stewart Brown Papers, WM&G.

8. Quoted in Thomas Bender, *New York Intellect: A History of Intellectual Life in New York City, from 1750 to the Beginnings of Our Own Time* (New York, 1987), 83.

9. Victorians also formed study clubs with both men and women members, but information on these clubs has not yet been collected and analyzed. For mention of one such club, see Moorhead, *Whirling Spindle*, 265–66.

10. For information on the Decatur club, see Theodora Penny Martin, *The Sound of Our Own Voices: Women's Study Clubs, 1860–1910* (Boston, 1987), especially 146–49.

11. See Claudia L. Bushman, *"A Good Poor Man's Wife": Being a Chronicle of Harriet Hanson Robinson and Her Family in Nineteenth-Century New England* (Hanover, N.H., 1981), 178–79.

12. Quoted in Martin, *Sound of Our Own Voices*, 118, 119; quoted in Bushman, *"A Good Poor Man's Wife,"* 178.

13. Quoted in Martin, *Sound of Our Own Voices*, 62.

14. P. T. Barnum, *Struggles and Triumphs*, ed. Carl Bode (New York, 1981), 335.

15. *Daily Cincinnati Gazette*, 15 March 1867, and *Cincinnati Daily Commercial*, 15 March 1867, and *Cincinnati Daily Commerical*, 15 March 1867, quoted in Mary Kupiec Cayton, "The Making of an American Prophet: Emerson, His Audiences, and the Rise of the Culture Industry in Nineteenth-Century America," *American Historical Review* 92 (1987): 617.

16. Quoted in David Mead, *Yankee Eloquence in the Middle West: The Ohio Lyceum, 1850–1870* (East Lansing, Mich., 1951), 204.

17. Thomas Wentworth Higginson, "The American Lecture-System," *Every Saturday* 5 (1868): 492.

18. Quoted in Mead, *Yankee Eloquence*, 103, 104, 107.

19. Ibid., 237.

20. Quoted in Huburt H. Hoeltje, "Notes on the History of Lecturing in Iowa, 1855–1885," *Iowa Journal of History and Politics* 25 (1927): 107; Mead, *Yankee Eloquence*, 232, 233.

21. Quoted in Daniel M. Fox, *Engines of Culture: Philanthropy and Art Museums* (Madison, Wis., 1963), 13.

22. Frederick Law Olmsted, *The Formative Years*, vol. 1 of *The Papers of Frederick Law Olmsted*, ed. Charles Capen McLaughlin, et al. (Baltimore, 1977), 275–76; see also Frederick Law Olmsted, *Defending the Union, 1861–1863*, vol. 4 of *The Papers of Frederick Law Olmsted*, ed. Jane Turner Censer (Baltimore, 1986), 466–71.

23. In cities with many citizens of German ancestry, such as Pittsburgh and Cincinnati, the German-Americans took the lead in founding orchestras and chorales.

24. Quoted in Frederick Law Olmsted, *Creating Central Park, 1857–86*, vol. 3 of *The Papers of Frederick Law Olmsted*, ed. Charles E. Beveridge and David Schuyler (Baltimore, 1983), 273–74.

25. Quoted in *History of Washington, New Hampshire* (1886; reprint, Somersworth, N.H., 1976), 257; see also Olmsted, *Creating Central Park*, 279.

26. Quoted in Winifred E. Howe, *A History of the Metropolitan Museum of Art: With a Chapter on the Early Institutions of Art in New York* (New York, 1913), 102.

27. Quoted in Elizabeth W. Stone, "A Historical Approach to American Library Development: A Chronological Chart," *University of Illinois Graduate School of Library Science: Occasional Papers*, no. 83 (May 1967), 52, and Howe, *History of the Metropolitan Museum of Art*, 199.

28. Quoted in Neil Harris, "The Gilded Age Revisited: Boston and the Museum Movement," *American Quarterly* 14 (1962): 554, 555.

29. Quoted in *History of Washington, New Hampshire*, 256; Evelyn Geller, *Forbidden Books in American Public Libraries, 1876–1939: A Study in Cultural Change* (Westport, Conn., 1984), 27; the journal of Martha Fletcher of Delanco, New Jersey, WM&G.

30. Quoted in Lawrence W. Levine, *Highbrow, Lowbrow: The Emergence of Cultural Hierarchy in America* (Cambridge, Mass., 1988), 159.

31. Geller, *Forbidden Books*, 20, 24.

32. Quoted in Geoffrey Blodgett, "Frederick Law Olmsted: Landscape Architecture as Conservative Reform," *Journal of American History* 62 (1976): 881.

33. Quoted in Daniel M. Bluestone, "From Promenade to Park: The Gregarious Origins of Brooklyn's Park Movement," *American Quarterly* 39 (1987): 529.

34. Walter Muir Whitehill, *The Museum of Fine Arts, Boston: A Centennial History* (Cambridge, Mass., 1970), 40–41.

35. Lawrence H. Larsen, *The Urban West at the End of the Frontier* (Lawrence, Kans., 1978), 58; quoted in Bluestone, "From Promenade to Park," 540; *Phrenological Journal* 46 (1867): 109.

36. Whitehill, *Museum of Fine Arts*, 188.

Chapter Four

1. W. Buck Yearns and John C. Barrett, *North Carolina Civil War Documentary* (Chapel Hill, N.C., 1980), 234.

2. John W. Alvord, *Eighth Semi-Annual Report on Schools for Freedmen* (Washington, D.C., 1869), 83, reprinted in Alvord *Semi-Annual Report on Schools for Freedmen*, vol. 1 of *Freedmen's Schools and Textbooks*, ed., Robert C. Morris (New York, 1980).

3. There were many common school textbooks besides *McGuffey's Readers* in use during the Civil War and Reconstruction years. *McGuffey's Readers* were most popular west of the Allegheny Mountains; Charles W. Sanders's readers were more popular east of them. Most differences among these texts were superficial. All common school readers affirmed, and none contradicted, the behaviors and values taught in *McGuffey's* lessons.

4. *The Freedman's Spelling-Book* (1865–66; reprint, New York, 1980), "Note," n.p.; *The Freedman's Second Reader* (1865–66; reprint, New York, 1980), "Note," n.p.

5. Jacqueline Jones, *Soldiers of Light and Love: Northern Teachers and Georgia Blacks, 1865–1973* (Chapel Hill, N.C., 1980), 229.

6. Alvord, *Eighth Semi-Annual Report*, 82.

7. John W. Alvord, *Sixth Semi-Annual Report on Schools for Freedmen* (Washington, D.C., 1868), 76–75, reprinted in Alvord, *Semi-Annual Report on Schools for Freedmen*.

8. John W. Alvord, *Third Semi-Annual Report on Schools for Freedmen* (Washington, D.C., 1867), 16, reprinted in Alvord, *Semi-Annual Report on Schools for Freedmen*; quoted in Henry Allen Bullock, *A History of Negro Education in the South from 1619 to the Present* (Cambridge, Mass., 1967), 42.

9. Quoted in Katherine Smedley, *Martha Schofield and the Re-education of the South, 1939–1916* (Lewiston, N.Y., 1987), 85; Alvord, *Third Semi-Annual Report*, 23–24.

10. John W. Alvord, *Inspector's Report* (Washington, D.C., 1866), 9, 9–10, reprinted in Alvord, *Semi-Annual Report on Schools for Freedmen*.

11. George N. Comer, *Penmanship Made Easy* (Boston, 1864), n.p.; Noah Porter,

"Science and Sentiment," with Other Papers, Chiefly Philosophical (New York, 1882), 36–37.

12. *McGuffey's Fourth Eclectic Reader,* rev. ed. (New York, 1879), 62.

13. Carl E. Seashore, "The District School," *Palimpsest* 23 (1942): 106.

14. Comer, *Penmanship,* 4.

15. Valentine Kimmel, salutatory address in C. W. Unger Papers, WM&G.

16. *McGuffey's Fifth Eclectic Reader,* rev. ed. (New York, 1879), 40, 41, 42.

17. Valentine Kimmel, miscellaneous writings, in C. W. Unger Papers, WM&G.

18. *McGuffey's First Eclectic Reader,* rev. ed. (New York, 1879), 51, 73, 83.

19. *Freedman's Spelling-Book,* 109; *Freedman's Second Reader,* 35, 36; *Freedman's Third Reader* (1865–66; reprint, New York, 1980), 31, 32.

20. *Freedman's Spelling-Book,* 109; *Freedman's Second Reader,* 38, 39; *Freedman's Third Reader,* 209.

21. *Freedman's Spelling-Book,* 141; quoted in Alvord, *Third Semi-Annual Report,* 15–16.

22. *Freedman's Spelling-Book,* 15; *Freedman's Second Reader,* 63–64.

23. *Freedman's Spelling-Book,* 54, 85; *Freedman's Second Reader,* 71.

24. Joe M. Richardson, "The Negro in Post Civil-War Tennessee: A Report by a Northern Missionary," *Journal of Negro Education* 34 (1965): 421; quoted in Smedley, *Schofield,* 82.

25. Alvord, *Eighth Semi-Annual Report,* 83.

26. Quoted in Joe M. Richardson, *Christian Reconstruction: The American Missionary Association and Southern Blacks, 1861–1890* (Athens, Ga., 1986), 44.

27. Quoted in Smedley, *Schofield,* 85; John W. Alvord, *Fourth Semi-Annual Report on Schools for Freedmen* (Washington, D.C., 1867), 64, reprinted in Alvord *Semi-Annual Report on Schools for Freedmen.*

28. J. A. Congdon, *The Normal and Commercial System of Penmanship* (Philadelphia, 1868), n.p.; Daniel T. Ames, *Ames' Compendium of Practical and Ornamental Penmanship,* new ed. (New York, 1883), 9.

29. Reward of merit, in C. W. Unger Papers, WM&G; scrapbook of school rewards, Mendsen Collection, WM&G.

30. *McGuffey's First Reader,* 94.

31. Quoted in Richardson, *Christian Reconstruction,* 47.

32. For a wonderful account of a school spelling bee, see Edward Eggleston, *The Hoosier Schoolmaster: A Story of Backwoods Life in Indiana* (New York, 1871), ch. 4.

33. *Freedman's Spelling-Book,* 109, 110.

34. *Freedman's Third Reader,* 132.

35. *Freedman's Third Reader,* 132.

35. "The Little Chimney Sweep," *McGuffey's First Eclectic Reader,* 95, reprinted in Stanley W. Lindberg, *The Annotated McGuffey: Selections from the McGuffey Eclectic Readers, 1836–1920* (New York, 1976), 17.

36. *McGuffey's Sixth Eclectic Reader,* rev. ed. (New York, 1879), 266–69.

37. *Freedman's Second Reader,* 157; *Freedman's Third Reader,* 47.

38. *McGuffey's Sixth Reader,* rev. ed., 256–57.

39. *McGuffey's New Sixth Eclectic Reader* (New York, 1867), 458, 459.

40. *McGuffey's Sixth Reader,* rev. ed., 253.

41. *The First Reader, for Southern Schools* (Raleigh, N.C., 1864), 16–17; Albert D. Kirwan, ed., *The Confederacy: A Social and Political History in Documents* (New York, 1959), 94; quoted in Lawrence F. London, "Confederate Literature and Its Publishers," in *Studies in Southern History*, ed. J. Carlyle Sitterson (Chapel Hill, N.C., 1957), 13; *First Reader*, 46.

42. William Naylor McDonald and J. S. Blackbum, *A Southern School History of the United States of America* (Baltimore, 1869), passim.

43. Thomas Wentworth Higginson, *Young Folks' History of the United States* (New York, 1875), iv; William D. Swan, *First Lessons in the History of the United States by a Practical Teacher* (Boston, 1861), 77.

44. John C. Ridpath, *History of the United States Prepared Especially for Schools* (1876; reprint, New York, 1974), 12–14.

45. William Swinton, *A Condensed School History of the United States* (Boston, 1868), iv.

46. Ridpath, *History of the United States*, 338.

47. Ames, *Ames' Compendium*, 9; exercise books of Helen M. Putnam of Atkinson, N.H., 1854, WM&G.

48. Quoted in Alvord, *Eighth Semi-Annual Report*, 84.

49. Ibid.

50. Joseph Downs Manuscript Collection.

Chapter Five

1. Burton J. Bledstein, *The Culture of Professionalism: The Middle Class and the Development of Higher Education in America* (New York, 1976), 278; Colin Burke, *American Collegiate Populations: A Test of the Traditional View* (New York, 1982), 218; Louise L. Stevenson, "Preparing for Public Life: The Collegiate Students at New York University, 1832–1881," in Thomas Bender, ed., *The University and the City from Medieval Origins to the Present* (New York, 1988), 158; Barbara Miller Solomon, *In the Company of Educated Women: A History of Women and Higher Education in America* (New Haven, Conn., 1985), 127.

2. Burke, *Collegiate Populations*, 216.

3. Quoted in Stephen M. Clement, "Aspects of Student Religion at Vassar College, 1861–1914" (Ed. D. diss., Harvard University, April 1977), 44.

4. Quoted in George E. Peterson, *The New England College in the Age of the University* (Amherst, Mass., 1964), 37.

5. Quoted in Louise L. Stevenson, *Scholarly Means to Evangelical Ends: The New Haven Scholars and the Transformation of Higher Learning in America, 1830–1890* (Baltimore, 1986), 73.

6. James Dwight Dana, *Manual of Mineralogy*, quoted in Stevenson, *Scholarly Means*, 76,

7. Quoted in Stevenson, *Scholarly Means*, 60; Stevenson, "Preparing for Public Life," 161.

8. Quoted in Stevenson, *Scholarly Means*, 53.

9. William S. Powell, *The First State University: A Pictorial History of the University of North Carolina* (Chapel Hill, N.C., 1972), 84, 91.

10. Quoted in Stevenson, "Preparing for Public Life," 163, 168.

11. Quoted in ibid., 150.

12. Quoted in Peterson, *New England College*, 31.

13. Quoted in Stevenson, *Scholarly Means*, 127, 61.

14. Quoted in ibid., 40.

15. Charles William Eliot, "The New Education," *Atlantic Monthly* 23 (1869): 218.

16. Charles William Eliot, inaugural address as president of Harvard University (1869), reprinted in Richard Hofstadter and Wilson Smith, eds., *American Higher Education: A Documentary History* (Chicago, 1961), 623.

17. The Morrill Act of 1862, reprinted in Hofstadter and Smith, *American Higher Education*, 568.

18. Inaugural address of John Milton Gregory, reprinted in Richard A. Hatch, ed., *Some Founding Papers of the University of Illinois* (Urbana, Ill., 1967), 100, 112.

19. Quoted in Robin Brabham, "Defining the American University: The University of North Carolina, 1865–1875," *North Carolina Historical Review* 57 (October 1980): 434.

20. Burke, *Collegiate Populations*, 222.

21. Hatch, *Papers of the University of Illinois*, 87.

22. Quoted in Hugh Hawkins, *Between Harvard and America: The Educational Leadership of Charles W. Eliot* (New York, 1971), 174.

23. Ibid., 94.

24. James T. Moore, "The University and the Readjusters," *Virginia Magazine of History and Biography* 78 (January 1970): 91; quoted in Stevenson, "Preparing for Public Life," 168.

25. See Ollinger Crenshaw, *General Lee's College: The Rise and Growth of Washington and Lee University* (New York, 1869), 202.

26. Quoted in Stevenson, "Preparing for Public Life," 167.

27. John W. Alvord, *Fourth Semi-Annual Report on Schools for Freedmen* (Washington, D.C., 1867), 63, reprinted in Alvord, *Semi-Annual Report on Schools for Freedmen*; Alvord, *Fifth Semi-Annual Report on Schools for Freedmen* (Washington, D.C., 1868), 11, reprinted in Alvord, *Semi-Annual Report on Schools for Freedmen*, Alvord, *Ninth Semi-Annual Report on Schools for Freedmen* (Washington, D.C., 1870), 63, reprinted in Alvord, *Semi-Annual Report on Schools for Freedmen*.

28. Cynthia Griggs Fleming, "A Survey of the Beginnings of Tennessee's Black Colleges and Universities, 1865–1920," *Tennessee Historical Quarterly* 39 (1980): 203.

29. Smedley, *Schofield*, 181.

30. Quoted in James D. Anderson, *The Education of Blacks in the South, 1860–1935* (Chapel Hill, N.C., 1988), 30.

31. Matthew Vassar quoted in Clement, "Aspects of Student Religion," 44; Association for the Advancement of Women *Annual Report for 1873* (New York, 1874), 93; quoted in Mabel Newcomer, *A Century of Higher Education for American Women* (New York, 1959), 26.

32. Address of Henry W. Sage, in *Proceedings at the Laying of the Corner Stone of the Sage College of Cornell University* (Ithaca, N.Y., 1873), 15, 10.

33. Ibid., 11, 14.

34. W. Paul Gamble, "Westminster College: Pioneer in Co-education and Participant in the 1850–1900 Curriculum Revolution," paper presented at the Duquesne History Forum, Pittsburgh, Pa., 21 October 1983, 5.

35. Charlotte Williams Conable, *Women at Cornell: The Myth of Equal Education* (Ithaca, N.Y., 1987), 87.

36. Quoted in William Hall Cate, "The Development of Higher Education for Women in Virginia," (Ph.D. diss., University of Virginia, 1941), 162, 163.

37. Quoted in Winton U. Solberg, *The University of Illinois, 1867–1894: An Intellectual and Cultural History* (Urbana, Ill., 1968), 162.

38. M. Carey Thomas, *The Making of a Feminist: Early Journals and Letters of M. Carey Thomas*, ed. Marjorie Housepian Dobkin (Kent, Ohio, 1979), 103.

39. Quoted in Dorothy Gies McGuigan, *A Dangerous Experiment: 100 Years of Women at the University of Michigan* (Ann Arbor, Mich., 1970), 32, 33–34.

40. Quoted in ibid., 49.

41. Quoted in Conable, *Women at Cornell*, 118.

42. Carol Bleser, ed. *The Hammonds of Redcliffe* (New York, 1981), 189; Thomas, *Making of a Feminist*, 121.

43. Newcomer, *Century of Higher Education*, 49.

44. Quoted in Alice Hackett Harter, *Wellesley: Part of the American Story* (Lexington, Mass., 1949), 39; quoted in Cornelia M. Raymond, *Memories of a Child of Vassar* (Poughkeepsie, N.Y., 1940), 45.

45. Solberg, *University of Illinois*, 158.

46. Newcomer, *Century of Higher Education*, 92.

47. Association for the Advancement of Women, *Annual Report for 1880* (Boston, 1881), 9; quoted in Edward T. James and Janet Wilson James, eds., *Notable American Women, 1607–1950*, (Cambridge, Mass., 1971), s.v. "Maria Mitchell."

48. Quoted in Harter, *Wellesley*, 39.

49. Quoted in Clement, "Aspects of Student Religion," 144.

50. Quoted in Frances A. Wood, *Earliest Years at Vassar* (Poughkeepsie, N.Y., 1909), 90, 97.

51. Quoted in Patricia Palmieri, "*Incipit Vita Nuova*: Founding Ideals of the Wellesley College Community," *History of Higher Education* 3 (1983): 65; Raymond, *Memories of a Child*, 5.

52. Quoted in Newcomer, *Century of Higher Education*, 225.

53. Quoted in Palmieri, "*Incipit Vita Nuova*," 69.

54. Quoted in Clement, "Aspects of Student Religion," 132; quoted in Raymond, *Memories of a Child*, 63.

55. William Watts Folwell, *University Addresses* (Minneapolis, 1909), 27.

Chapter Six

1. Quoted in Mary Kelley, *Private Woman, Public Stage: Literary Domesticity in Nineteenth-Century America* (New York, 1984), 214.

2. Smedley, *Schofield*, 66.

3. Alice Cary, "On Seeing a Wild Bird," in *Ballads, Lyrics, and Hymns* (New York, 1876), 159.

4. For descriptions of various revivals, see D. L. Moody, *The Great Redemption, Containing Sermons, Bible Readings, Addresses, etc.* 10th ed. (Chicago, 1893).

5. Henry Ward Beecher, *Yale Lectures on Preaching* (New York, 1873), 40; Phillips Brooks, *Lectures on Preaching Delivered before the Divinity School of Yale College* (New York, 1877), 244.

6. Maris A. Vinovskis, "Have Historians Lost the Civil War: Some Preliminary Demographic Speculations," *Journal of American History* 76 (1989): passim.

7. Quoted in Colleen McDannell, *The Christian Home in Victorian American, 1840–1900* (Bloomington, Ind., 1986), 83; *Civil War Songbook*, 86.

8. Elizabeth Stuart Phelps, *The Gates Ajar* (1868; reprint, Cambridge, Mass., 1964), 66.

9. Ibid., 54.

10. Ibid., 38, 109, 110.

11. Phillips Brooks, *The Life and Death of Abraham Lincoln* . . . (Philadelphia, 1865), 17, 18, and passim.

12. Henry Ward Beecher, *Norwood, or, Village Life in New England* (1867; reprint, New York, 1895), 494.

13. Quoted in Earl J. Hess, *Liberty, Virtue, and Progress: Northerners and Their War for the Union* (New York, 1988), 33.

14. Crawford, *Civil War Songbook*, 2–3.

15. Quoted in Hess, *Liberty, Virtue, and Progress*, 35, 36.

16. Crawford, *Civil War Songbook*, 18–19.

17. Gail Hamilton (Mary Abigail Dodge), "A Call to My Country-Women," *Atlantic Monthly* 11 (1863): 348, 349.

18. Quoted in Randall C. Jimerson, *The Private Civil War: Popular Thought during the Sectional Conflict* (Baton Rouge, La., 1988), 20, 21.

19. Roy P. Basler, ed., *The Collected Works of Abraham Lincoln*, 9 vols. (New Brunswick, N.J., 1953), 8:333.

20. Louisa May Alcott, *Hospital Sketches and Campfire Stories* (New York, 1872), 314, 316.

21. Quoted in Drew Gilpin Faust, *A Sacred Circle: The Dilemma of the Intellectual in the Old South, 1840–1860* (Baltimore, 1977), 139.

22. Quoted in Gaines M. Foster, *Ghosts of the Confederacy: Defeat, the Lost Cause, and the Emergence of the New South, 1865 to 1913* (New York, 1987), 36.

23. Quoted in Louise L. Stevenson, ed., *The School and Its Students, 1847–1900*, vol. 1 of *Miss Porter's School: A History in Documents, 1847–1948* (New York, 1987), 47.

24. John William Draper, *History of the Conflict between Religion and Science* (New York, 1874), 367.

25. Quoted in D. H. Meyer, "The Victorian Crisis of Faith," in Howe, *Victorian America*, 63.

26. (Edward L. Youmans), "Purpose and Plan of Our Enterprise," *Popular Science Monthly* 1 (1872): 113; (Youmans), "Aim of Science Education," ibid. 3 (1873): 640.

27. (Youmans), "The Accusation of Atheism," ibid. 11 (1877): 369; (Youmans), "The Conflict of Ages," ibid. 8 (1876): 494.

28. Harriet Beecher Stowe, *We and Our Neighbors* (New York, 1875), 47.

29. Quoted in (Youmans), *Popular Science Monthly* 15 (1879): 413; quoted in Darrel M. Robertson, *The Chicago Revival, 1876: Society and Revivalism in a Nineteenth-Century City* (Metuchen, N.J., 1989), 186.

30. *The Countryman*, 14 June 1864.

31. *Mr. Moody's Methods: Reports of His Lectures and Work in Baltimore* (Baltimore, 1879); quoted in James F. Findlay, Jr., *Dwight L. Moody: American Evangelist, 1837–1899* (Chicago, 1969), 259.

32. Brooks, *Lectures on Preaching*, 225; Phillips Brooks, *Essays and Addresses* (1892), as quoted in Allen Johnson, ed., *Dictionary of American Biography*, (New York, 1929), s.v. "Phillips Brooks."

33. Charles Hodge, *What Is Darwinism?* quoted in George M. Marsden, *Fundamentalism and American Culture: The Shaping of Twentieth-Century Evangelicalism, 1870–1925* (New York, 1980), 19.

34. Quoted in Stevenson, *Scholarly Means*, 80.

35. For arguments against woman suffrage, see Horace Bushnell, *Women's Suffrage: The Crime against Nature* (New York, 1869), and Catharine Beecher, *Woman's Profession as Mother and Educator* (Hartford, 1872); for arguments in favor of woman suffrage, see Josiah Allen's Wife (Marietta Holley), *Josiah Allen's Wife as a P.A. [Promiscuous Advisor] and P.I. [Private Investigator]: Samantha at the Centennial* (Hartford, 1877), and Isabella Beecher Hooker, *A Mother's Letters to a Daughter on Woman's Suffrage* (Hartford, 1870).

36. Quoted in Judith Papachristou, *Women Together: A History in Documents of the Women's Movement in the United States* (New York, 1976), 75.

37. Quoted in ibid., 76.

38. Cary, *Ballads, Lyrics, and Hymns*, 230.

Chapter Seven

1. Harriet Beecher Stowe, *My Wife and I* (New York, 1871), 139.

2. *Scribner's Monthly* 1 (November 1870): 106.

3. *Chautauqua Assembly Herald* (June 1880).

4. Quoted in James H. McBath, "The Emergence of Chautauqua as a Religious and Educational Institution, 1874–1900," *Methodist History* 20 (1981): 3.

5. Quoted in James H. McBath, "Darwinism at Chautauqua," *Methodist History* 24 (1986): 231.

6. Quoted in Association for the Advancement of Women, *Report for 1878–1879* (Boston, 1879), 1.

7. Quoted in Helen Lefkowitz Horowitz, *Alma Mater: Design and Experience in the Women's Colleges from Their Nineteenth-Century Beginnings to the 1930s* (Boston, 1984), 60.

8. William Gilmore Simms, ed., *War Poetry of the South* (New York, 1866), 55.

9. Quoted in Mary Elizabeth Massey, *Bonnet Brigades* (New York, 1966), 125.

10. Quoted in Smedley, *Schofield*, 66–67.

11. Jennie June (Jane Cunningham Croly), *Sorosis: Its Origins and History* (1886; reprint, New York, 1975), 31; *Constitution and Bylaws of the Association for the Advancement of Women* (Boston, 1877), 3.

12. Quoted in *Papers of the Association for the Advancement of Women* (New York, 1874), 184.

13. Elizabeth Cady Stanton, "Coeducation," *Papers and Letters Presented at the First Woman's Congress of the Association for the Advancement of Women* (New York, 1874), 52.

14. *The Countryman*, 11 October 1862.

15. Quoted in Kirwan, *The Confederacy*, 101, 100.

16. "Southern War Poetry," *Southern Review*, new series, (1867): 283.

17. Quoted in Brooks, "The *Magnolia*," 155.

18. Quoted in E. Merton Coulter, "The New South: Benjamin H. Hill's Speech before the Alumni of the University of Georgia," *Georgia Historical Quarterly* 57 (1983): 182. See also Jack Claiborne, *The Charlotte Observer: Its Time and Place, 1869–1986* (Chapel Hill, N.C., 1986), which reveals how southern ideas began to change.

19. Quoted in Claiborne, *Charlotte Observer*, 9.

20. "Beadle's Dime Books," *North American Review* 99 (1864): 309.

21. Augusta Jane Evans (Wilson), *St. Elmo* (1867; reprint, New York, 1896), 491.

22. Ibid., 321.

23. Augusta Jane Evans (Wilson), *Macaria* (1864; reprint, New York, 1896), 347.

24. Ibid., 411; Wilson, *St. Elmo*, 404.

25. Ibid., *Nation* 1 (1865): 404.

26. See, for instance, Stowe, *My Wife and I*, 264–65.

27. *Nation* 1 (1865): 260.

28. "The Political South Hereafter," *Nation* 24 (1877): 202.

29. "The Educational Influences of Free Soup," *Nation* 24 (1876): 154–56; "The Late Riots," ibid. 25 (1877): 68.

30. "The Late Riots," ibid., 68–69.

31. Advertisement for the *New York Times* in *Harper's Weekly*, 15 December 1877.

32. "The Condition of Art in America," *North American Review* 102 (1866): 15.

33. "Chromo-Civilization," *Nation* 19 (1874): 202.

34. "Our First Year's Work," *Popular Science Monthly* 2 (1873): 746.

35. John W. Draper, *History of the Intellectual Development of Europe*, rev. ed. 2 vols. (New York, 1876), 2:392; Jacobi, quoted in William Leach, *True Love and Perfect Union: The Feminist Reform of Sex and Society* (New York, 1980), 141.

36. *"My Cave Life in Vicksburg," North American Review* 99 (1864): 309; John W. Draper, *Thoughts on the Future Civil Policy of America*, 4th ed. (New York, 1865), 252, 260, 261; *Life and Letters of Mary Putnam Jacobi*, (New York, 1915), quoted in Leach, *True Love*, 141.

37. Quoted in Thomas L. Haskell, *The Emergence of Professional Social Science: The American Social Science Association and the Nineteenth-Century Crisis of Authority* (Urbana, Ill., 1977), 98, 105.

38. C. E. Norton, ed., *Orations and Addresses of George William Curtis*, 3 vols. (New York, 1894), 2:196, 170, 27–28.

39. Gail Hamilton (Mary Abigail Dodge), "Civil Service Reform," *New-York Daily Tribune*, 10 August 1878.

40. Daniel Coit Gilman, inaugural address, in *Addresses at the Inauguration of Daniel Coit Gilman . . .* (Baltimore, 1876), 44.

41. Croly, *Sorosis*, 43.

42. *Harper's Weekly*, 20 January 1877, 664.

43. (Edward L. Youmans) "The Family and the State," *Popular Science Monthly* 11 (1877): 370.

44. Josiah Allen's Wife (Marietta Holley), *My Opinions and Betsey Bobbet's* (Hartford, 1872), 359.

Chapter Eight

1. My analysis draws on the 900 pages of Fourth of July speeches collected in Frederick Saunders, ed., *Our National Centennial Jubilee: Orations, Addresses, and Poems* (New York, 1877). Speakers on the Fourth came from all regions, from big cities and small towns, and from both the Republican and Democratic parties. Only two women (Miss Sarah Doughtery and Miss Clara B. Heath) contributed pieces because of the accepted exclusion of women from public life. Some orators were Irish, some Catholic, and some Jewish.

2. W. T. Avery, ibid., 559.

3. Rev. Morgan Dix, ibid., 346.

4. Rev. Hugh Miller Thompson, ibid., 635.

5. Rev. R. A. Holland, ibid., 627.

6. Ibid., 362.

7. Rev. Jeremiah Taylor, ibid., 476; Rev. Henry Ward Beecher, ibid., 362.

8. Ibid., 339.

9. Henry George, *Progress and Poverty: An Inquiry into the Cause of Industrial Depressions, and of the Increase of Want with Increase of Wealth* (New York, 1879), 496.

10. *Centennial Eagle*, no. 11 (1876): 225–26; James D. McCabe, *The Illustrated History of the Centennial Exhibition* (1876; reprint, Philadelphia, 1975), 111.

11. Saunders, *Our National Centennial*, 13, frontispiece.

12. Ibid., 376.

13. Quoted in John Hope Franklin, *George Washington Williams: A Biography* (Chicago, 1985), 107.

14. Quoted in Philip S. Foner, "Black Participation in the Centennial of 1876," *Phylon* 39 (1978): 287.

15. "A Declaration of Rights for Women," reprinted in Mari Jo and Paul Buhle, eds., *The Concise History of Woman Suffrage: Selections from the Classic Work of Stanton, Anthony, Gage, and Harper*, 297–303 (Urbana, Ill., 1978), 302, 303.

16. Holley, *Josiah Allen's Wife as a P.A. and P.I.*, 529–30.

Suggested Reading

Historians have written so many books on the Civil War and Reconstruction that a comprehensive bibliographical essay would fill an entire volume. Readers who wish more information on political, economic, and social topics should consult James M. McPherson, *Ordeal by Fire: The Civil War and Reconstruction* (New York, 1982), his *Battle Cry of Freedom: The Civil War Era* (New York, 1988), or Eric Foner's *Reconstruction: America's Unfinished Revolution* (New York, 1988). All contain extensive bibliographical essays.

The following essay includes articles and books that I found helpful while writing this book. It should give readers a starting point for independent investigation of cultural and intellectual life during the years 1860–80.

For The Introduction

Works useful for defining "middle class" and "Victorianism" are Stuart M. Blumin, "The Hypothesis of Middle-Class Formation in Nineteenth-Century America," *American Historical Review* 90 (1985): 299–338; his recently published *The Emergence of the Middle Class: Social Experience in the American City, 1760–1900* (New York, 1989); and Daniel Walker Howe, "Victorian Culture in America," in Daniel Walker Howe, ed., *Victorian America* (Philadelphia, 1976). Daniel D. Sutherland's *The Expansion of Everyday Life, 1860–1876* (New York, 1989) provides a brief, general discussion of the everyday life of non-Victorians as well as Victorians. Peter Gay, *The Bourgeois Experience: Victoria to Freud*, 2 vols. (New York, 1984) provides a transatlantic perspective and a look at life in middle-class bedrooms.

For Chapter One

Starting points for an investigation of Victorian homes and their parlors are the appropriate chapters of Clifford Edward Clark, Jr., *The American Family Home, 1830–1960* (Chapel Hill, N.C., 1986), and Colleen McDannell, *The Christian Home in Victorian America, 1840–1900* (Bloomington, Ind., 1986). For more detail and analysis, see Harvey Green, *The Light of the Home: An Intimate View of the Lives of Women in Victorian America* (New York, 1983), and Katherine C. Grier, *Culture and Comfort: People, Parlors, and Upholstery, 1850–1930* (Rochester, N.Y., 1988). For parlor behavior, see also Karen Halttunen, *Confidence Men and Painted Women: A Study of Middle-Class Culture in America, 1830–1870* (New Haven, Conn., 1982), though I am always suspicious of such highly interpretive analysis. Green and Grier tend to see women as captives of Victorianism and emphasize their subordination in the household. Harold L. Peterson, *American Interiors from Colonial Times to the Late Victorians* (New York, 1971), and William Seale, *The Tasteful Interlude: American Interiors through the Camera's Eye, 1860–1917* (New York, 1975) provide a visual overview of parlor decoration, and their texts and illustrations allow comparisons with earlier and later periods. See also Sally McMurry, *Families and Farmhouses in Nineteenth-Century America: Vernacular Design and Social Change* (New York, 1988), and George W. McDaniel, *Hearth and Home: Preserving a People's Culture* (Philadelphia, 1982), which covers southern African-American life in the postwar period. These books suggest that parlors were not found exclusively in the residences of urban whites. Martha Crabill McClaugherty, "Household Art: Creating the Artistic Home, 1868–1893," *Winterthur Portfolio* 18, no. 1 (Spring 1983): 1–26, introduces the major arbiters of household taste.

On pianos and parlor organs, see McDannell, *Christian Home*, Kenneth L. Ames, "Material Culture as NonVerbal Communication: A Historical Case Study," *Journal of American Culture* 3 (1980): 619–41, and Bruce Carlson, ed., *The Piano—A Mirror of American Life* (St. Paul, Minn., 1981). On reading, see Mary Lynn Stevens Heininger, *At Home with a Book: Reading in America, 1840–1940* (Rochester, N.Y., 1986). And on photography and stereographs, see William C. Darrah, *The World of Stereographs* (Gettysburg, Pa., 1977), Edward W. Earle, ed., *Points of View: The Stereograph in America—A Cultural History* (Rochester, N.Y., 1979), Peter B. Hales, *William Henry Jackson and the Transformation of the American Landscape* (Philadelphia, 1988), and Richard N. Masteller, "Western Views in Eastern Parlors: The Contribution of the Stereograph Photographer to the Conquest of the West," *Prospects* 6 (1981): 55–71.

Advanced students and scholars of the period and of Victorian material culture may also want to explore some of the theses produced by students of the Winterthur Program of the University of Delaware. See especially Gail Lorene Dennis, "American Factory-Made Parlor Suites, 1871–1901" (Master's thesis, University of Delaware, 1982); Susan Ruth Finkel, "Victorian Photography and Cartes de Visite Albums" (Master's thesis, University of Delaware, 1979); Donald B. Pierce, "Mitchell and Rammelsberg: Cincinnati Furniture Makers, 1847–1881" (Master's thesis, University of Delaware, 1976); Richard Henry Saunders, "American Decorative Arts Collecting in New England, 1840–1920" (Master's thesis, University of Delaware, 1973).

For Chapter Two

Contemporary historians are devoting much attention to the subjects of books and reading. See Heininger, *At Home with a Book*, and Barbara Sicherman, "Sense and Sensibility: A Case Study of Women's Reading in Late-Victorian America," in Cathy N. Davidson, ed., *Reading in America: Literature and Social History* (Baltimore, 1989). Frank Luther Mott, *Golden Multitudes: The Story of Best Sellers in the United States* (New York, 1947), and James D. Hart, *The Popular Book: A History of America's Literary Taste* (New York, 1950) catalog popular reading. Dee Garrison describes the "immoral" best-sellers that Victorians were reading and suggests why women were reading them in "Immoral Fiction in the Late Victorian Library," in Howe, *Victorian America*. For newspapers, see Dan Schiller, *Objectivity and the News: The Public and the Rise of Commercial Journalism* (Philadelphia, 1981), and for magazine reading, see the appropriate volumes of Frank Luther Mott, *A History of American Magazines*, 5 vols. (Cambridge, Mass., 1938–68). Mott's work is so thorough that it is still one of the best introductions to the literary culture of the years 1860–80. In *Mechanic Accents: Dime Novels and Working-Class Culture in America* (New York, 1987), Michael Denning describes and analyzes the reading interests of working people. On obscenity laws and Anthony Comstock, Paul S. Boyer, *Purity in Print: The Vice Society Movement and Book Censorship in America* (New York, 1968), and Frederick F. Schauer, *The Law of Obscenity* (Washington, D.C., 1976) provide essential information.

On the subject of reading during the war years, there are few books that focus on the North. George Winston Smith and Charles Judah, *Life in the North during the Civil War* (Albuquerque, N.M., 1966) is somewhat helpful. Mary Elizabeth Massey tells what women in the North and the South were doing to help the war effort, including being authors, in *Bonnet Brigades* (New York, 1966). For southern reading, see John Austin Edwards's encyclopedic dissertation, "Social and Cultural Activities of Texans during the Civil War and Reconstruction, 1861–1873" (Ph.D. diss., Texas Technical University, 1985), and Mary Elizabeth Massey, *Refugee Life in the Confederacy* (Baton Rouge, La., 1964).

Bell Irvin Wiley discusses soldiers' reading in *The Life of Johnny Reb: The Common Soldier of the Confederacy* (Baton Rouge, La., 1978), and *The Life of Billy Yank: The Common Soldier of the Union* (Garden City, N.Y., 1971). Other historians are less skeptical about soldiers' pursuing serious entertainment. See Fletcher Melvin Green, "Johnny Reb Could Read," in Fletcher Melvin Green, *Democracy in the Old South and Other Essays*, ed. J. Isaac Copeland (Nashville, 1969); David Kaser, *Books and Libraries in Camp and Battle: The Civil War Experience* (Westport, Conn., 1984); Lawrence F. London, "Confederate Literature and Its Publishers," in J. Carlyle Sitterson, ed., *Studies in Southern History* (Chapel Hill, N.C., 1957); and Annette Woolard, "Camp Life of Delaware Troops in the Union Army," *Delaware History* 21 (1984): 1–21.

For Chapter Three

As yet, historians have not fully and completely described urban life during the Civil War and Reconstruction. See Michael H. Frisch, *Town into City: Springfield, Massachusetts, and the Meaning of Community, 1840–1880* (Cambridge, Mass., 1972). Don Harrison Doyle, *The Social Order of a Frontier Community: Jacksonville, Illinois, 1825–*

1870 (Urbana, Ill. 1978), and Richard Sennett, *Families against the City: Middle-Class Homes of Industrial Chicago, 1872–1890* (Cambridge, Mass., 1970) take middle-class urban life as their subject. For the development of southern cities, see Doyle, *New Men, New Cities, New South: Atlanta, Nashville, Charleston, Mobile, 1860–1910* (Chapel Hill, N.C., 1990).

Historians are giving non-Victorian urban populations increasing attention. See especially Francis G. Couvares, *The Remaking of Pittsburgh: Class and Culture in an Industrializing City, 1877–1919* (Albany, N.Y., 1984). For the leisure pursuits of working people, see Roy Rosenzweig, *Eight Hours for What We Will: Workers and Leisure in an Industrial City, 1870–1920* (New York, 1983). Christine Stansell describes the experiences of poor and working women in *City of Women: Sex and Class in New York, 1789–1860* (New York, 1986).

For lyceums and lectures, see Mary Kupiec Cayton, "The Making of an American Prophet: Emerson, His Audiences, and the Rise of the Culture Industry in Nineteenth-Century America," *American Historical Review* 92 (1987): 597–620; Donald M. Scott, "The Popular Lecture and the Creation of a Public in Mid-Nineteenth-Century America," *Journal of American History* 66 (1980): 791–809; and his "Print and the Public Lecture System, 1840–1860," in Walter L. Joyce, et al., eds., *Printing and Society in Early America* (Worcester, Mass., 1983), 278–99. Older publications that include more anecdotes and color are David Mead, *Yankee Eloquence in the Middle West: The Ohio Lyceum, 1850–1870* (East Lansing, Mich., 1951), and Huburt H. Hoeltje, "Notes on the History of Lecturing in Iowa, 1855–1885," *Iowa Journal of History and Politics* 25 (1927): 62–131.

The starting point for a women's clubs is Jane C. Croly, *The History of the Woman's Club Movement in America* (New York, 1898). Recent studies include Theodora Penny Martin, *The Sound of Our Own Voices: Women's Study Clubs, 1860–1910* (Boston, 1987); and Karen J. Blair, *The Clubwoman as Feminist: True Womanhood Redefined, 1868–1914* (New York, 1980).

Neil Harris provides an overview of the development of urban cultural institutions in "Four Stages of Cultural Growth: The American City," in Arthur Mann, Neil Harris, Sam Bass Warner, Jr., *History and the Role of the City in American Life, Indiana Historical Society Lectures, 1971–72* (Indianapolis, 1972), 24–49. For the politics of cultural reform, see Geoffrey Blodgett, "Frederick Law Olmsted: Landscape Architecture as Conservative Reform," *Journal of American History* 62 (1976): 869–89. Although it focuses on Olmsted, Blodgett's article has broad relevance for understanding mid-century liberal reformers and the cultural institutions they sponsored. Helen Lefkowitz Horowitz discusses the background and rationale behind the founding of Chicago cultural institutions in the first four chapters of *Culture and the City: Cultural Philanthropy in Chicago from the 1880s to 1917* (1976; reprint, Chicago, 1989). Lawrence W. Levine emphasizes the role of elites in sponsoring cultural institutions in his *Highbrow, Lowbrow: The Emergence of Cultural Hierarchy in America* (Cambridge, Mass., 1988). David D. Hall reconstructs the transatlantic network of literary liberals in "The Victorian Connection," in Howe, *Victorian America*.

On parks as related to urban design, see David Schuyler's *The New Urban Landscape: The Redefinition of City Form in Nineteenth-Century America* (Baltimore, 1986), which focuses on the urban planning of Frederick Law Olmsted. In "From Promenade to Park: The Gregarious Origins of Brooklyn's Park Movement," *American Quarterly* 39

(1987): 529–50, Daniel M. Bluestone argues that parks provided a specialized locale for social interaction. See also the informative introduction to Frederick Law Olmsted, *Creating Central Park, 1857–1861*, vol. 3 of *The Papers of Frederick Law Olmsted*, ed. Charles E. Beveridge and David Schuyler (Baltimore, 1983).

Two helpful books on libraries are Dee Garrison, *Apostles of Culture: The Public Librarian and American Society, 1876–1920* (New York, 1979), and Evelyn Geller, *Forbidden Books in American Public Libraries, 1876–1939: A Study in Cultural Change* (Westport, Conn., 1984). Geller provides a full and fair explanation of why Victorians considered some books undesirable reading.

An overview of museum history can be found in Daniel M. Fox, *Engines of Culture: Philanthropy and Art Museums* (Madison, Wis., 1963). Readers should also consult Neil Harris's *Humbug: The Art of P. T. Barnum* (1973: reprint, Chicago, 1981) to gain a more complete view of museums at midcentury. A. H. Saxon, *P. T. Barnum: The Legend and the Man* (New York, 1989) provides a wealth of information on Barnum and urban amusements. Harris provides a provocative study of change in the mission of museums in "The Gilded Age Revisited: Boston and the Museum Movement," *American Quarterly* 14 (1962): 545–66, though my research suggests that midcentury museums were more selective in their collections than Harris allows. Narrative histories of the two most important museums of the period are Winifred E. Howe, *A History of the Metropolitan Museum of Art: With a Chapter on the Early Institutions of Art in New York* (New York, 1913), and Walter Muir Whitehill, *The Museum of Fine Arts, Boston: A Centennial History* (Cambridge, Mass., 1970).

For Chapter Four

There is a wealth of information on African-American education in the South. James D. Anderson, *The Education of Blacks in the South, 1860–1935* (Chapel Hill, N.C., 1988) supplements Henry Allen Bullock, *A History of Negro Education in the South: From 1619 to the Present* (Cambridge, Mass., 1967) as the standard history of southern African-American education starting in 1860. Anderson emphasizes the contributions of African-Americans to their own education. The one recent history of freedmen's education is Robert C. Morris, *Reading, 'Riting, and Reconstruction: The Education of Freedmen in the South, 1861–1870* (1976; reprint Chicago, 1981). Joe Martin Richardson, *Christian Reconstruction: The American Missionary Association and Southern Blacks, 1861–1890* (Athens, Ga., 1986) offers additional information on freedmen's schools as well as on colleges for African-Americans.

The efforts of northerners to educate freed men and women have evoked much historical controversy. In his *Northern Schools, Southern Blacks, and Reconstruction: Freedmen's Education, 1862–1875* (Westport, Conn., 1980), Ronald E. Butchart criticizes the organizers and teachers of freedmen's schools for their ethnocentric approach to southern African-American culture. In *Soldiers of Light and Love, Northern Teachers and Georgia Blacks, 1865–1973* (Chapel Hill, N.C., 1980), Jacqueline Jones judges the teachers more sympathetically. Katherine Smedley, *Martha Schofield and the Re-education of the South, 1839–1916* (Lewiston, N.Y., 1987) is another balanced treatment of a white educator's efforts in the postwar South.

Surveys of white attitudes toward African-Americans may be found in Guy C. McElroy, *Facing History: The Black Image in American Art, 1710–1940* (San Francisco, 1990), and George M. Fredrickson, *The Black Image in the White Mind: The Debate on Afro-American Character and Destiny, 1817–1914* (New York, 1971), which covers the attitudes of academics, ministers, scientists, and men of letters. For images of African-Americans in everyday American life, see Sam Dennison, *Scandalize My Name: Black Imagery in American Popular Music* (Westport, Conn., 1982).

A starting point for further reading on common schools should be Carl F. Kaestle, *Pillars of the Republic: Common Schools and American Society, 1780–1860* (New York, 1983). For a rich analysis, as well as nuggets of information, see Lawrence A. Cremin, *American Education: The National Experience, 1783–1876* (New York, 1982). Lee Soltow and Edward Stevens reveal what literacy meant in common schools in their *The Rise of Literacy and the Common School in the United States: A Socioeconomic Analysis to 1870* (Chicago, 1981). Reconstruction of the classroom experience of the common school can be found in Jean H. Baker, *Affairs of Party: The Political Culture of Northern Democrats in the Mid-Nineteenth Century* (Ithaca, N.Y., 1983). ch. 2, and Wayne E. Fuller, *The Old Country School: The Story of Rural Education in the Middle West* (Chicago, 1982). The notes to both these books also contain references to memoirs and autobiographical writings that discuss daily life in common schools. For southern schoolbooks, see the works on southern reading cited in the chapter 2 section above. For the cultural and political tasks that southerners assigned to their schools, see Drew Gilpin Faust, *The Creation of Confederate Nationalism: Ideology and Identity in the Civil War South* (Baton Rouge, La., 1988).

For Chapter Five

An exploration of the history of higher education could profitably begin with an understanding of the relationship between the development of professionalism and collegiate and university reform. Introductions to these subjects appear in Burton J. Bledstein, *The Culture of Professionalism: The Middle Class and the Development of Higher Education in America* (New York, 1976); Thomas L. Haskell, *The Emergence of Professional Social Science: The American Social Science Association and the Nineteenth-Century Crisis of Authority* (Urbana, Ill., 1977); and Laurence R. Veysey, *The Emergence of the American University* (Chicago, 1965).

Until recently, historians of American collegiate and university education have emphasized the backwardness of colleges; they have located change and reform at state universities and at one or two private institutions, namely, Harvard and Johns Hopkins University. The following books belong to this tradition of historiography but are worthwhile surveys nonetheless. George E. Peterson, *The New England College in the Age of the University* (Amherst, Mass., 1964) is an excellent introduction to the meaning of liberal arts in the last half of the nineteenth century, and Veysey, *Emergence of the American University* is an equally valuable and thought-provoking introduction to reform in higher education. Veysey's discussion of Harvard and Johns Hopkins should be supplemented by Hugh Hawkins's studies of those institutions, *Between Harvard and America: The Educational Leadership of Charles W. Eliot* (New York,

1971), and *Pioneer: A History of Johns Hopkins University, 1874–1889* (Ithaca, N.Y., 1960).

Notable studies disputing the necessary association of religious conviction and educational backwardness include David J. Hoeveler, Jr., *James McCosh and the Scottish Intellectual Tradition: From Glasgow to Princeton* (Princeton, N.J. 1981), and Winton U. Solberg, *The University of Illinois, 1867–1894: An Intellectual and Cultural History* (Urbana, Ill, 1968). Other revisionist works include Colin Burke, *American Collegiate Populations: A Test of the Traditional View* (New York, 1982), and Louise L. Stevenson, *Scholarly Means to Evangelical Ends: The New Haven Scholars and the Transformation of Higher Learning in America, 1830–1890* (Baltimore, 1986). Two articles by Bruce Leslie, "Localism, Denominationalism, and Institutional Strategies in Urbanizing America: Three Pennsylvania Colleges, 1870–1915," *History of Education Quarterly* (Fall 1977): 235–56, and "The Re-emergence of the American College: A Multiple-Case Study, 1870–1920," *Liberal Education* 62 (1976): 507–26, suggest that the story of the development of collegiate curricula presented in Frederick Rudolph, *Curriculum: A History of the American Undergraduate Course of Study since 1636* (San Francisco, 1976) may overgeneralize and misrepresent academic life at liberal arts colleges.

There is no reliable comprehensive picture of nineteenth-century student life at colleges and universities. I turned to the histories of individual colleges and universities named in this bibliography and to my own "Preparing for Public Life: The Collegiate Student at New York University, 1832–1881," in Thomas Bender, ed., *The University and the City from Medieval Origins to the Present* (New York, 1988). Three articles that discuss student life at southern colleges are Alden G. Bigelow, "Student Life at Hampden-Sydney College, 1872–1876," *Virginia Magazine of History and Biography* 87 (1979): 448–54; Calvin Dickinson, "Collegiate Life in Nineteenth Century Texas," *Texana* (Winter 1969): 313–21; and Stanley J. Folmsbee, "Campus Life at the University of Tennessee, 1794–1879," *East Tennessee Historical Society Publications* 45 (1973): 25–50. Monroe H. Little describes African-American student life in "The Extra-Curricular Activities of Black College Students, 1868–1940," *Journal of Negro History* 65 (1980): 135–48. Readers in need of a broad survey may turn to Helen Horowitz, *Campus Life: Undergraduate Cultures from the End of the Eighteenth Century to the Present* (New York, 1987).

Higher education in the postwar South has been undeservedly ignored by historians who write about national educational trends. As an introduction to southern developments, Thomas G. Byer, "Higher Education in the South since the Civil War: Historiographical Issues and Trends," Walter J. Fraser, Jr., et al., ed., *The Web of Southern Social Relations: Women, Family, and Education* (Athens, Ga., 1985) is valuable. The best studies of individual institutions are Robin Brabham, "Defining the American University: The University of North Carolina, 1865–1875," *North Carolina Historical Review* 57 (October 1980): 427–55; Paul K. Conkin, *Gone with the Ivy: A Biography of Vanderbilt University* (Knoxville, Tenn., 1985); and Ollinger Crenshaw, *General Lee's College: The Rise and Growth of Washington and Lee University* (New York, 1869). Other publications that reveal the diversity of the southern educational experience are James R. Montgomery, et. al., *To Foster Knowledge; A History of the University of Tennessee, 1794–1970* (Knoxville, Tenn., 1984); Arthur Ben Chitty, Jr., *Reconstruction at Sewanee: The Founding of the University of the South and Its First Administration, 1857–*

1872 (Sewanee, Tenn., 1954); and James T. Moore, "The University and the Read-justers," *Virginia Magazine of History and Biography* 78 (January 1970): 87–101.

The book that most closely approaches being a survey of southern African-American colleges and universities in the postwar period is Richardson, *Christian Reconstruction*. Its focus on the activities of the American Missionary Association precludes, however, its being comprehensive. Cynthia Griggs Fleming, "A Survey of the Beginnings of Tennessee's Black Colleges and Universities, 1865–1920," *Tennessee Historical Quarterly* 39 (1980): 195–207, catalog developments in one state. Useful histories of individual institutions include Clarence A. Bacote, *The Story of Atlanta University: A Century of Service, 1865–1965* (Atlanta, 1969); John K. Bittersworth, "The Cow in the Front Yard: How a Land Grant University Grew in Mississippi," *Agricultural History* 53 (1979): 62–70; and Joe M. Richardson, *A History of Fisk University, 1865–1946* (University, Ala., 1980). Historians who address the issue of vocational education are Anderson, *Education of Blacks*; Louis R. Harlan, *Booker T. Washington: The Making of a Black Leader, 1856–1901* (New York, 1972); Richardson, *Christian Reconstruction*; and Smedley, *Martha Schofield*.

Historians studying coeducational colleges and universities and women's colleges have a recent, comprehensive survey to draw on, namely, Barbara Miller Solomon, *In the Company of Educated Women: A History of Women and Higher Education in America* (New Haven, Conn., 1985). A useful anthology is John Mack Faragher and Florence Howe, eds., *Women and Higher Education in American History: Essays from the Mount Holyoke College Sesquicentennial Symposia* (New York, 1988). These works supersede two others that are still useful for their extensive detail: Mabel Newcomer, *A Century of Higher Education for American Women* (New York, 1959), and Thomas Woody, *A History of Women's Education in the United States*, vol. 2 (1929; reprint, New York, 1974). Helen Lefkowitz Horowitz, *Alma Mater: Design and Experience in the Women's Colleges from Their Nineteenth-Century Beginnings to the 1930s* (Boston, 1984) attempts to show how the architecture of women's colleges embodies their educational purposes.

On the experience of coeducation, see especially Charlotte Williams Conable, *Women at Cornell: The Myth of Equal Education* (Ithaca, N.Y., 1987); Dorothy Gies McGuigan, *A Dangerous Experiment: 100 Years of Women at the University of Michigan* (Ann Arbor, Mich., 1970); Lynn D. Gordon, "Coeducation on Two Campuses: Berkeley and Chicago, 1890–1912," in Mary Kelley, ed., *Woman's Being, Woman's Place: Female Identity and Vocation in American History* (Boston, 1979); and Joan G. Zimmerman, "Daughters of Main Street: Culture and the Female Community at Grinnell, 1884–1917," in Kelley, *Woman's Being*.

Other studies include Alice Hackett Harter's somewhat dated *Wellesley: Part of the American Story* (Lexington, Mass., 1949), and Patricia Palmieri's "Incipit Vita Nuova: Founding Ideals of the Wellesley College Community," *History of Higher Education* 3 (1983): 59–78. Jeanne L. Noble has written a brief history, *The Negro Woman's College Education* (New York, 1956).

For Chapter Six

The history of intellectuals is far from completely written. Women intellectuals do not yet have their own history in this or any other period of American history. William Leach discusses the activities of the more advanced women thinkers of 1860–80 in *True Love and Perfect Union: The Feminist Reform of Sex and Society* (New York, 1980). Women authors' contribution to the war effort is catalogued in Massey, *Bonnet Brigades* and analyzed by Drew Gilpin Faust in "Altars of Sacrifice: Confederate Women and the Narratives of War," *Journal of American History* 76 (1990): 1200–28. In *Private Woman, Public Stage: Literary Domesticity in Nineteenth-Century America* (New York, 1984), Mary Kelley suggests the tension between the professional life and personal life of best-selling women authors. Individual biographies are also useful for understanding how women reached their publics. For example, see Lois Banner, *Elizabeth Cady Stanton: A Radical for Woman's Rights* (Boston, 1980). Edward T. James and Janet Wilson James, eds., *Notable American Women, 1607–1950: A Biographical Dictionary*, 2 vols. (Cambridge, Mass., 1971) is an indispensable source of information.

Theoretical essays about intellectuals, their identity, and their role in society are usually about male intellectuals exclusively. The following works are helpful in thinking about their identity: Thomas Bender, "The Erosion of Public Culture: Cities, Discourses, and Professional Disciplines," in Thomas L. Haskell, ed., *The Authority, of Experts: Studies in History and Theory* (Bloomington, Ind., 1984); Bender, *New York Intellect: A History of Intellectual Life in New York City, from 1750 to the Beginnings of Our Own Time* (New York, 1987); Lewis Perry, *Intellectual Life in America: A History* (New York, 1984); David Hall, "Victorian Connection," in Howe, *Victorian America*; and Haskell, *Emergence of Professional Social Science*. Editors Alexandra Oleson and John Voss assembled essays about significant institutions of intellectual life in *The Organization of Knowledge in Modern America, 1860–1920* (Baltimore, 1979).

Smith and Judah show the issues that concerned intellectuals during the war in *Life in the North*. And George M. Fredrickson suggests how northern intellectuals changed their thinking during the war and afterward in *The Inner Civil War: Northern Intellectuals and the Crisis of the Union* (New York, 1965).

Readers interested in Darwinism, social Darwinism, and science in the postwar period may start with Richard Hofstadter's clear and readable presentation in *Social Darwinism in American Thought*, rev. ed. (Boston, 1955). But then, without delay, they should read Donald C. Bellomy's "'Social Darwinism' Revisited," *Perspectives in American History*, new series 1 (1984): 131–86, as a corrective to Hofstadter's misrepresentations and overstatements. This article also clarifies the issues raised by Robert C. Bannister, *Social Darwinism: Science and Myth in Anglo-American Social Thought* (Philadelphia, 1979). Charles D. Cashdollar brilliantly elucidates the issues presented by modern science—and specifically, the controversies generated by positivism—in *The Transformation of Theology, 1830–1890: Positivism and Protestant Thought in Britain and America* (Princeton, N.J., 1989). Two biographies of key modern science figures are Milton Berman, *John Fiske: The Evolution of a Popularizer* (Cambridge, Mass., 1961), and Donald Fleming, *John William Draper and the Religion of Science* (1950; reprint, New York, 1972).

The relationship between religion and culture is one of the many issues that Clifford E. Clark, Jr. tackles in *Henry Ward Beecher: Spokesman for a Middle-Class America* (Urbana, Ill., 1978); it also occupies William G. McLoughlin, Jr. in *The Meaning of Henry Ward Beecher: An Essay on the Shifting Values of Mid-Victorian America; 1840–1870* (New York, 1970).

James F. Findlay, Jr. cogently explains the intellectual content of Dwight L. Moody's theology and its appeal to postwar Americans in *Dwight L. Moody: American Evangelist, 1837–1899* (Chicago, 1969). Two other valuable books on revivalism are Darrel M. Robertson's case study of one Moody-inspired revival, *The Chicago Revival, 1876: Society and Revivalism in a Nineteenth-Century City* (Metuchen, N.J., 1989), and Sandra S. Sizer's explication of the cultural meanings of gospel hymns, *Gospel Hymns and Social Religion: The Rhetoric of Nineteenth-Century Revivalism* (Philadelphia, 1978).

Intellectuals are said to have lost their religious faith after the Civil War. The most sophisticated and sustained discussion of this development appears in James Turner, *Without God, Without Creed: The Origins of Unbelief in America* (Baltimore, 1985), though Stevenson, *Scholarly Means* suggests that unbelief was but one among several paths available to intellectuals confronting modern thought. Also helpful is D. H. Meyer, "The Victorian Crisis of Faith," in Howe, *Victorian America*. Paul A. Carter, *The Spiritual Crisis of the Gilded Age* (DeKalb, Ill., 1971) is an entertaining survey of the subject.

Two very readable and well-researched books discuss the postwar South and the meaning of its defeat: Gaines M. Foster, *Ghosts of the Confederacy: Defeat, the Lost Cause, and the Emergence of the New South, 1865 to 1913* (New York, 1987), and Charles Reagan Wilson, *Baptized in Blood: The Religion of the Lost Cause, 1865–1920* (Athens, Ga., 1980).

The meaning of the war is often discussed through examination of the published writings of prominent Americans. Two historians who depart from this practice are Earl J. Hess, *Liberty, Virtue, and Progress: Northerners and Their War for the Union* (New York, 1988), and Randall C. Jimerson, *The Private Civil War: Popular Thought during the Sectional Conflict* (Baton Rouge, La., 1988).

For Chapter Seven

Historians of intellectual life during the Civil War and Reconstruction have given most attention to those intellectuals labeled either liberal or "genteel." For the liberal intellectuals connected with *The Nation* and other reform projects, the most reliable authorities are Bender, *New York Intellect*; Hall, "Victorian Connection"; and Hall, "The 'Higher Journalism' and the Politics of Culture in Mid-Nineteenth-Century America" (unpublished paper, Davis Center, Princeton University, 4 March 1988). Haskell is the authority on the American Social Science Association; see his *Emergence of Professional Social Science*. Leach, *True Love* can be consulted for snippets of information on the Association for the Advancement of Women.

From 1880 on, voices proposing alternatives to liberal and genteel thought became louder and more conspicuous. John L. Thomas stimulates thinking about social thought in *Alternative America: Henry George, Edward Bellamy, Henry Demarest Lloyd, and the Adversary Tradition* (Cambridge, Mass., 1983).

Until a contemporary cultural historian recognizes the richness of the Chautauqua movement as a subject, readers should consult the following works, each of which presents a fragmentary picture: Victoria Case and Robert Ormond Case, *We Called it Culture: The Story of Chautauqua* (Chautauqua, N.Y. 1948), and Joseph E. Gould, *The Chautauqua Movement: An Episode in the Continuing American Revolution* (Binghamton, N.Y., 1961). Relief from the boosterism found in these two works is available in Theodore Morrison, *Chautauqua: A Center for Education, Religion, and the Arts in Amer-*

ica (Chicago, 1974), and in James H. McBath's two articles, "Darwinism at Chautauqua," *Methodist History* 24 (1986): 227–37, and "The Emergence of Chautauqua as a Religious and Educational Institution, 1874–1900," *Methodist History* 20 (1981): 3–12.

The history of southern intellectuals during the Civil War and Reconstruction years has to be gleaned from a variety of works, including Clement Eaton, *A History of the Southern Confederacy* (New York, 1954); Faust, *Confederate Nationalism*; Foster, *Ghosts of the Confederacy*; Lawrence F. London, "Confederate Literature and Its Publishers," in Sitterson, *Studies in Southern History*; Michael O'Brien, *Rethinking the South: Essays in Intellectual History* (Baltimore, 1988); Sam G. Riley, *Magazines of the American South* (Westport, Conn., 1986); Emory M. Thomas, *The Confederate Nation, 1861–1865* (New York, 1979); and Wilson, *Baptized in Blood*.

For Chapter Eight

Essays by Lillian Miller, Walter T. K. Nugent, and H. Wayne Morgan provide an overview of the Centennial year and raise vital questions. They are collected in *1876—The Centennial Year* (Indianapolis, 1973). Robert W. Rydell, *All the World's a Fair: Visions of Empire at American International Expositions, 1876–1916* (Chicago, 1984) puts the Centennial Exhibition into the context of international expositions. But the Centennial Exhibition awaits its own historian; in the meantime, readers may consult John Maass, *The Glorious Enterprise: The Centennial Exhibition of 1876 and H. J. Schwarzmann, Architect-in-Chief* (Watkins Glen, N.Y., 1973). Dee Alexander Brown, *The Year of the Century* (New York, 1966) is a somewhat dated overview of the history and culture of 1876. Also useful are contemporary guidebooks, among which are James D. McCabe, *The Illustrated History of the Centennial Exhibition* (1876; reprint, Philadelphia, 1975); J. S. Ingram, *The Centennial Exposition . . .* (Philadelphia, 1876); and *What Ben Beverley Saw at the Great Exposition: A Souvenir of the Centennial* (Chicago, 1877). Articles describing the contributions of various groups are Mary Francis Cordato, "Towards a New Century: Women and the Philadelphia Centennial Exhibition, 1876," *Pennsylvania Magazine of History and Biography* 107 (1983): 113–36; Philip S. Foner, "Black Participation in the Centennial of 1876," *Phylon* 39 (1878): 235–64; and Judy Brown Zegas, "The North American Indian Exhibit at the Centennial Exposition," *Curator* 19 (1976): 162–73.

Cultural historians are giving increased attention to the history of public holidays and celebrations. Readers should refer to Couvares, *Remaking of Pittsburgh* and Rosensweig, *Eight Hours* for descriptions of Fourth of July festivities. See also Susan G. Davis, *Parades and Power: Street Theatre in Nineteenth-Century Philadelphia* (Berkeley, Calif., 1988). These authors, especially Davis, tend to emphasize the differences between the celebrations of working people and Victorians and never mention the similarities. See also Mary P. Ryan, *Women in Public: Between Banners and Ballots, 1825–1880* (Baltimore, 1990) for more information on civic festivals and women's place in them.

The meaning of equal rights in state and national political debate is discussed ably by Earl Maltz in "Reconstruction without Revolution: Republican Civil Rights Theory in the Era of the Fourteenth Amendment," *Houston Law Review* 24 (1987): 221–79, and "Fourteenth Amendment Concepts in the Antebellum Era," *American Journal of Legal History* 32 (1988): 305–46.

Index

Act for the Suppression of Trade in, and Circulation of, Obscene Literature and Articles of Immoral Use, 41, 53, 173, 194

African Americans: and Centennial Exhibition, 188, 191–98; images of, 98–100; literacy rates, 74; and Reconstruction, 92–93, 192–94; and schools, 74, 76. *See also* higher education, African-American

Alcott, Louisa May, 25, 46, 147, 163–64

Alger, Horatio, Jr., 39

Alvord, John, 71–72, 74, 76, 98

American Social Science Association, 103, 172, 175, 176, 177–79, 180

Anthony, Susan B., 153, 194, 195

Art, 26, 60–61, 64–65. *See also* cultural life

Association for the Advancement of Women, 161, 164–65, 170, 175–76

Barnum, P. T., 22, 50, 51–52, 56, 61, 63

Beecher, Catharine E., xxii, 123, 132

Beecher, Henry Ward, 56, 140, 141, 142, 144, 145, 151, 174, 183, 185

Bible, xix, 2, 8–9, 12–13, 35, 83, 96

Books, 22–25; ownership, 30. *See also* reading

Boston Public Library, 49. *See also* libraries

Brooks, Phillips, 136, 140, 141, 144, 151, 157

Cartes-de-visite albums, 2, 15–16, 22, 27

Cary, Alice, 139, 155, 157

Centennial Exhibition. *See* International Centennial Exhibition

Central Park (New York City), 49, 63, 66, 68, 69. *See also* Olmsted, Frederick Law

Chautauqua Assembly, 157–61, 164

Chestnut, Mary, xix, 43, 151

Chicago Public Library, 49, 66

Chromolithographs, 5–6, 26, 60, 65

Civil Service reform, 114, 178–79

Civil War, 22–23; casualty rates, 143; *See also* common schools; freedmen's schools; lyceums

Civil War Amendments (Thirteenth, Fourteenth, and Fifteenth), 59, 62, 153, 172, 190–91

Clemens, Samuel (Mark Twain), xix, 59, 171

Common schools, 72–73; and Civil War, 90, 92–93; curriculum, 77, 78, 79, 82–83, 86–89, 99, 173

Comstock Act. *See* Act for the Suppression of Trade in, and Circulation of, Obscene Literature and Articles of Immoral Use

Comte, Auguste, 148, 149, 176–77, 180. *See also* modern science; positivism

Confederacy: colleges, 110; defeat, 147; intellectual life, 166–67; reading, 44–45, 46; schooling, 71, 94–95

Cornell University, 111; women's education, 122–24
Croly, Jane Cunningham (Jennie Juneiana), 27, 162
Cultural institutions, 59–70; and democratic values, 61–64, 69; and mission of cultivation, 64–68; and public response, 66, 68–69. *See also* Chautauqua Assembly; common schools; libraries; lyceums; parlor; women's study clubs
Cultural life: antebellum, 49–50, 52; reformed, 51–52, 69–70; rural, 48, 50; urban, 49–52, 59–61, 68–70; wartime, 51
Culture: definition of, 64–65
Curtis, George W., 178, 183, 190, 198

Darwin, Charles, 5, 96, 105, 151
Dodge, Mary Abigail (Gail Hamilton), 146, 162, 163, 178–79
Draper, John W., 149
Du Bois, W. E. B., 119

Eastlake, Charles, 26–27
Edison, Thomas, 28
Eliot, Charles, W.: and electives, 109–10, 113, 114; and Greek language requirement, 112–13
Emerson, Ralph Waldo, 56, 57, 58

Family: definition of, xxiii, 11–12
Fort Sumter, xiii
Fourth of July celebration, 182–83, 186–87, 191
Freedmen's Bureau, 71
Freedmen's schools, 73, 74–76; and lessons, 77, 82–83, 84–86, 89, 97–98; and meaning of Civil War, 90–92
Freedmen's school teachers, 75–76, 84–85
Freedom: meaning of, 47, 84

George, Henry, 186
Godkin, E. L., 171. *See also* liberals
Golden Gate Park (San Francisco), 49, 69

Hampton Institute, 119–20
Harper's Weekly, xiv, 25, 42, 43, 156

Higher Education
African-American: 115–21; college life, 116–17; curriculum, 118–19, practical versus classical education, 119–21;

reasons for founding, 115–16; women's, 118
Men's: 101, 109; and liberalism, 114–15; and professions, 101, 103, 109, 112; curriculum, 104–6, 108–10; admissions requirements, 112–13; elective courses, 113; extracurriculum, 106–8; ideal man, 108; old-time college, 104–6; practical education, 111–12; southern postwar, 111
Women's: 54, 121–36; and professions, 125, 128, 136; at coed institutions: curriculum, 124; college life, 125–27; domestic science, 125; hostility to women, 125–27; ladies' course, 124–25; at single-sex colleges: 127, college life, 134–36; curriculum, 127–28; ideal woman, 135–36; religious life at, 133

Holland, J. G., xx, 56
Holley, Marietta, 151, 180, 198
Homer, Winslow, 28, 60

Immigrants, xix, 188. *See also* working people
Integration, 97–100, 102
Intellectual life: definition of, xv–xvi
Intellectuals, 156–57, 180–81; identified, 137–38; males, 102–3, 138; northern, 163–64; southern, 162–63, 166–71; women, 138, 161–65. *See also* Chautauqua Assembly; liberals; lyceums
International Centennial Exhibition, 182, 187–94; and South, 189; and women, 195–98

Ku Klux Klan, 117, 192

Land Grant Act (Morrill Act), 110, 121
Levine, Lawrence W., xvii
Liberalism, 185; definition of, 114–15, 171–72
Liberals: and culture, 60–65, 174–75, 180–81; identified, 171–72; social and political thought, 172–76
Libraries, 40, 49, 61, 65–66; domestic, 24–25
Lincoln, Abraham, 78, 92, 102, 144, 145, 146
Literacy rates, 30
Literary societies: collegiate, 107–8; men's 51–53, 54. *See also* women's study clubs

Lyceums, 56–59, 166

Magazines. *See* periodical literature
Men, middle-class: ideal, xxi, 6–7, 9;
   intellectual life of, 53–54; as leaders of
   intellectual life, 102–4; and urban life,
   50–52
Middle class: and cultural institutions, 64–
   65; definition of, xxi–xxv; and suburbs,
   48–49
Mitchell, Maria, 122, 133
Metropolitan Museum of Art (New York
   City), 49, 62, 65, 68
Modern science, 148–52, 160
Moody, Dwight, 97, 140, 141–42, 144, 151
Museum of Fine Arts (Boston), 49, 61, 65,
   68
Museums. *See* cultural institutions and
   specific names

Napoleon, 8, 108
Nativism, 96
Newspapers, 42
Norton, Charles Eliot, 26, 171

Olmsted, Frederick Law, 62, 64, 66, 68,
   103; as new style leader, 103, 104, 171

Parlor: change in parlor form, 25–29; and
   cultural institutions, 64–65; definition of,
   1–2; and discourse of, 38, 139; and
   reading, 22–25; and Victorian thought,
   139–40
Parlor decorations and furnishings, 2–29;
   hair art, 10; lighting, 2, 28; naturalistic
   decor, 4–5; photographs, 4–5; portraits
   and portrait busts, 6–7
Parlor games, 33
Parlor organ, 10–11, 27
Pendleton Act. *See* Civil Service reform
Periodical literature, 42–43, 156–57;
   southern, 166–67, 171. *See also* story
   papers
Phelps, Elizabeth Stuart, 24, 143–44
Phillips, Wendell, 58–59
Phrenological Journal, xiv, 31
Pianos, 27, 180
Politics: national, 184, 192–94; urban, 63–
   64
Popular Science Monthly, 149, 174
Popular songs, 11–12, 143, 145, 146, 166

Poor and poverty, xx–xxi, 15, 90, 179–80,
   185
Porter, Noah, 33, 77, 105, 107, 152
Positivism, 176–77, 180–81. *See also* modern
   science
Protestantism, xviii, 9–10, 11–13, 96–97;
   theory of atonement, 142

Racism, 97–100
Reading: and family, 31–32; how to read,
   34–35; and parlor, 22–25; and parlor
   discourse, 33, 35, 38–39; on the
   homefront, 43–44; on the warfront, 45–
   47; oral reading, 78–79; what not to read,
   41, 65–66; what to read, 35–36, 37–40,
   66; and women, 28. *See also* women,
   readers
Reading advisers, 30–31, 32–33
Religious life, xii–xxiii, 11–13; collegiate,
   107, 132–33; domestic, 8–13, 27; urban,
   145, 154
Republican thought, 1–29, 74–75, 102–3,
   114–15, 184, 195. *See also* women,
   republican motherhood

Schofield, Martha, 120–21, 138
Smith College, 54, 121, 127
Social unrest, 94, 173, 186
South: literature of, 167–71; postwar, 49,
   69, 147, 189, 192–94. *See also*
   Confederacy
Spencer, Herbert, 148, 149, 152, 180
Stanton, Elizabeth Cady, 153
Stereographs, 2, 14–15
Story papers, 31, 38–39, 41
Stowe, Harriet Beecher, xxii, 24, 36, 37,
   82, 150, 156, 180

Taylor, Bayard, 56, 57
Thomas, M. Carey, 124, 125–26, 127
Trade catalogs, xiv, 7–8, 206n2
Twain, Mark. *See* Clemens, Samuel

Urban form, xxiii, 48–49

Vassar, Matthew, 102, 122
Vassar College, 54, 121, 127, 128, 132
Victorian America, definition of, xviii–xxi
Victorian thought, xix–xxi, 14–15, 77, 96–
   100, 154–55; death, 142, 143, 145;
   individualism, 2, 28, 33; love, 140;

Victorian thought (*Continued*)
  optimism, 183–84; truth, 105, 133, 139,
  151, 154, 155, 199. *See also* modern
  science; positivism

Washington, Booker T., 119
Wellesley College, 121, 127, 128, 132
White, Andrew Dickson, 111
Wilson, Augusta, Jane Evans, xiv, 164,
  168–71
Woman's rights, xxiv, 152–54, 194–96
Women, xxi–xxii, 6–7, 9, 12–13; and parlor
  decor, xxii–xxv, 10–11; republican
motherhood, xxiv, 7, 122; urban cultural
  life of, 51–52; readers, 28, 36–37, 79–82.
  See also higher education, women's;
  intellectuals, women
Women's study clubs, 53–56
Woodhull, Victoria, 153–55, 160, 174
Working people, xxi–xxiii, 38, 52–53, 68,
  90, 110, 173, 185, 186, 187. *See also*
  immigrants; story papers

Yale College, 104, 105
Youmans, Edward L., 56, 149, 150, 180

The Author

Louise L. Stevenson received her B.A. in American studies from Barnard College, her M.A. in history from New York University, and her Ph.D. in American and New England studies from Boston University. For the past nine years she has taught at Franklin and Marshall College, where she is associate professor of American studies and history. A specialist in nineteenth-century cultural and intellectual history, including women's history, Stevenson is the author of *Scholarly Means to Evangelical Ends: The New Haven Scholars and the Transformation of Higher Learning in America, 1830–1890* (1986) and contributed the article "Preparing for Public Life: The Collegiate Students at New York University, 1832–1881" to *The University and the City from Medieval Origins to the Present*, edited by Thomas Bender (1985). Stevenson is a frequent contributor to such scholarly journals as *Book Research Quarterly, Journal of American History, New England Quarterly,* and *Reviews in American History.* She served on the Merle Curti Prize Committee of the Organization of American Historians and is a regional officer of the American Studies Association. She lives with her husband and their two daughters in Newark, Delaware.